IMAGES of America

Aquarena Springs

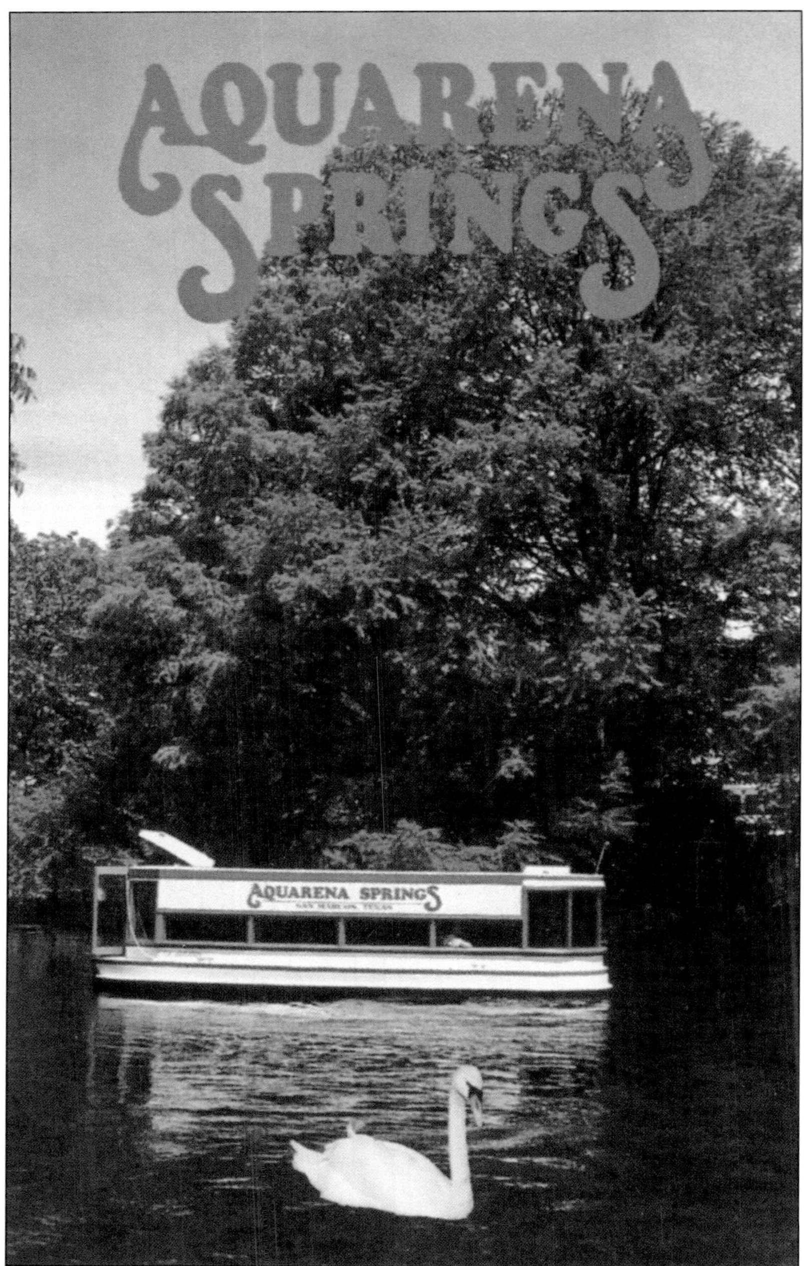

This photograph captures the essence of Aquarena Springs. The glass bottom boats were the park's first attraction, and they remain at the center of Aquarena today. The swan underscores the beauty that is to be found on the San Marcos River and, more importantly, beneath the river's surface. (Courtesy the Rogers family.)

ON THE COVER: Aquamaids Margaret Russell (left) and Shirley Rogers smile for the camera while perched at an underwater picnic table. Russell developed the submarine theater's underwater show and trained the Aquamaids. Rogers, daughter of Aquarena's founder, enjoyed performing in the show along with her sister Jean. (Courtesy San Marcos-Hays County Collection [SMHCC]-San Marcos Public Library.)

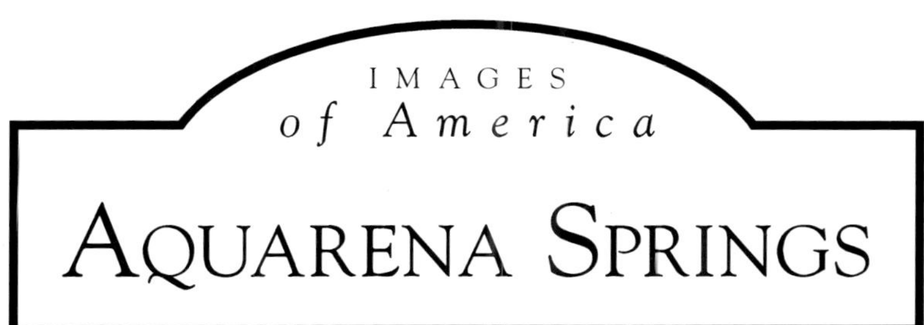

Aquarena Springs

Doni Weber

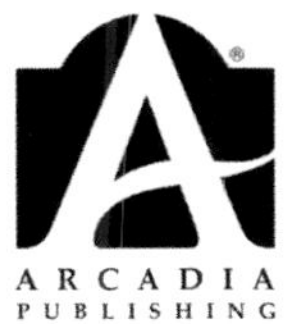

ISBN 978-0-7385-7187-4

Published by Arcadia Publishing
Charleston, South Carolina

Printed in the United States of America

Library of Congress Control Number: 2009928043

For all general information contact Arcadia Publishing at:
Telephone 843-853-2070
Fax 843-853-0044
E-mail sales@arcadiapublishing.com
For customer service and orders:
Toll-Free 1-888-313-2665

Visit us on the Internet at www.arcadiapublishing.com

*To all those enchanted by the
San Marcos River—past, present, and future*

Contents

Acknowledgments

It truly took a village to assemble the images included in this book. Numerous individuals compiled, sorted, scanned, explained, and graciously granted permissions. Special thanks go to my family members—Shirley Rogers, Ann Mary Carney, Cindy Carroll, Dan Carney, and Roland Carroll. The late Jean Rogers Carney was surely with us in spirit. I am particularly grateful for the invaluable assistance I received from the following people: Sandra Cortez and Stephanie Langenkamp at the San Marcos Public Library; Doris Howdeshell, Kathy Murphy, and Anne Cook of the Travel Information Division at the Texas Department of Transportation (TxDOT); Ron Coley and Deborah Lane at Aquarena Center; Andrew Sansom at the Texas River Systems Institute; and Aquarena veterans Carole McCarley and Scott McGehee. Thanks, also, to everyone who shared information and fond memories involving Aquarena Springs.

My editor at Arcadia Publishing, Kristie Kelly, provided much-appreciated guidance and patiently responded to my relentless inquiries.

My husband, Jim, spent countless hours helping me comb through and organize information for the captions in this book, supporting and encouraging me as he does in everything. Thank you, Jaime.

Unless otherwise noted, all images appear courtesy of the Rogers family. Numerous images in this volume appear courtesy of the San Marcos-Hays County Collection at the San Marcos Public Library (SMHCC) and the Texas Department of Transportation (TxDOT).

Introduction

Aquarena was the dream of two men in San Marcos, Texas, Arthur Birch (A. B.) Rogers and his son Paul Rogers. In 1926, A. B. Rogers purchased 125 acres of land around the headwaters of the San Marcos River with the goal of creating "one of the great playgrounds of Texas and the Southwest." Rogers wanted visitors to enjoy and appreciate the natural beauty of the river, and he embarked on a three-year mission to build a first-class resort with the river at its center.

On April 22, 1929, Rogers Spring Lake Park Hotel opened with much fanfare. From 9:00 a.m. to midnight, guests at the "Premier Opening" were invited to stroll on the grounds; swim in Spring Lake, the newly cleared area at the head of the river; play golf on the new course; and dine in style in the luxurious hotel. Dancing on the hotel's roof continued until 1:30 a.m.

The hotel has had a storied history since its opening. During the Depression years, the building was re-equipped as a hospital. The Brown Schools for children with educational and emotional difficulties occupied the structure from 1940 to 1960. In 1961, Paul Rogers remodeled the building and opened the Aquarena Springs Motor Hotel, which operated until 1994, when Southwest Texas State University (now Texas State University) purchased the Aquarena Springs property.

Meanwhile, Paul Rogers had spent almost two decades creating the attraction known as Aquarena, later Aquarena Springs. In 1946, Rogers launched a 16-foot electric-powered glass bottom boat on Spring Lake. The boat proved popular with guests, and by 1947, Rogers was able to treat more than 50 newspapermen to a cruise in a larger version. Through the boat's glass bottom, passengers could see the bubbling springs in the river's headwaters, as well as the aquatic life that flourished in the underwater gardens.

Inspired by the boats' popularity, in 1949 Rogers, accompanied by his wife and two daughters, embarked on a fact-finding trip to Florida. Rogers and family enjoyed the glass bottom boats at Silver Springs and the underwater "mermaids" at Weeki Wachee Springs. By trip's end, Rogers was convinced he could create a first-class tourist attraction in San Marcos. Impressed by Don Russell, a young manager he met at the Weeki Wachee Springs resort, Rogers persuaded Russell to move to Texas and become Aquarena's first manager. Russell's wife, Margaret, brought with her the expertise to create and develop the underwater show that would become an integral part of the attraction.

Back in San Marcos, Rogers began arduous construction. The river was dredged to create an underwater performance area, and offices, a gift shop, and a snack bar were added. However, the two main attractions of Aquarena were to be the glass bottom boats, launched from newly constructed docks, and the submarine theater, a submersible structure that was the only one of its kind in the world. On October 3, 1950, A. B. Rogers and Paul Rogers saw the fruition of all their plans with the grand opening of Aquarena.

Although the underwater shows at Aquarena would evolve through the years, the submarine theater itself was the main attraction. An engineering marvel featured on the cover of *Popular Mechanics* magazine in 1952, the theater allowed guests to sit in dry comfort as the submarine submerged, giving them a fish-eye view of the performances. Audiences were delighted by beautiful "Aquamaids," who performed underwater ballet, taking occasional "sips" of air from hoses, and consumed underwater picnics of celery and soft drinks. In the early days, the clowns Glurpo and Glurpette entertained visitors with their antics, including blowing underwater "smoke rings" and attempting to duplicate the ballet movements of the Aquamaids. During the 1960s, Ralph the Swimming Pig became a popular feature of the show. As the theater submerged, Ralph would perform his signature "swine dive" from the stage platform and then swim, coaxed by an Aquamaid with a milk bottle, across the surface of the water. Ralph remains one of the most memorable symbols of Aquarena Springs. In 1967, the theme of the underwater show changed when a giant fiberglass volcano was added to the stage. Performers now became members of a "native village" complete with thatched huts and a giant clam, from which an Aquamaid would emerge on cue.

In 1958, Paul Rogers added Texana Village to the Aquarena landscape. The "village" was a remarkable frontier town exhibit for which Rogers and manager Don Russell amassed everything from complete buildings to the smallest items of jewelry or clothing from frontier times. Visitors meandered through painstakingly reconstructed structures, including a saloon, the barbershop where Gene Autry shined shoes as a boy, a general store, a blacksmith shop, a livery stable, and even a jail. In addition, Rogers moved San Marcos' oldest house, the Merriman cabin, to Texana Village log by log, restoring and preserving it for posterity. Former visitors may remember the small arcade area at the village's entrance, complete with fun-house mirrors and a basketball-playing chicken. However, the intent behind Texana Village was a serious one, and it was considered one of the most impressive frontier town exhibits in the country.

The year 1963 saw the addition of the sky ride to Aquarena. A Swiss engineer oversaw the project, and when it was completed, 15 gondolas were ready to carry visitors from the launch area, across the river over the submarine theater, to the gardens on the river's west bank. One of the tallest such rides in the world, the sky ride soared 110 feet above Spring Lake. Visitors who disembarked on the river's west side could wander through the Hanging Gardens, visit a bell tower reflecting the influence of the Spanish missions, see a working gristmill produce corn meal, watch an ancient *noria* (Mexican water-pumping device) powered by donkeys, or visit an old-fashioned general store to purchase corn meal or candy before boarding the sky ride for the return trip. By the late 1960s, a ferryboat had been added to Aquarena's fleet, and now guests could cross the river via ferry or sky ride. The ferry operated from "Pirate's Cove," a landing on the east side of the river that featured a pirate-themed gift shop.

Despite its many attractions, the focus of Aquarena has always been, and continues to be, the beautiful San Marcos River. From historic floods to the discovery of ancient Paleo-Indian artifacts beneath its muddy bottom, the river has remained the very heart of Aquarena's life and its purpose. The Rogers family sold the attraction to a private individual in 1985, and in 1994, the property was purchased by Southwest Texas State University. The university (now Texas State University) converted the old hotel into the headquarters for the Texas Rivers Center, a partnership that, according to its Web site, is dedicated to "the study and protection of Texas waters." Visitors to the new Aquarena Center can still take a ride in a glass bottom boat, enjoying and learning about the beauty that glides beneath them. "Ecotourism" was an unfamiliar word in the 1940s, but the original dream of both A. B. Rogers and Paul Rogers was to pay homage to the glories of the San Marcos River. Aquarena's evolution shows that their dream continues to be realized.

One

The Vision

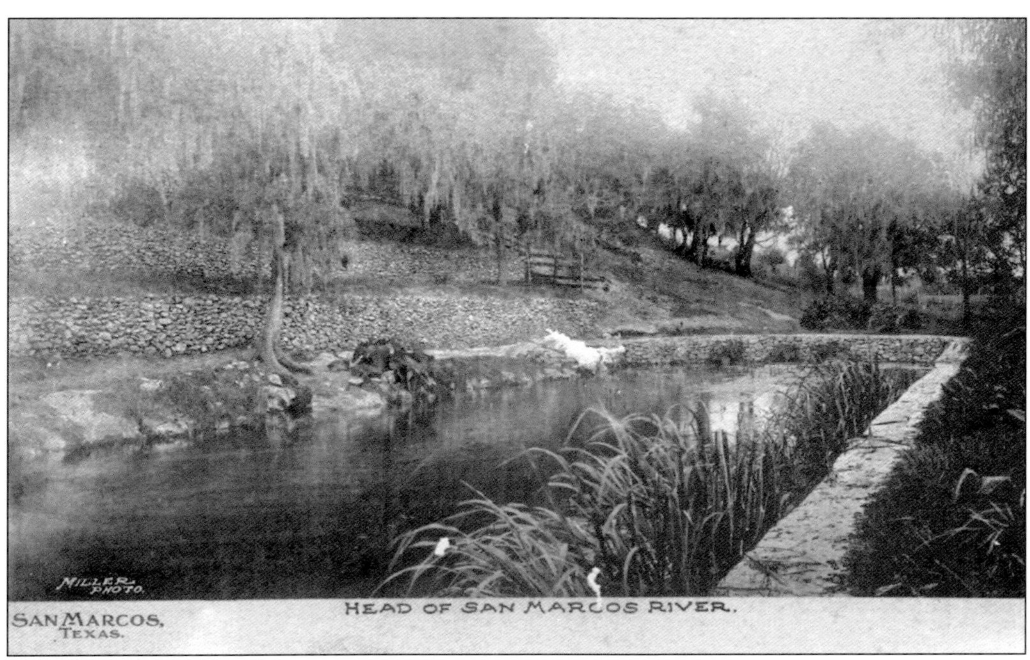

On March 12, 1926, the *San Marcos Record* reported that Arthur Birch (A. B.) Rogers of San Marcos had purchased 125 acres from the San Marcos Utilities Company with the intention of creating "one of the great playgrounds of Texas and the Southwest." Rogers, the article noted, planned to clear the growth from the headwaters (shown here in 1911) to make way for "a delightful bathing pool and beach." (Courtesy SMHCC-San Marcos Public Library.)

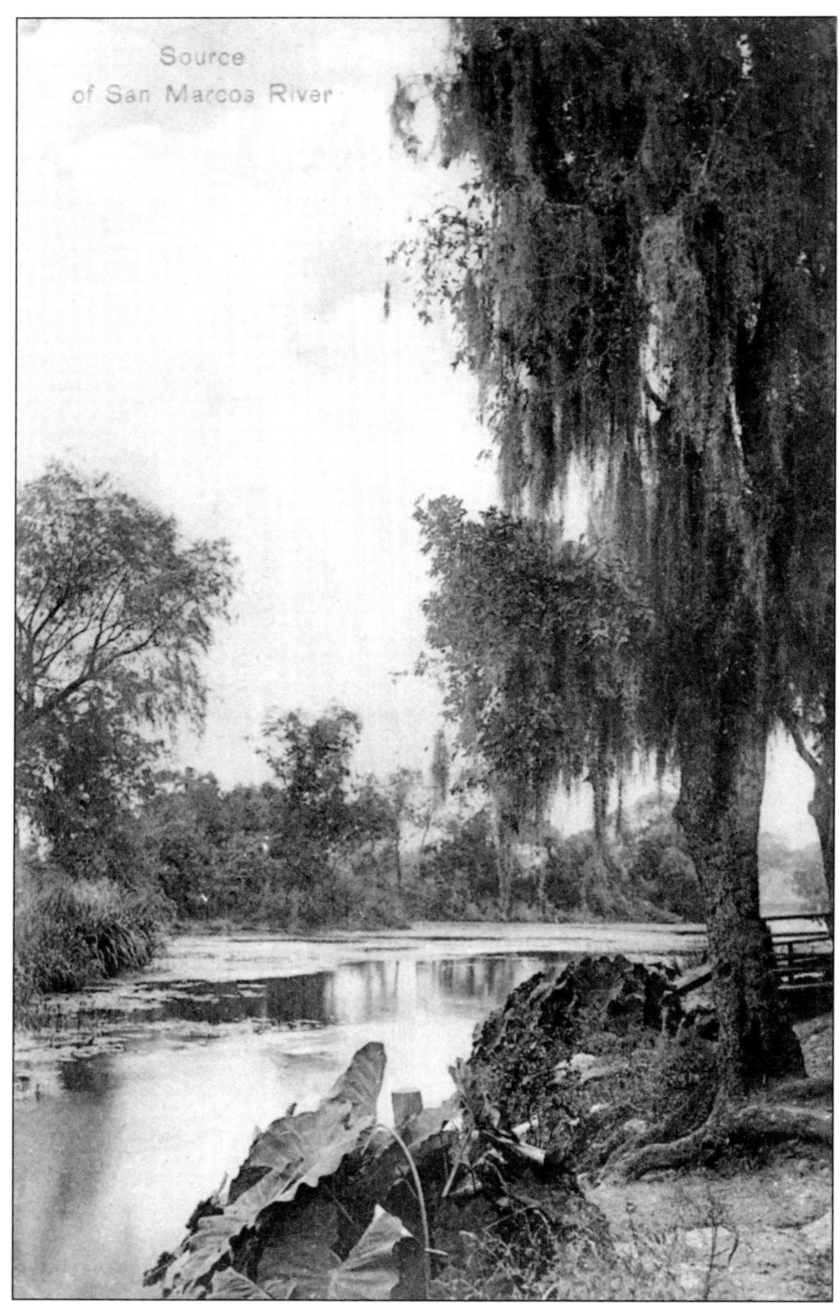

For centuries, the headwaters of the San Marcos River have been cherished for their pristine beauty. In 1821, Stephen F. Austin wrote in his journal that the valley of the San Marcos River was "the most beautiful" area he had ever seen. An 1890 traveler described "rambling over the embowered footpath that led to the brink of the river," admiring "the long tresses of Spanish moss dripping in profusion from the overhanging trees." Eventually, this traveler would come to the headwaters, where approximately 200 springs bubble up through three large fissures and countless smaller openings. He described the springs as "clear and sparkling" and the river as expanding into a "smooth and glassy" lake with islands of lily pads. Decades later, a San Marcos developer, A. B. Rogers, dreamed of sharing this beauty with visitors from Texas and beyond.

A 19th-century visitor described gliding over the river, noting that everything beneath the surface was visible to a depth of 30 feet: "It exceeds anything that our imagination could picture. It was as if we were floating over a fairy land. . . . Every rock or inequality of surface down in those depths of crystalline was covered with such growths of aquatic vegetation as we had never dreamed of before. Exquisite, plumy ferns and curious vegetable growths, long cones of strange plants reaching up toward the light. . . .Water lilies pushing their way to the air, their white stems looking like silver tubes." He concluded, "We shall never forget this peep at the underworld." This visitor never imagined that, thousands of years earlier, Native Americans had called this "fairy land" home. That discovery was yet to come.

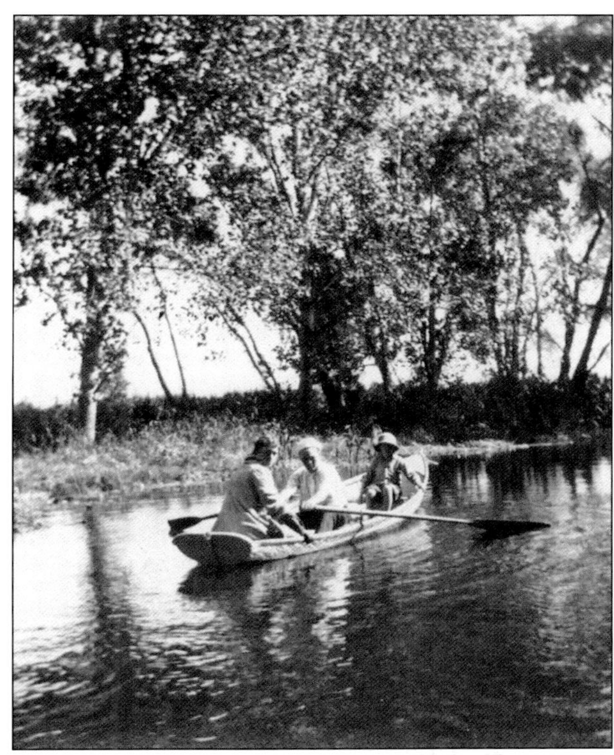

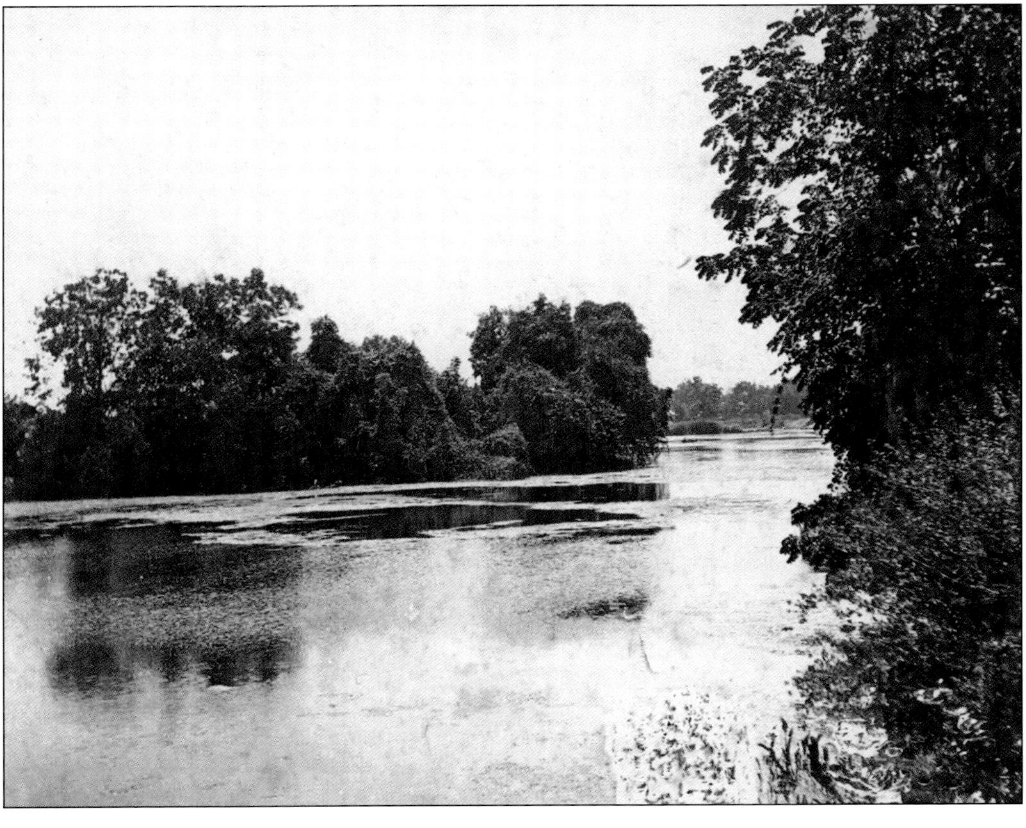

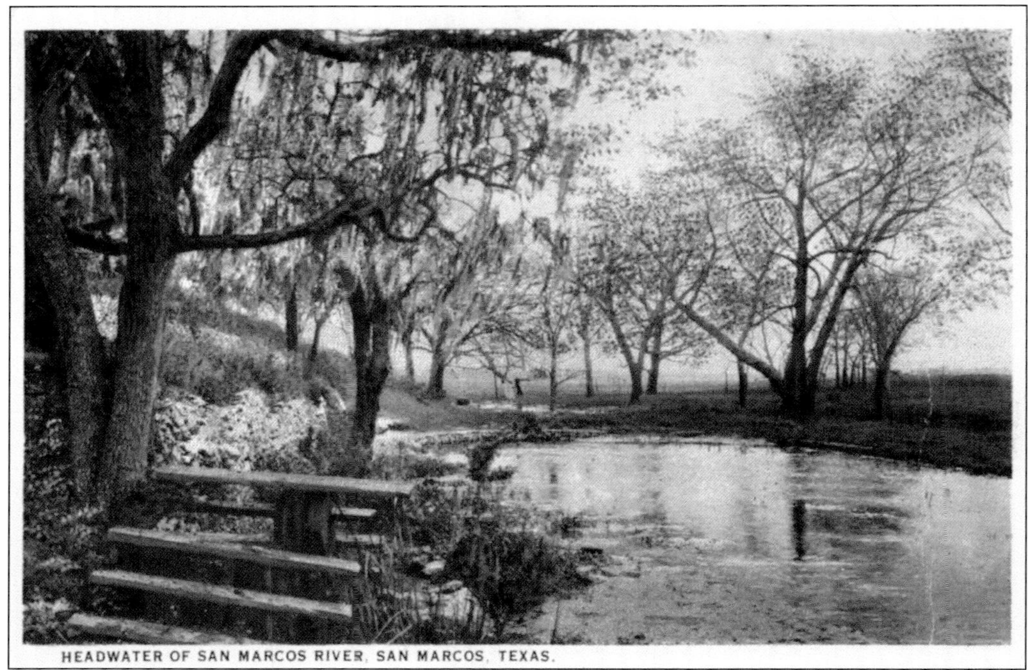

These early-20th-century photographs show the headwaters of the San Marcos River before development began. The reference to "State Normal" dates the photograph below to pre-1923, when Southwest Texas State Normal College was rechristened Southwest Texas State Teachers College. The building at the left, "Old Main," was the sole structure when the State Normal School opened in 1903 and today remains a revered part of the Texas State University campus. The proximity of the San Marcos River to the school has allowed generations of students to escape the rigors of study to sunbathe on the river's banks or cool off in its spring-fed waters. (Below, courtesy SMHCC-San Marcos Public Library.)

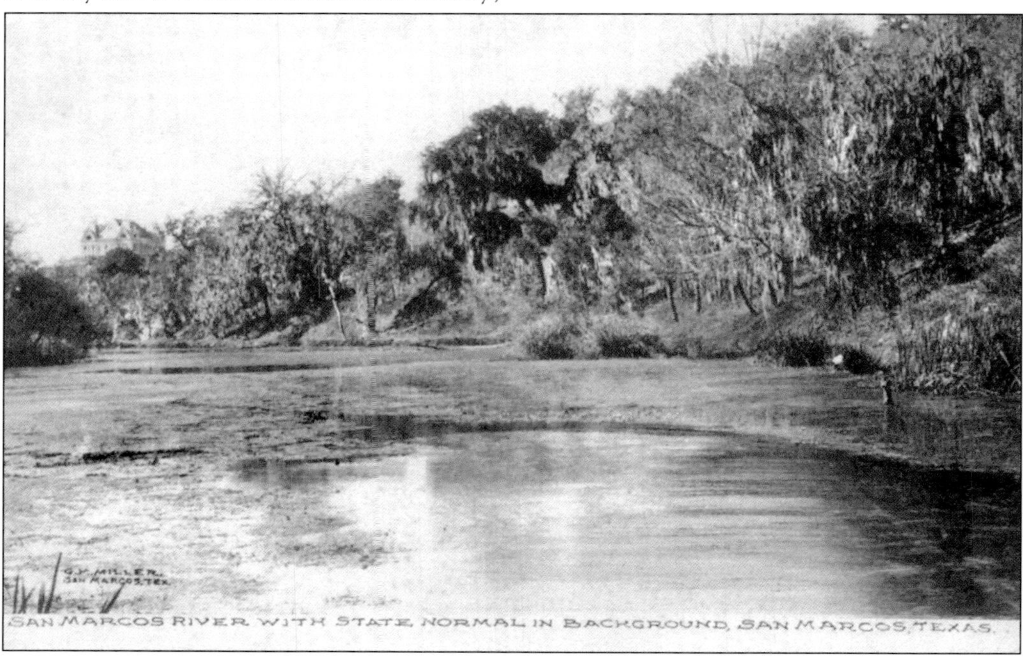

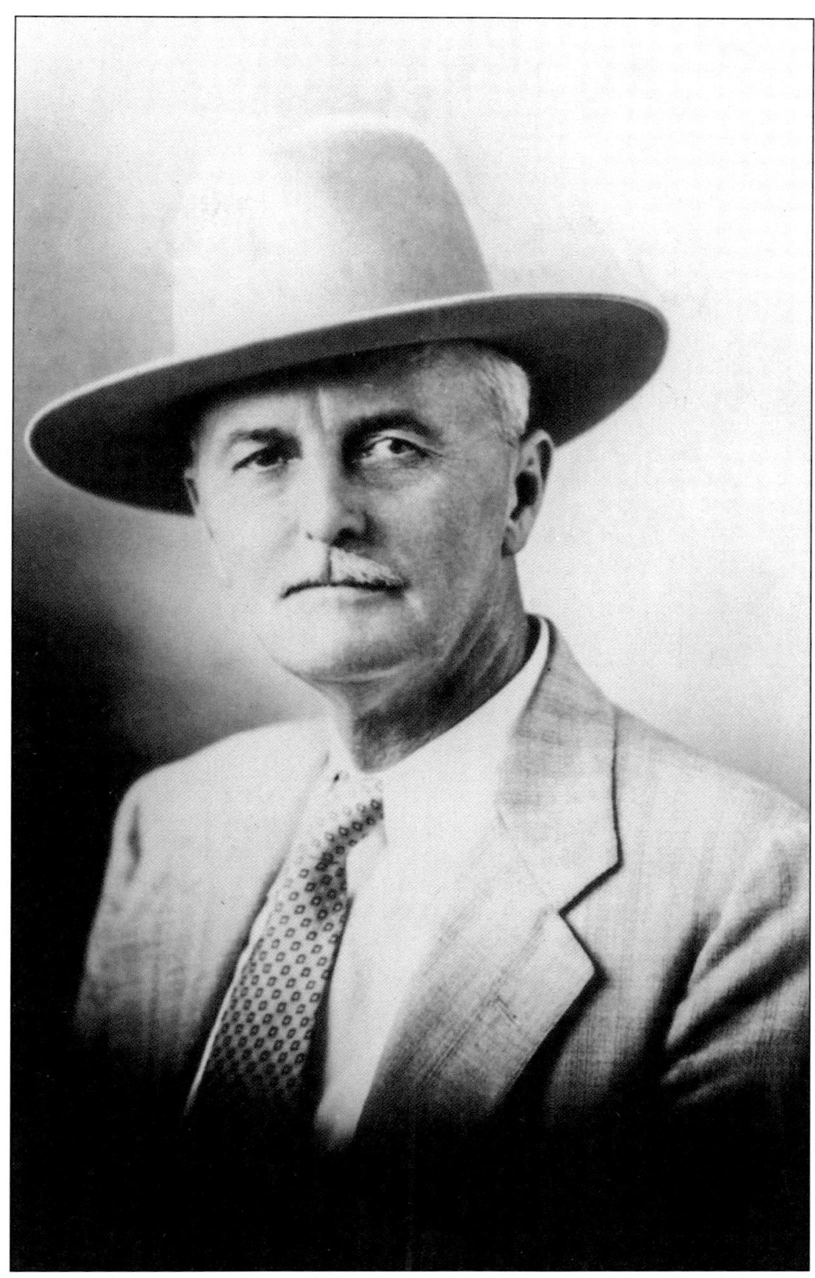

Arthur Birch (A. B.) Rogers, born in Ellis County, Texas, in 1871, moved with his family to San Marcos at the age of two. In 1950, the *San Marcos Record* characterized Rogers as "a rancher, a sportsman, a leading furniture dealer and undertaker, and a progressive citizen." Rogers' interest in tourism was lifelong, and he spent many years developing property along the San Marcos River, creating a playground for visitors. He developed Wonder Cave and Rogers Park, now Rio Vista Park. However, his ultimate dream was not fulfilled until he purchased the land around the headwaters of the San Marcos River, where he planned to build a resort hotel that would be the center of a major tourist attraction. With this 1926 purchase, Rogers was able to put his plan in motion, and in the decades that followed, Rogers, along with son Paul J. Rogers, would create the "waterful wonderland" that is Aquarena Springs.

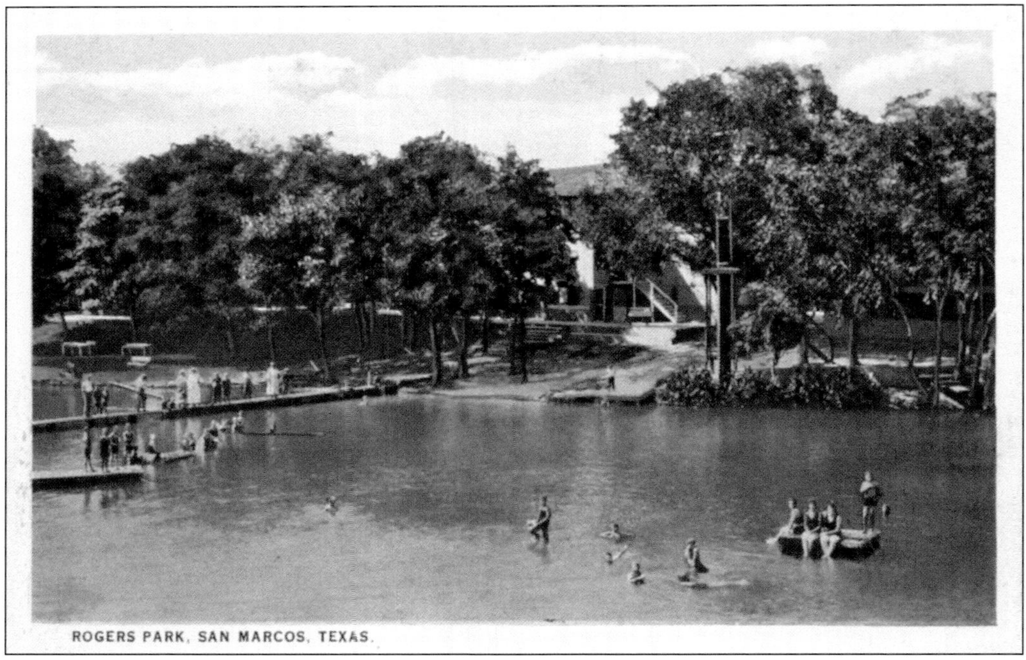

Rogers Park, also known as Rogers Resort, was A. B. Rogers' initial foray into tourism and recreation. In 1911, Rogers purchased land along the San Marcos River and created a mecca for young central Texans, who spent all day swimming, jumping into the river from a trolley cable attached to a tower, and sunbathing on the raft shown in the photograph. At night, dances were held in the park's pavilion.

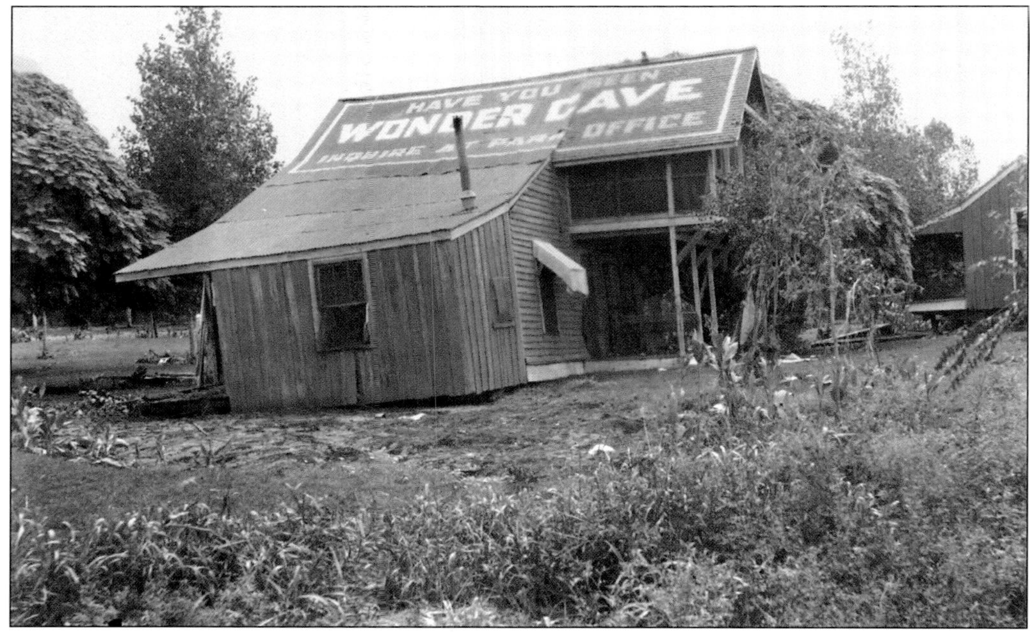

Wonder Cave is an outcrop of the Edwards Limestone at Balcones Fault. A. B. Rogers bought the cave in 1916 for the price of $50 and a gray horse. Visitors to Rogers' attraction toured the cave, enjoying rare formations of stalactites and stalagmites. This photograph from 1921 shows the original attraction headquarters.

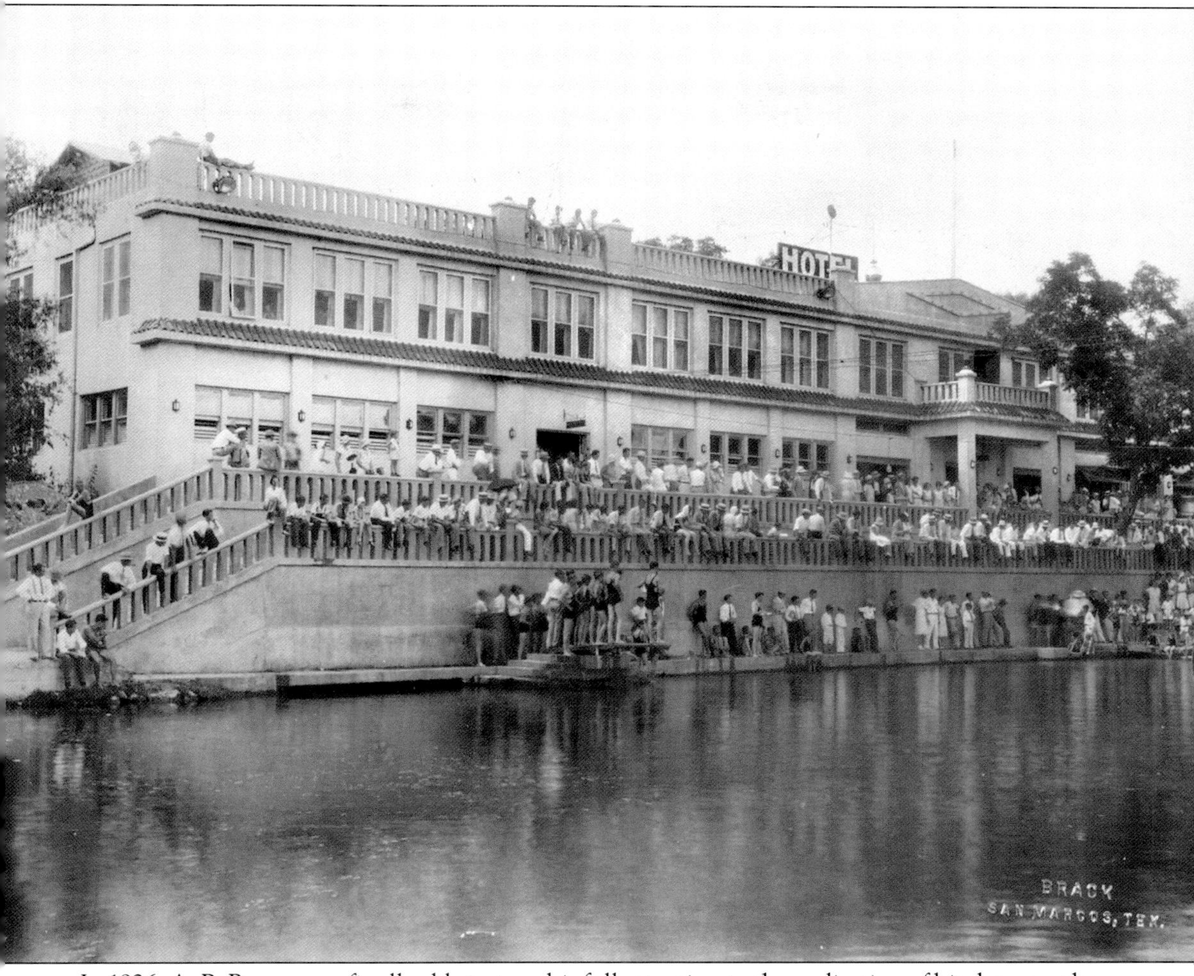

In 1926, A. B. Rogers was finally able to turn his full attention to the realization of his dream—the creation of a first-rate Texas tourist destination that would make the most of the natural beauty of the river's headwaters. That dream was largely realized in 1929 with the opening of the Rogers Spring Lake Park Hotel. At the grand opening on April 22nd, guests dined, danced on the hotel rooftop, played golf on the newly constructed course, swam in "the South's finest swimming pool," and enjoyed the beauty of the crystal clear waters that burst forth from the springs. Guests paid $2.50 for a double room with bath; a room without bath was a dollar less. A prominently posted announcement wished guests "a merry good time" but reminded them "to conduct themselves as ladies and gentlemen." The photograph shows the hotel and enthusiastic crowds at its opening.

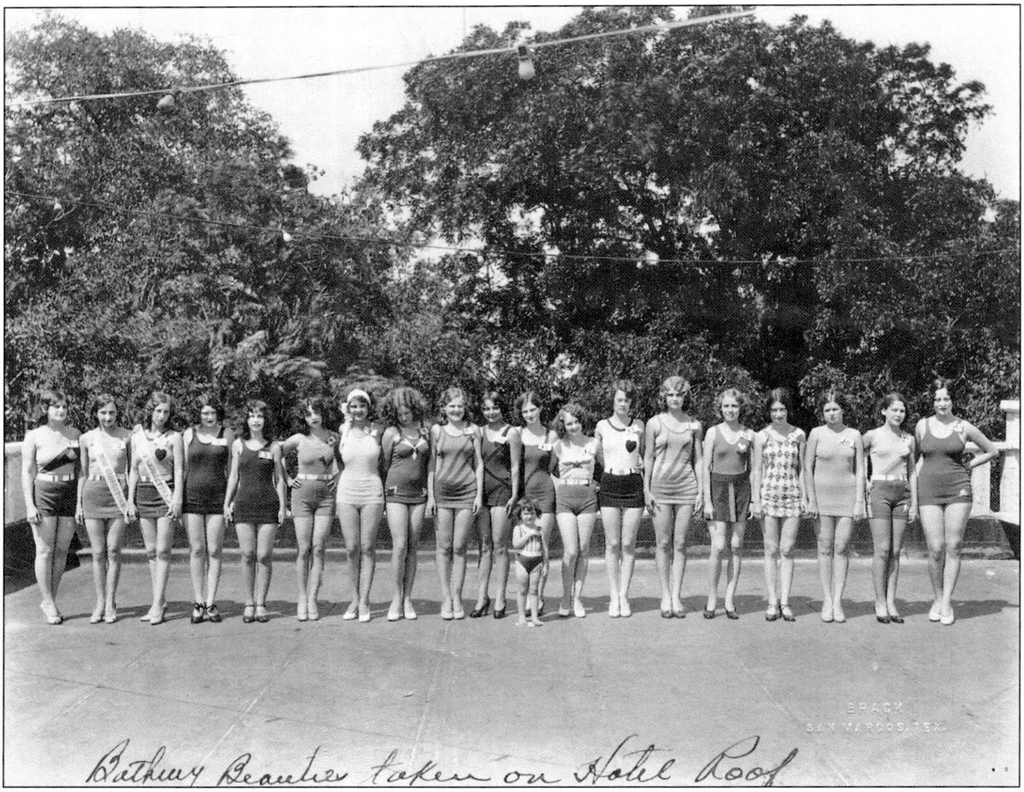

Bathing Beauties taken on Hotel Roof

Despite the deepening economic depression across America, the Rogers Spring Lake Park Hotel enjoyed relative prosperity in the early years. Local historian Albert McGehee notes that "beauty contests were popular spectator sports in the hotel's early days and furnished regular summer holiday diversion and entertainment." In the above photograph, bathing beauties pose on the hotel's rooftop in 1930. Guests could play bridge on the tree-covered veranda or dance on the rooftop dance floor. Swimming was available in front of the hotel in the river pool, and an ahead-of-its-time underwater elevator allowed guests to take underwater photographs. Golfers were promised year-round golfing on a course touted as "one of the finest in the Southwest." However, eventually, the deteriorating economic situation was bound to affect Spring Lake Park Hotel just as it did businesses throughout the country.

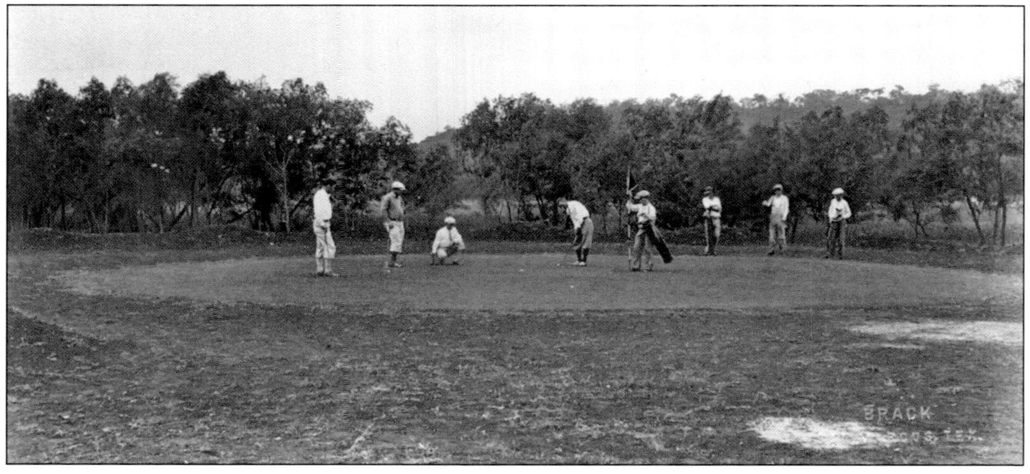

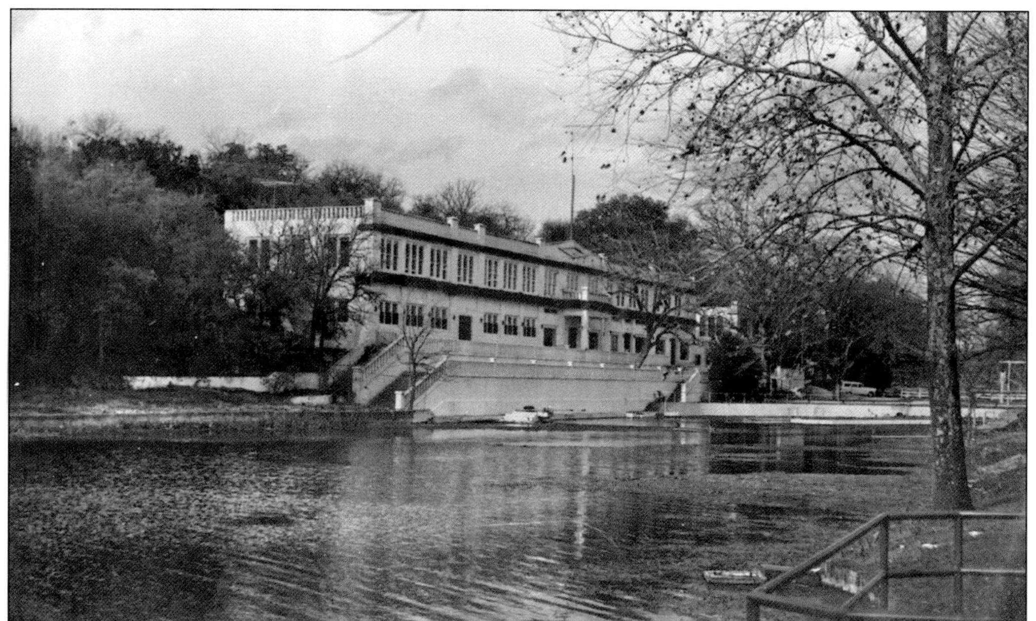

In 1934, the Spring Lake Park Hotel was sold to a group of investors whose plan it was to turn the hotel and park into a health resort and recuperative home. Recreational features, including the golf course and the swimming pool in front of the hotel, were focal points of the treatment center. San Marcos residents were allowed to enjoy the amenities of the center if they joined as club members.

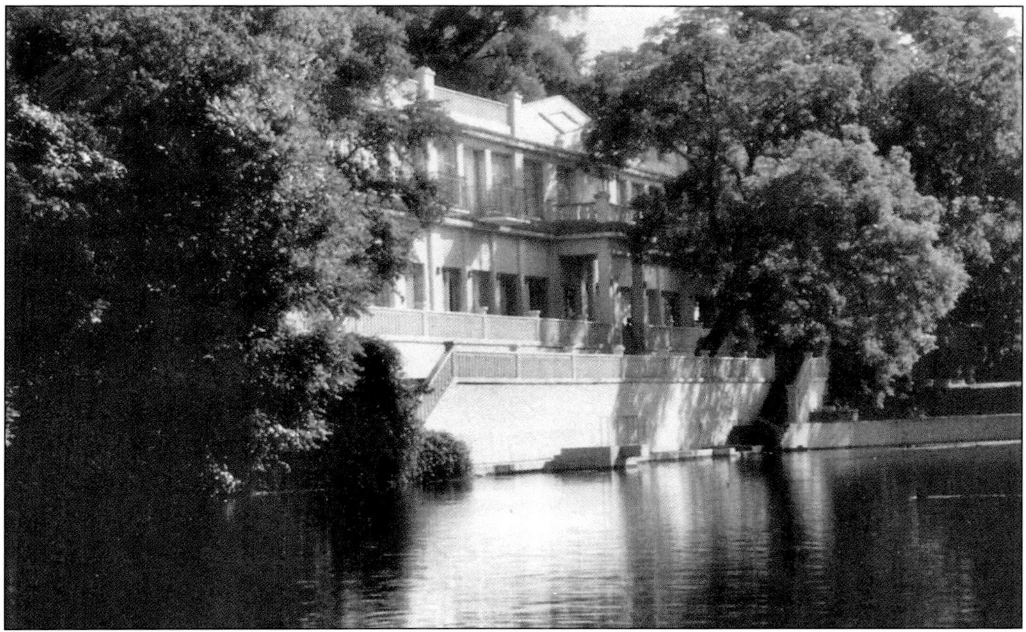

The hotel passed back into the hands of the Rogers family in 1939. A year later, the Brown Schools for children with educational and emotional difficulties signed a 20-year lease for the building. The local newspaper called the school "the loveliest of the Brown Schools units." The school operated until 1960, when A. B. Rogers' son Paul began the work of returning the building to its original use as a resort hotel.

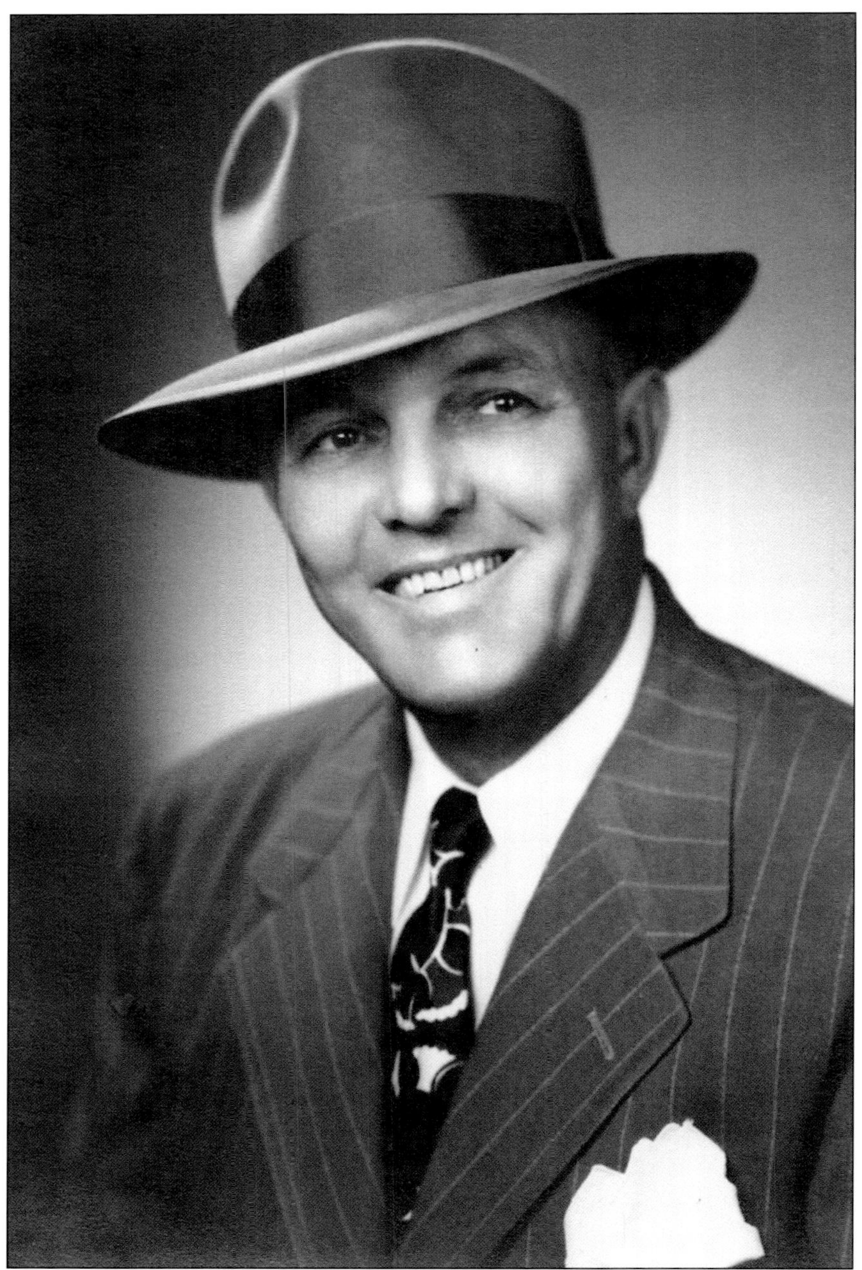

For some years, A. B. Rogers' son Paul Rogers (born February 11, 1898) had been a partner in the river-head resort development. At a young age, after attending Washington and Lee University and the University of Texas, Paul Rogers worked in oil interests in Mexico and mapped plans for a golf course in Mexico City. Upon returning to San Marcos, he developed several land tracts in the local area. In the 1940s, Rogers began implementing his vision to expand the resort development begun by his father, adding innovative elements that would encourage tourists to enjoy the river even more. Paul Rogers would become the founder of Aquarena, eventually expanding it into one of the largest tourist attractions in Texas. Rogers introduced, among other things, glass bottom boats, a submarine theater, a Swiss sky ride, and a frontier museum. One of Rogers' favorite quotations was, "He who never builds castles in the air never builds castles anywhere."

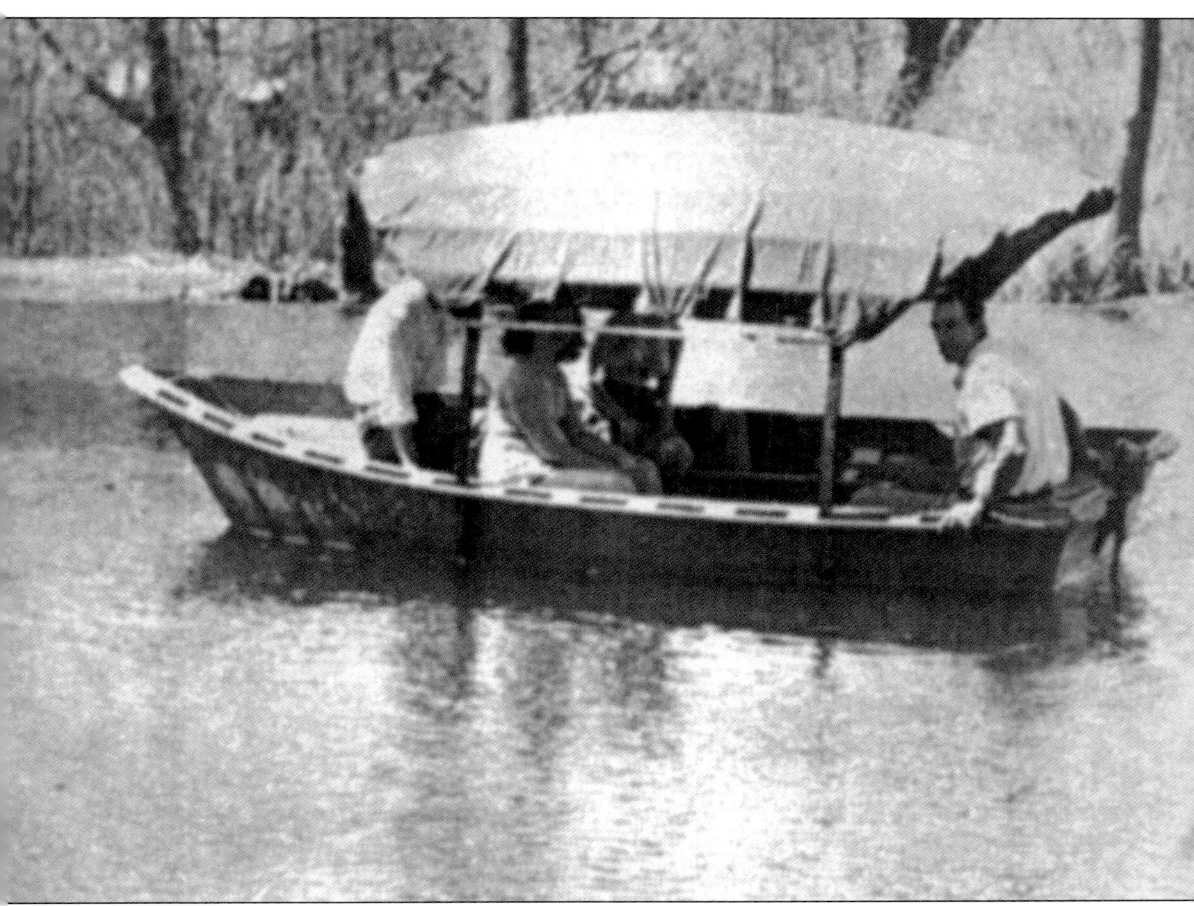

Paul Rogers grew up on the San Marcos River, and he had long dreamed of giving visitors a close-up view of the river's delights. His father had seen glass bottom boats on a trip to Catalina Island, California, years earlier and had interested his son in the concept. As early as 1938, Paul Rogers had plans to build a boat with a glass bottom. Finally, in May 1946, he built a small canvas-covered rowboat with a viewing glass panel in the bottom. The boat could carry several passengers, offering them a view of the springs and the varied plant life beneath Spring Lake. In the summer of 1947, he launched a larger vessel that could accommodate 25 passengers. On August 9, Rogers took 20 invited guests, including the mayor and a number of personal friends, on the boat's maiden voyage. Guests were enthusiastic about the crystal clear view of aquatic life and formations afforded by the boat's plate-glass bottom. This enthusiastic reception fired Rogers' imagination even more. (Courtesy River Systems Institute at Texas State University, San Marcos.)

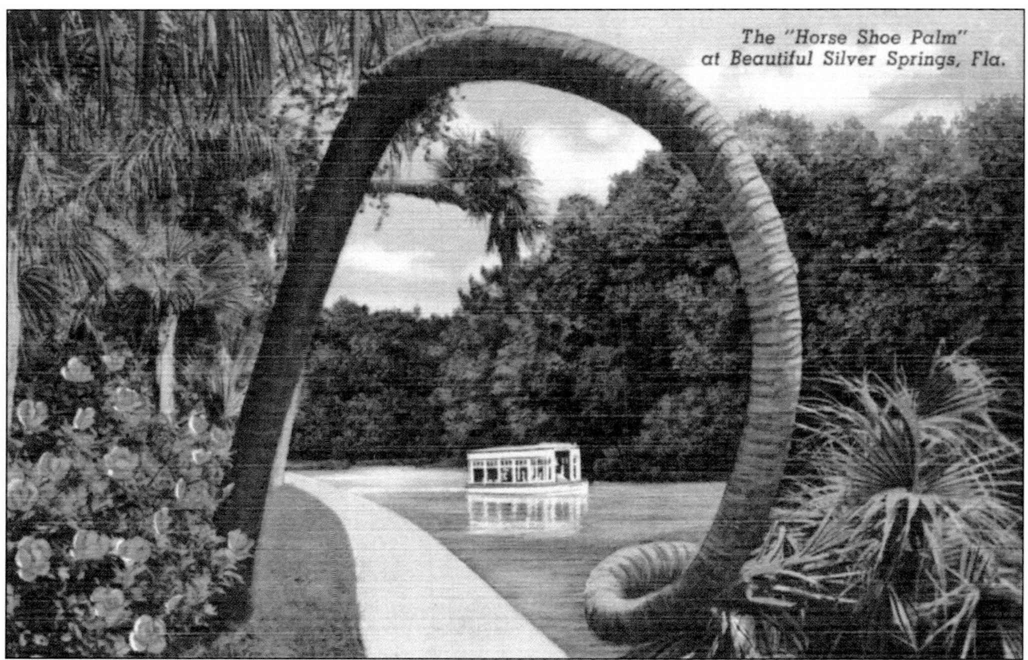

In 1949, Paul Rogers and his family visited Florida, where he spent three weeks studying resort operations at some of the most famous springs in the country. He visited Silver Springs, Weeki Wachee Springs, and other attractions, hoping to adopt some of their more advanced techniques. He was impressed by the electric-driven glass bottom boats at Silver Springs. At Weeki Wachee Springs, the entire Rogers family enjoyed the underwater theater, complete with beautiful "mermaids" who performed ballet moves and even enjoyed an underwater picnic. Also at Weeki Wachee, Rogers met Don Russell, a young manager who impressed him so much that Rogers eventually enticed him to move to Texas to oversee development of a submarine theater, an "aqua arena." Rogers returned to San Marcos ready to create Aquarena (later Aquarena Springs).

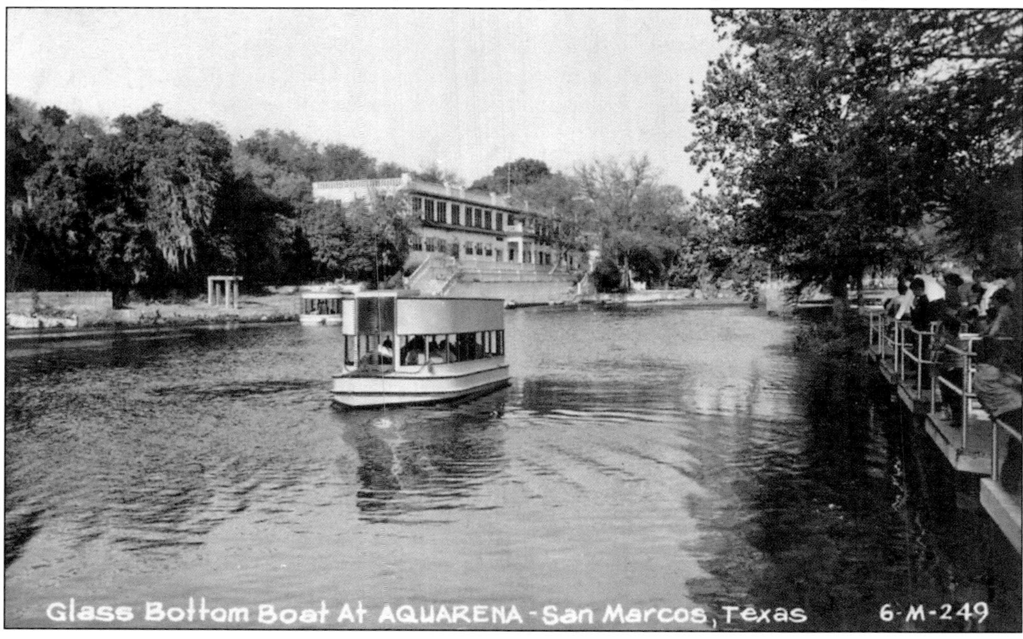

Two

The Glass Bottom Boats

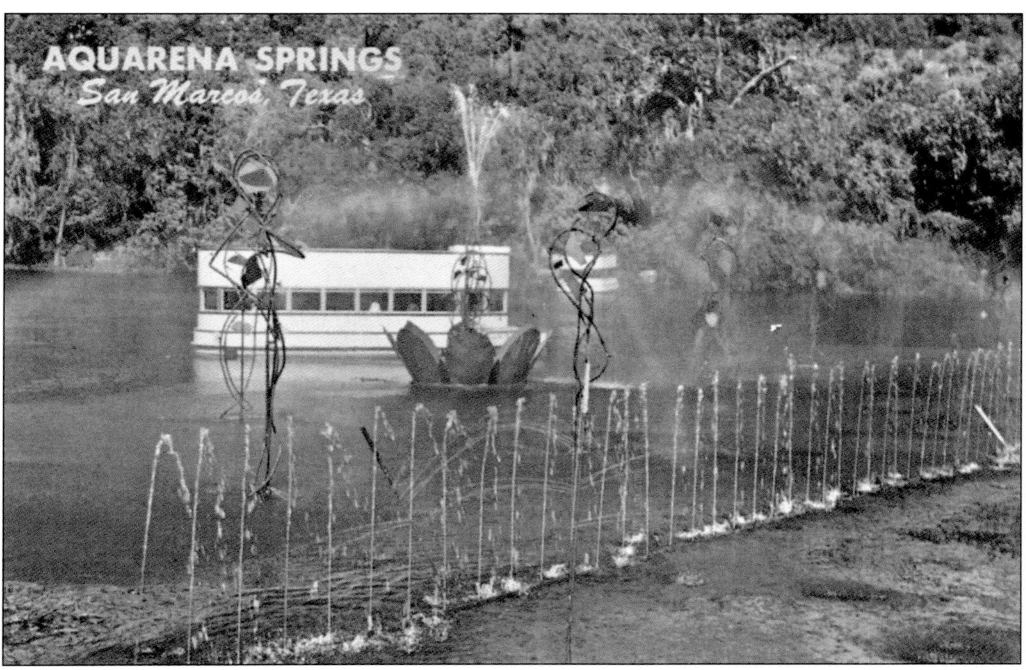

In the announcement for the grand opening of Aquarena in 1950, visitors were promised that a trip in a glass bottom boat would allow them to "explore a veritable fairyland and see aquatic life undisturbed in its natural habitat." A "restful, relaxing and educational trip over the headwaters of the picturesque San Marcos River" would provide spectators a view of "the widest variety of freshwater life in the nation."

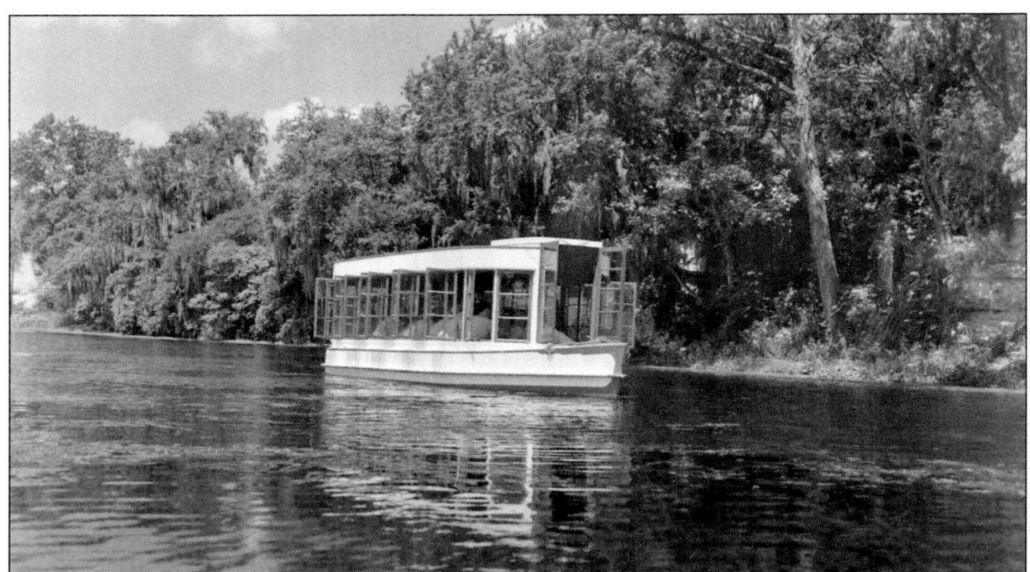

The early glass bottom boats, built by Jack Warner of San Marcos and launched with great fanfare from a newly built boat dock in 1950, were described by the *San Marcos Record* as "a model of convenience and comfort, as well as utility." Boasting beautiful mahogany interiors, the boats were enclosed and heated for winter use. Steel casement windows could be opened wide for comfort in warmer weather. (Courtesy TxDOT.)

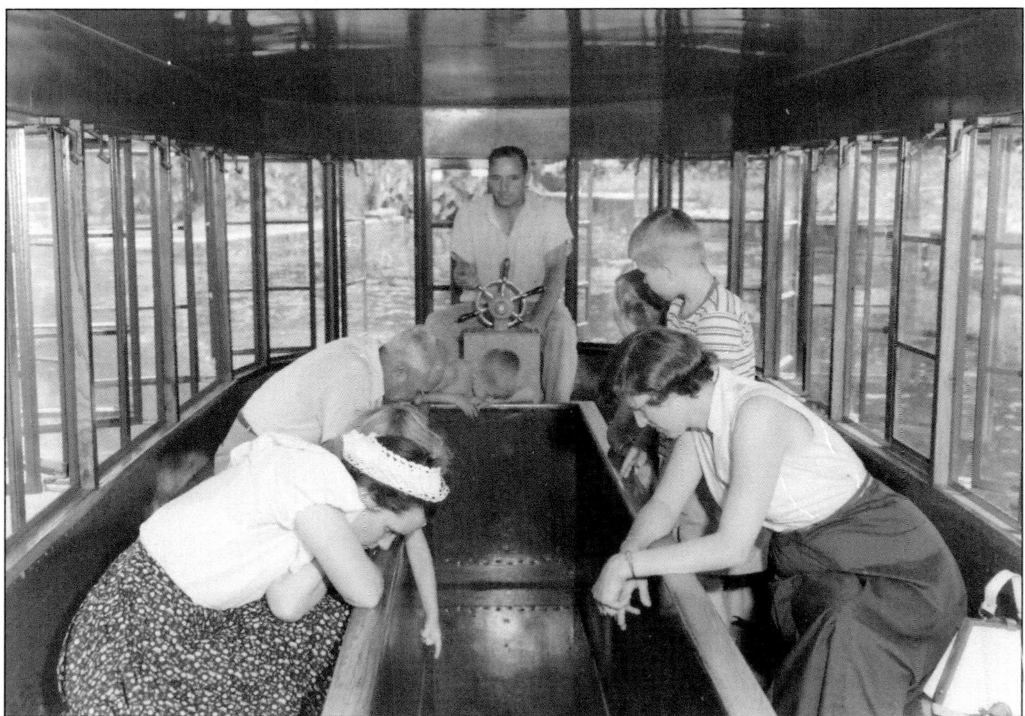

The boats were in use every day of the year except Christmas day. Paul Rogers accurately predicted that crowds would quickly increase in size as word spread about the beauty of the underwater gardens. The boats allowed visitors to view a living aquarium, observing fish in their natural habitat rather than in a glass tank. (Courtesy TxDOT.)

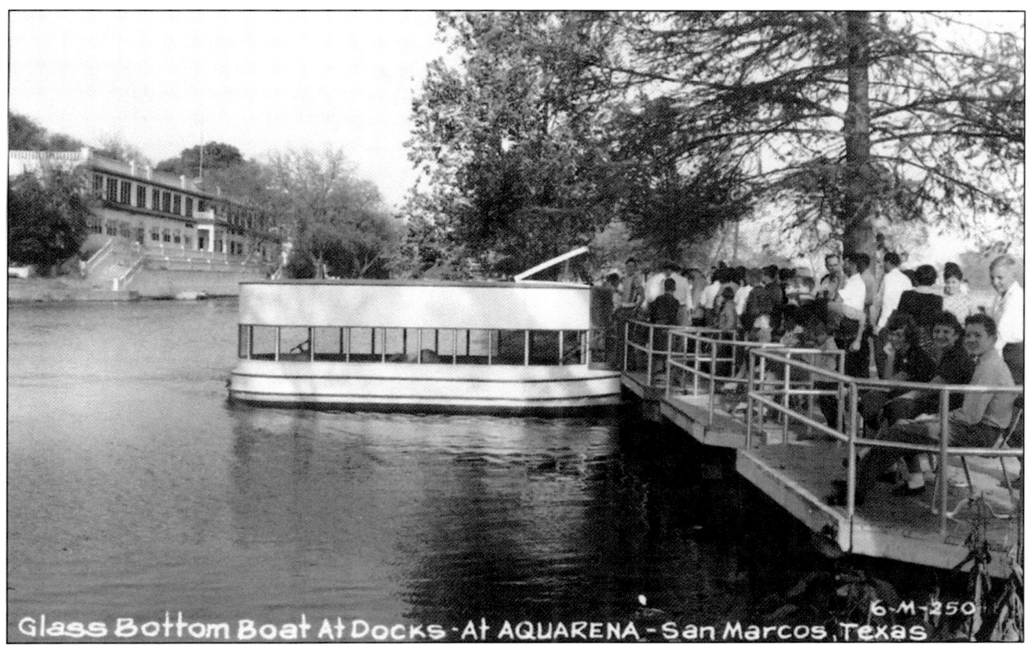

These photographs show the glass bottom boats and the boat dock as they existed in 1954. The former Spring Lake Hotel, seen in the background, was still being operated by the Brown Schools at this time. Summoned by a loudspeaker announcement that "a glass bottom boat will depart for its next fascinating journey in just five minutes," park visitors gathered at the dock until the boat captain invited them to board. During the half-hour trip, guests got a sense of the ever-changing panorama occurring just beneath the surface of the San Marcos River. A glass bottom boat passenger never sees the same show twice. In the photograph below, one of the fleet's older boats can be seen to the left of the newer model.

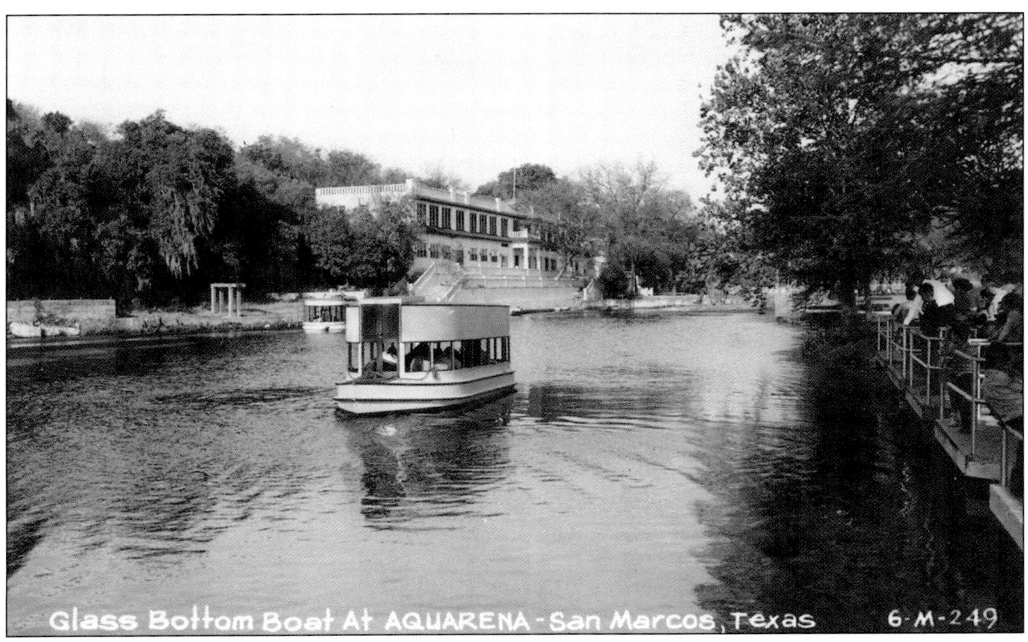

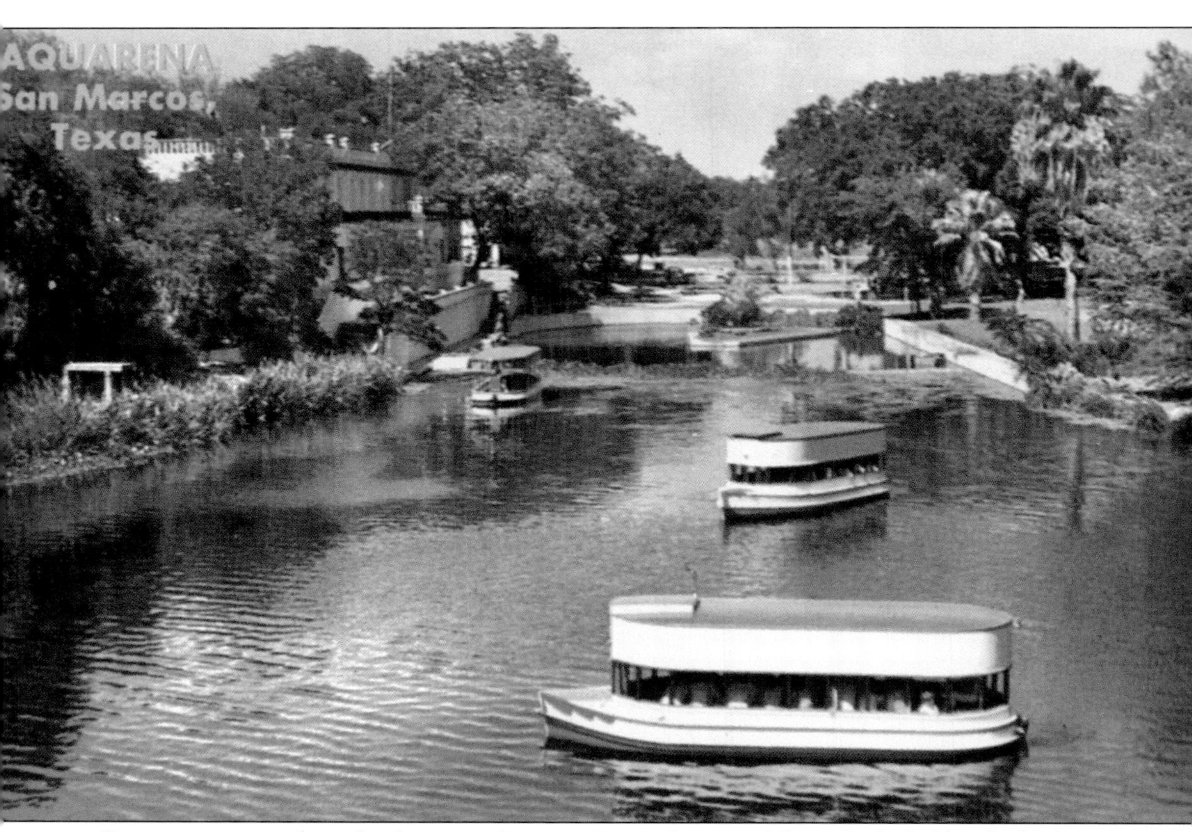

Boat captains conducted informative lectures during the tours. Through the half-inch-thick plate glass, visitors had clear views of hundreds of fish varieties, including Rio Grande perch, alligator gar, sun perch, black bass, turtles, and giant catfish darting among the nodding eelgrass. The captains pointed out major springs with descriptive names like Salt and Pepper and Cream of Wheat, names that derived from the springs' appearance as water boiled up from limestone caves. Captains also discussed the various marine flora and grasses, one of which was dubbed "mother-in-law tongue" because, as the pilots seemed to enjoy pointing out, it was "always wagging." The underwater plants grew so rapidly that they had to be mowed occasionally. In the early 1950s, Paul Rogers installed lights on the river bottom to allow for night rides during which, according to the December 1951 issue of *Texas Parade* magazine, lucky passengers might "see catfish bigger than a man." An exaggeration perhaps, but the giant catfish did prefer to come out at night because they were susceptible to sunburn.

These children are clearly fascinated by the teeming river life beneath their boat's glass bottom. The pilot narrates the voyage and, in this photograph, has quite possibly attracted fish by tossing a handful of fish food overboard. From the beauty of the clear, bubbling springs to various fish species that call the river's headwaters home, there is always something to marvel at on a glass bottom boat tour. (Courtesy SMHCC-San Marcos Public Library.)

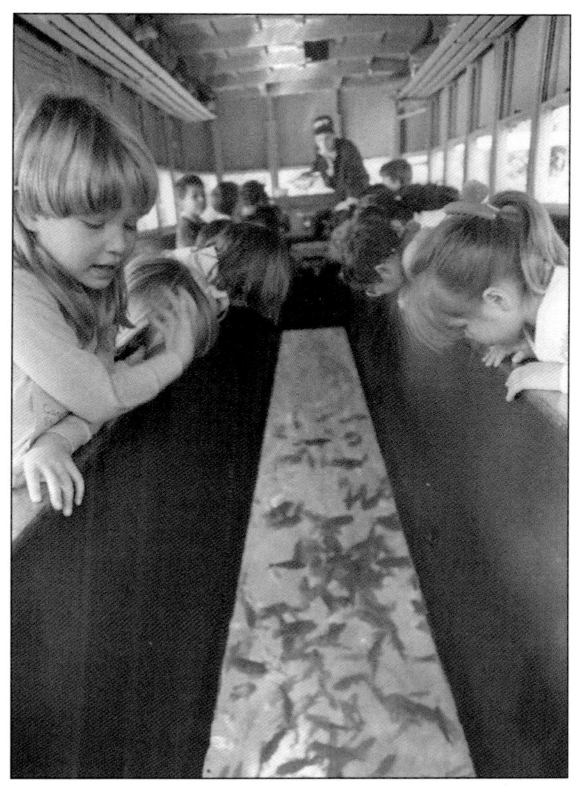

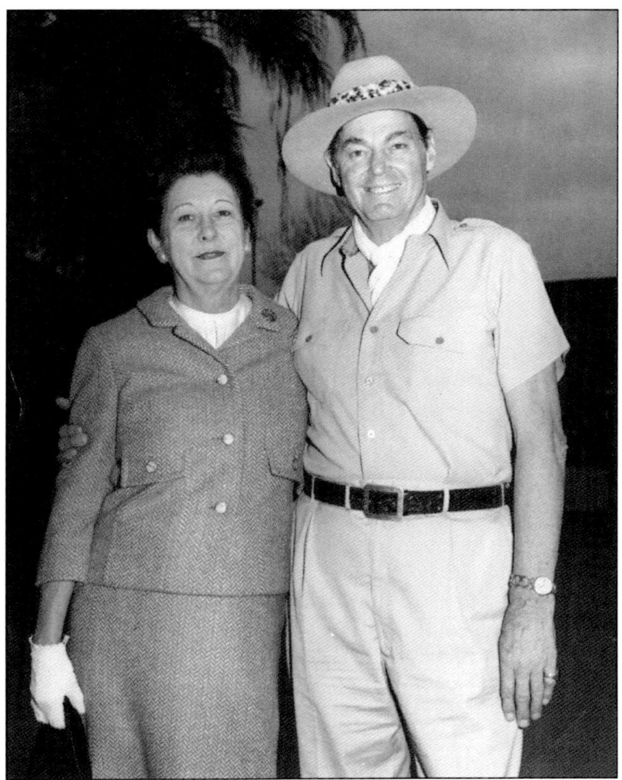

In 1960, a heretofore unknown spring was discovered. Four years later, Olympic swimmer and *Tarzan* star Johnny Weissmuller, pictured here with Penelope (Peny) Rogers, visited Aquarena and helped christen the spring. Johnny Weissmuller Spring took its place among Cream of Wheat and Salt and Pepper as a highlight of glass bottom boat tours.

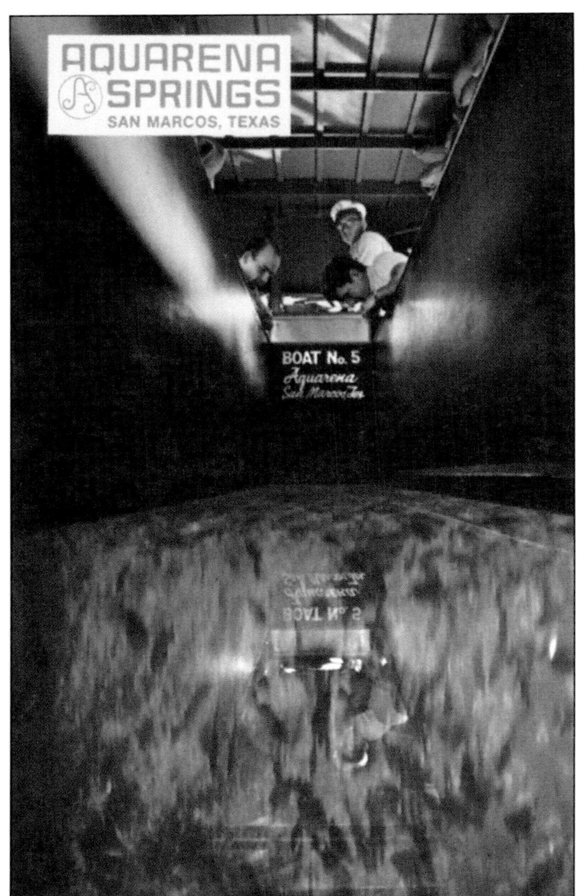

By 1970, the glass bottom boats were attracting 500,000 visitors per year. The fleet of eight boats, powered by batteries and golf-cart motors, with a top speed of 5 miles per hour, ran continuously from 7:00 a.m. to 8:00 p.m. Repeat visitors were the norm because each trip above the underwater world that seemed part jungle and part lunar landscape was a unique experience. The springs were a constant, as was "Catfish Hotel," a deep hole where the river's many catfish protected themselves from the sun during the day. This was the best spot to get a glimpse of these huge creatures.

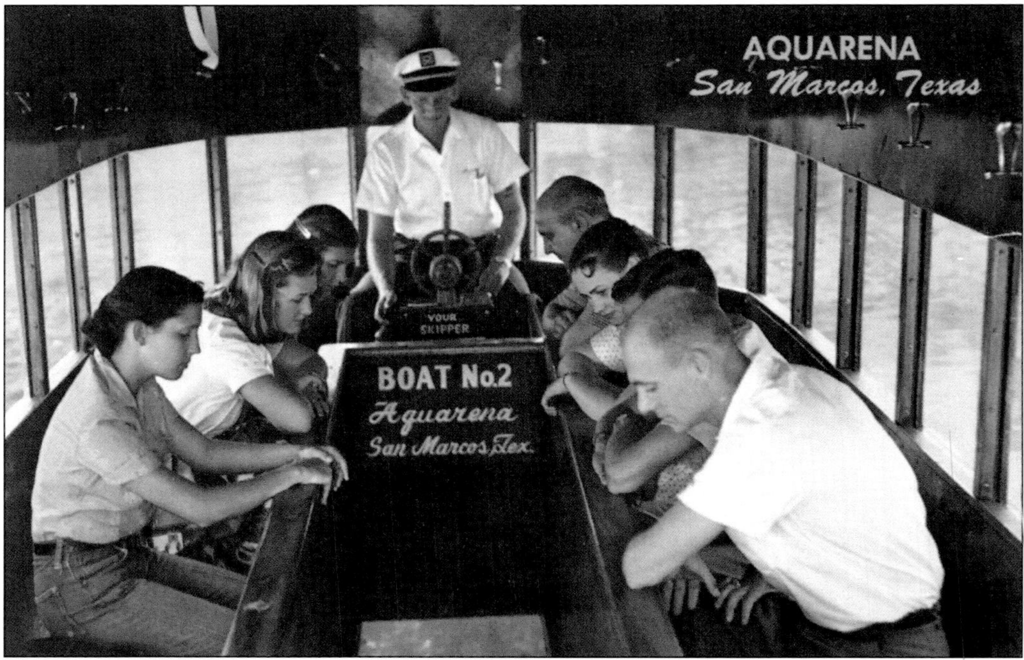

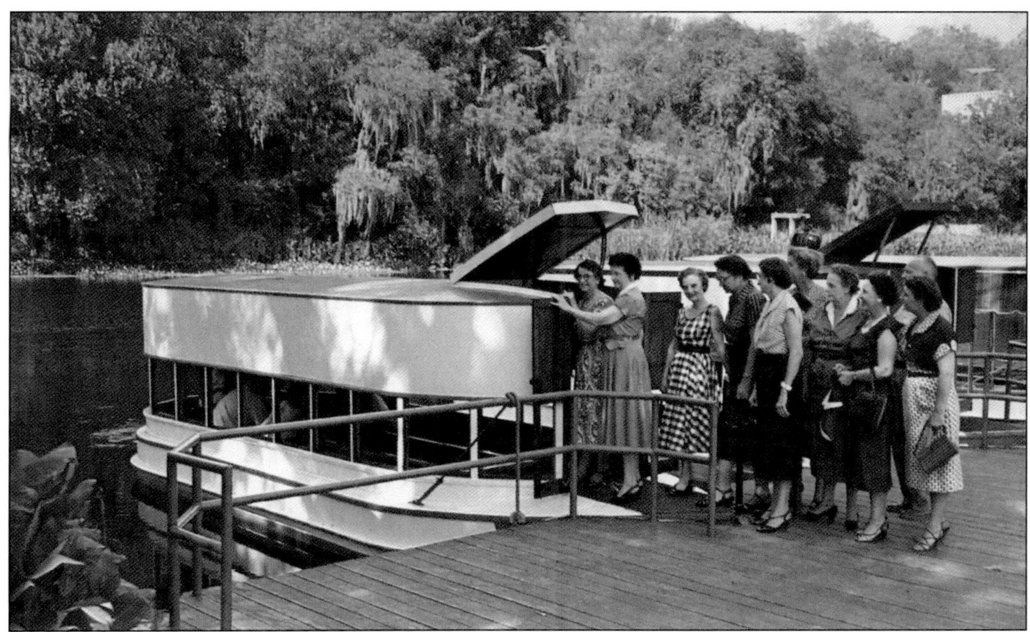

As these photographs suggest, the glass bottom boats remained popular throughout the decades in which Aquarena was operated as a tourist attraction. Visitors of all ages enjoyed the tours, which were both educational and entertaining. Boat captains usually injected some humor into their narratives. A frequent visitor recalls her many boat trips during the 1960s: "One of my favorite parts of the trip when I was a kid was the captain's announcement that we would soon see the elusive 'monkey fish.' Supposedly, this fish would wave back if the passengers waved to the glass. As we all started waving, the boat would enter a shaded area, and all we could see were the 'monkey fish' (ourselves) returning our own waves." (Above, courtesy SMHCC-San Marcos Public Library; below, photograph by John Suhrstedt; courtesy TxDOT.)

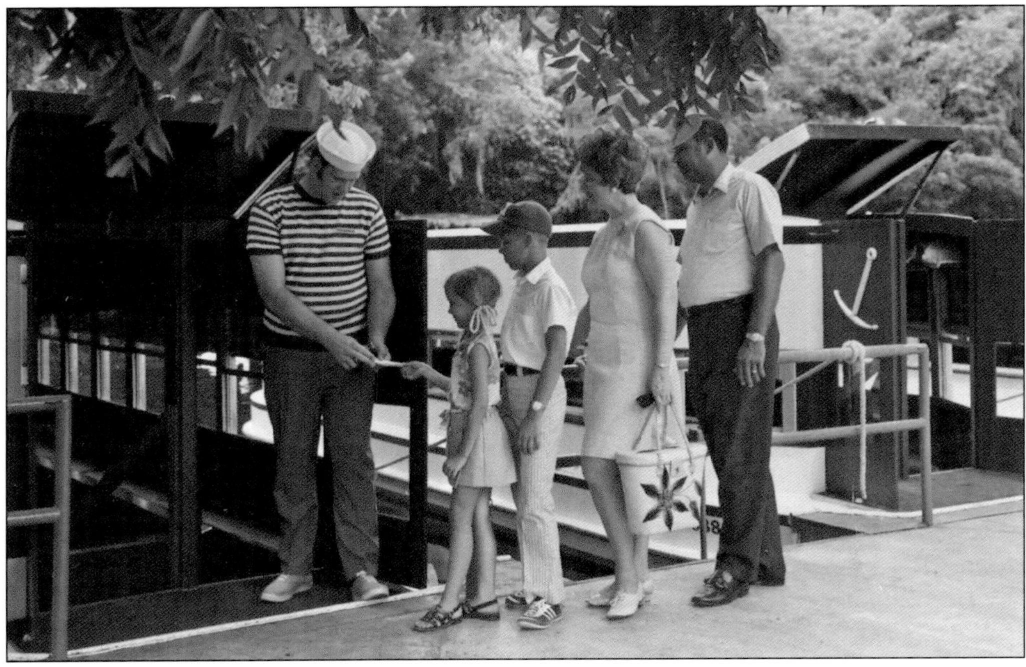

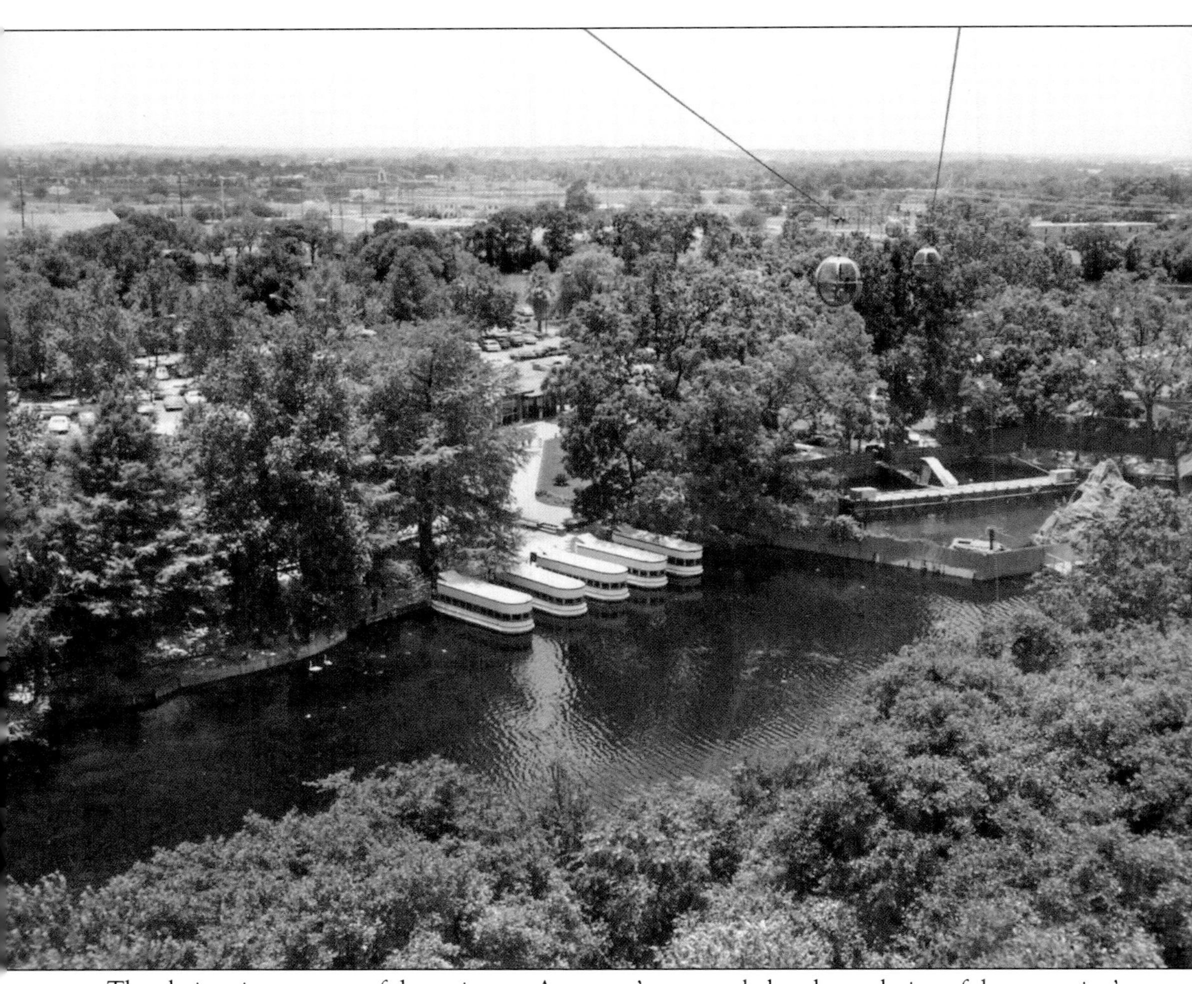

The obvious importance of the springs to Aquarena's purpose led to the evolution of the attraction's name from "Aquarena" to "Aquarena Springs," a change that had firmly taken root by the late 1960s. This 1970 photograph shows the glass bottom boats' place in context of Aquarena Springs as a whole. By this time, the boat Jack Warner unveiled in 1950 had undergone an evolution of its own, with bow shapes and exterior features changing for both practical and aesthetic reasons as needed, but Warner's original concept clearly stood the test of time. The submarine theater can be seen to the right of the boats, and the Swiss sky ride carries visitors high above the scene. The boats, the theater, and the sky ride were central features of Aquarena Springs, but it is the glass bottom boats and the access they afforded to the main attraction—the San Marcos River and its treasures—that were destined to endure throughout the many changes to come and that remain vitally significant today. (Photograph by John Suhrstedt; courtesy TxDOT.)

Three

THE SUBMARINE THEATER

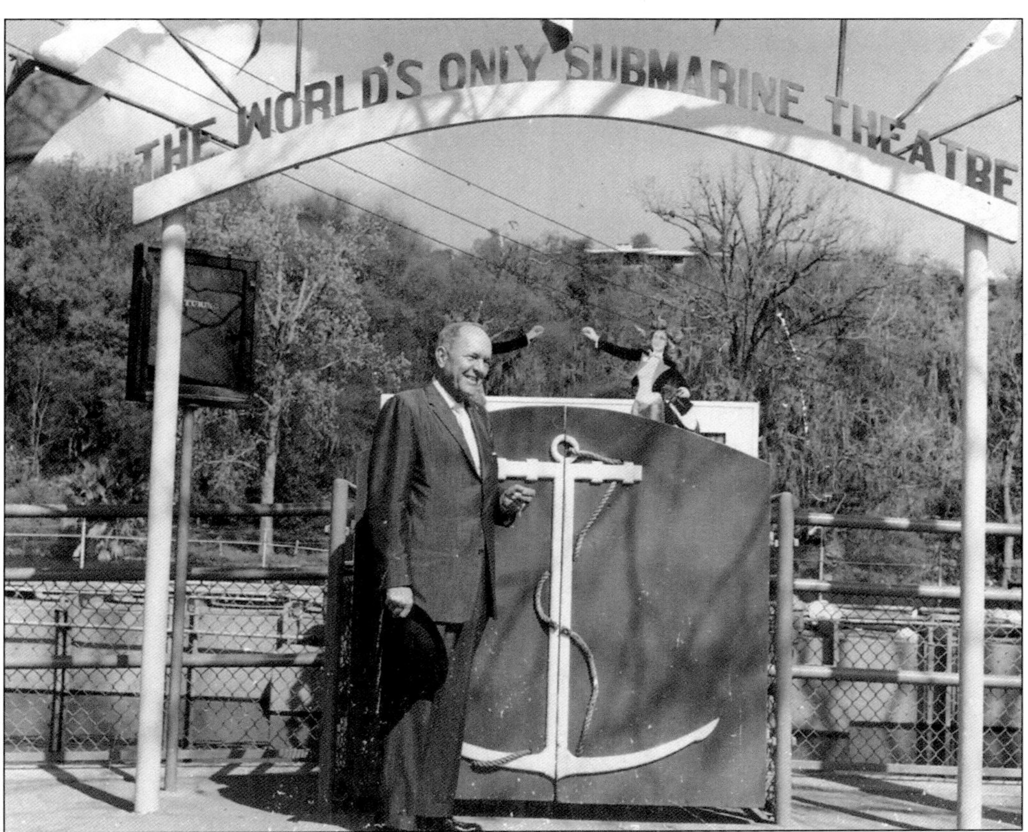

In 1948, Paul Rogers began dredging an area on the east shore of Spring Lake. Originally planning to model his theater after the one at Weeki Wachee Springs, Rogers was convinced that a submarine design by Marine Studios, Inc., of Florida was superior, and he agreed to let that company build his theater and to lease it from them. A year after its 1950 completion, Rogers purchased the theater.

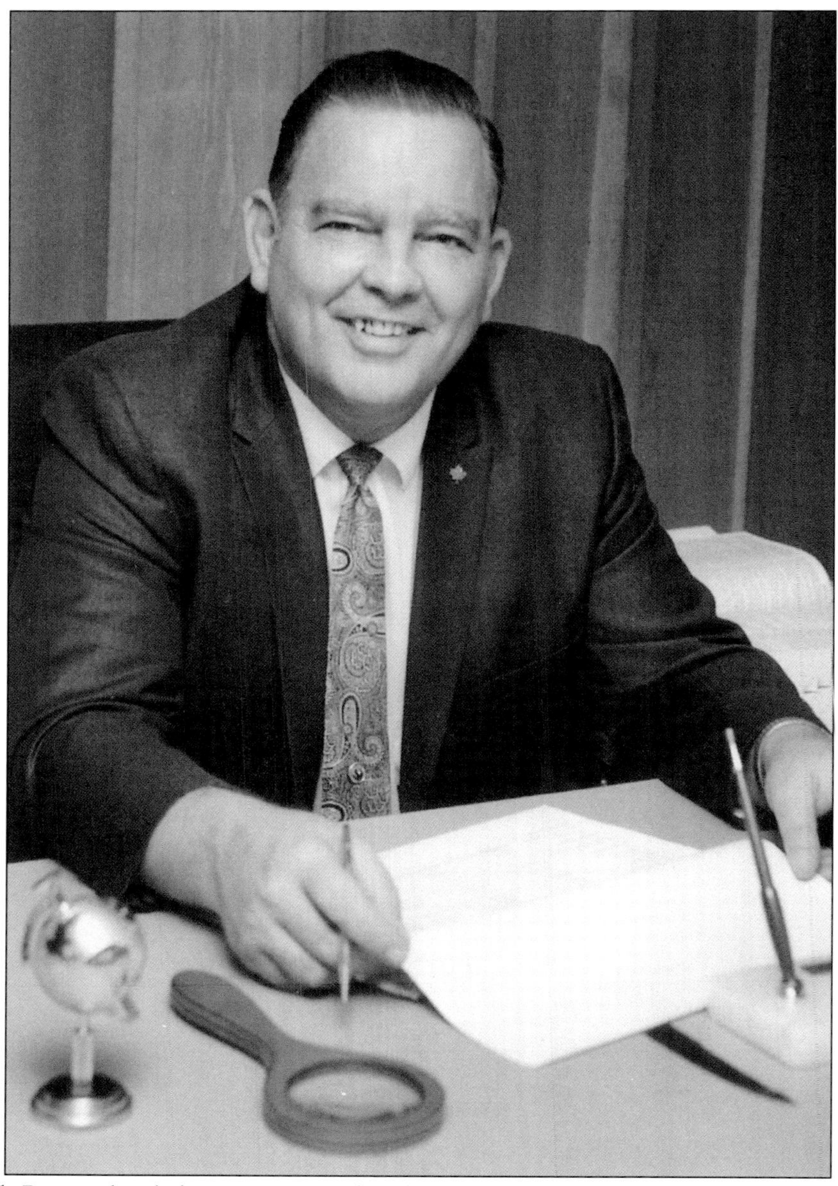

Although Rogers decided not to pattern his theater after the Weeki Wachee Springs idea, he enticed its young manager, and alligator wrestler, Don Russell, to leave that resort and move to Texas to oversee the submarine theater's creation. The Gainesville, Florida, company of Ebaugh and Goethe designed the theater, floating stage, diving tower, and various other structures. The John Broad Construction Company of Austin was the general contractor, and Tips Engine Works of Austin was the subcontractor and fabricated the theater's steel parts. The theater and supporting pontoons were produced in Austin and transported to San Marcos, where final assembly was completed. Russell saw the entire process through to its successful completion, and he became general manager of Aquarena, a position he would hold until Paul Rogers' death in 1965, at which time Russell succeeded Rogers as Aquarena's president. A significant bonus for Aquarena accompanied Russell to Texas. His wife, Margaret, was a swimmer, trainer, and choreographer for the underwater show at Weeki Wachee Springs, and her expertise was to prove invaluable to Aquarena's new venture. (Courtesy Carole McCarley.)

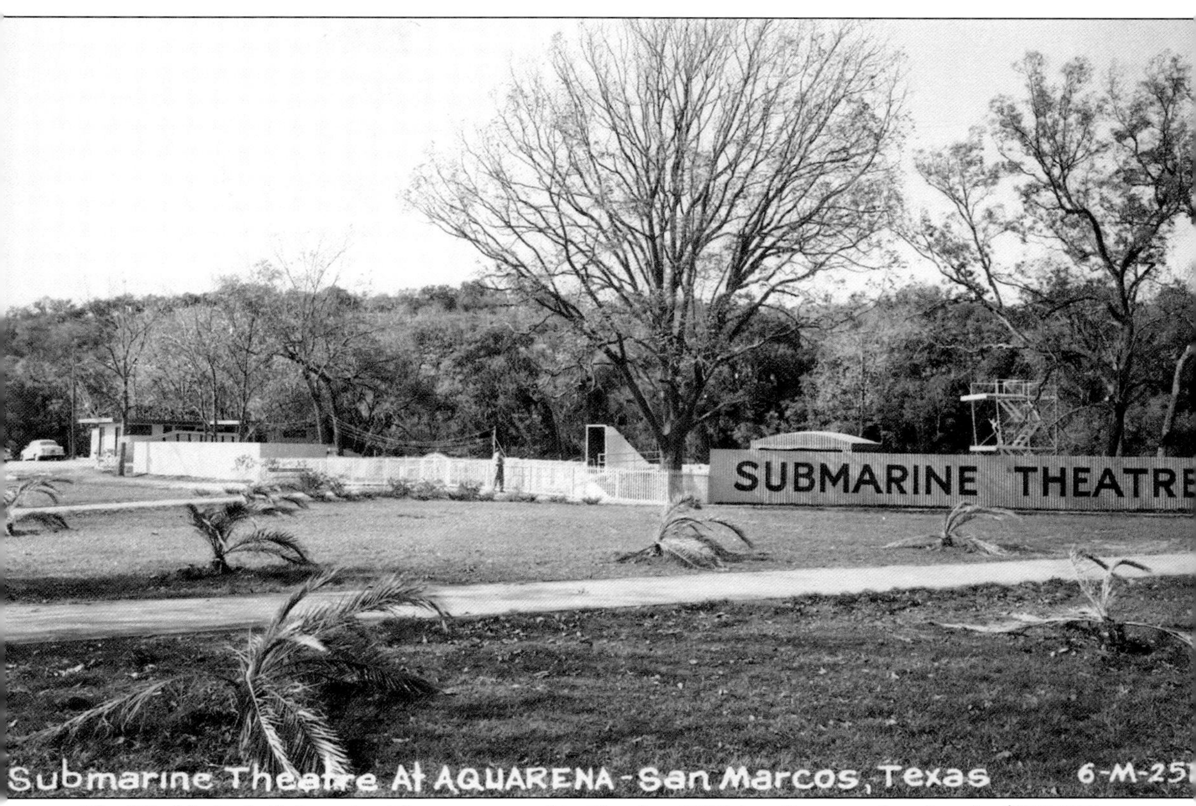

The World's Only Submarine Theater opened in October 1950, just five months after the $130,000 project was begun. The first sight greeting visitors was the theater's exterior, principally made of Cabin Creek ledgestone and corrugated transite painted green and brown to represent the water and the nearby trees. Guests entered the walkway through the opening shown in the center of the photograph. The diving platform from which performers entertained guests can be seen behind the theater's sign. Regardless of the weather, swimmers performed every day of the year except Christmas day.

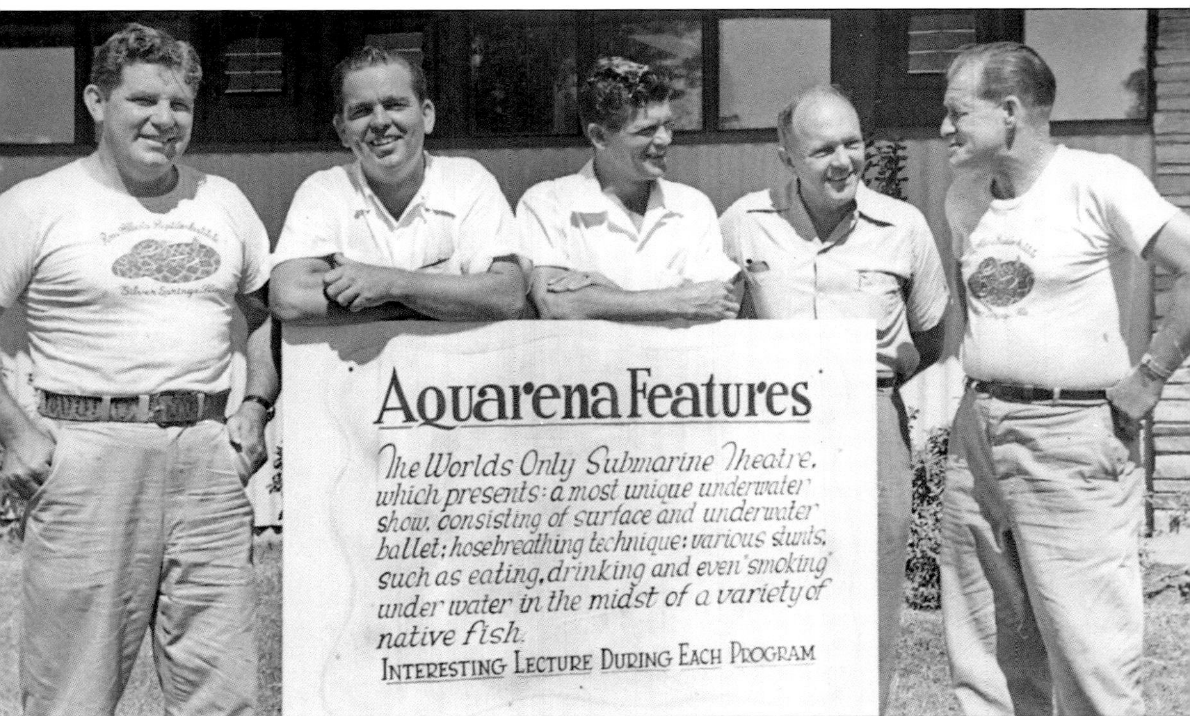

The smiles on these men's faces reflect pride and, no doubt, relief, that the project was successfully completed. The "lecture" touted by the sign consisted of explanations of the theater's ballast system, the performers' breathing techniques, and the various fish varieties spectators might see. Pictured are, from left to right, Ross Allen (famed reptile expert and understudy to Johnny Weissmuller in his *Tarzan* films), Don Russell (Aquarena general manager), Bush Ewing, Paul Rogers (Aquarena owner and president), and unidentified. (Courtesy SMHCC-San Marcos Public Library.)

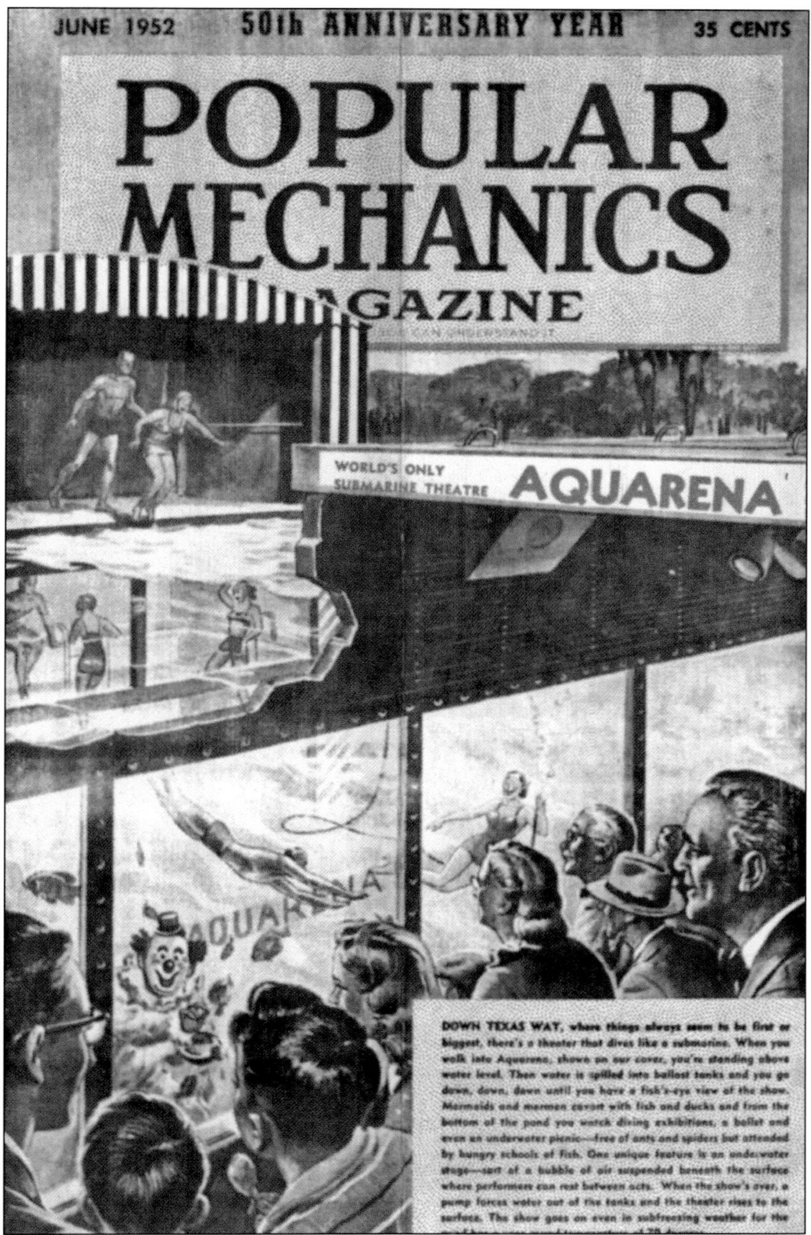

The cover story of the June 1952 issue of *Popular Mechanics* magazine paid tribute to the engineering marvel that was the submarine theater. The original theater was 80 feet long, 7 feet wide, and 14 feet deep. It was comprised of 50 tons of steel, 20 tons of concrete, and 1 ton of special, extra strong glass, and 15,500 gallons of water were required to submerge the theater to its proper depth of 42 inches. The theater submerged when water was permitted to flood its ballast tanks, removing the buoyancy equal to their displacement of water. It was raised by pumping the water out of the ballast tanks, thus restoring the buoyancy. The theater floated in the water at all times and was in reality a very rigid ship, according to the consulting engineers. General contractor John Broad noted that one of the challenges was constructing a subsurface fence, extending below the surface for 20 feet and above the surface for 6 feet. Broad hired only experienced World War II ship welders for the extensive welding work.

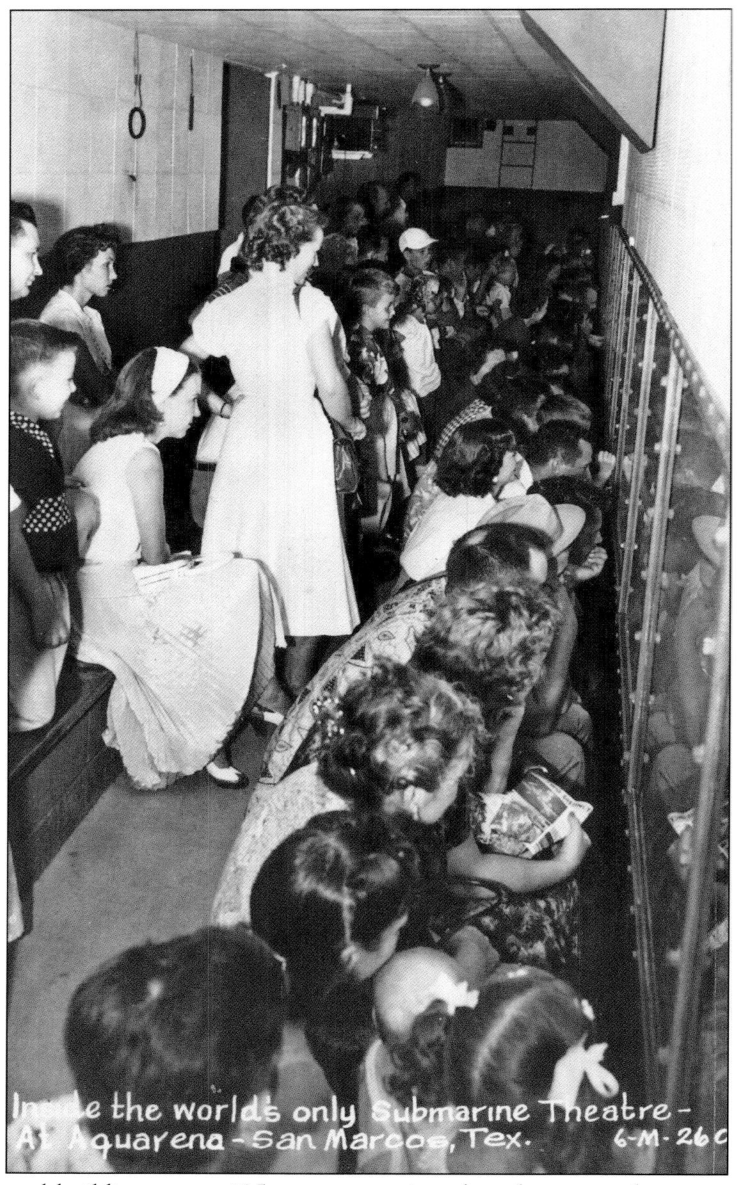

From the all-steel building, up to 125 spectators viewed performances by aquatic actors. An early brochure promised "a variety of water routines that constantly amaze visitors," including performances by "skillfully trained California sea lions and talented Aquamaids." The sea lions did not remain a feature of the shows for long. However, the Aquamaids, beautiful girls performing underwater ballet and even consuming underwater picnics, were favorites throughout the theater's existence. As the theater submerged, the audience watched the sea lions and performances from a high diving tower above the surface. Once the windows were completely under water, viewers were treated to a performance by Aquamaids as well as costumed clowns. A two-way amplifier system enabled the theater announcer and audience to maintain contact with the underwater stage, a small building that provided air and comfort for swimmers who stood 10 feet below the surface when inside. Although the submarine itself was submerged, the entrance always remained above the water. Visitors could relax and watch the show, knowing that they could exit the theater onto dry land any time they wished.

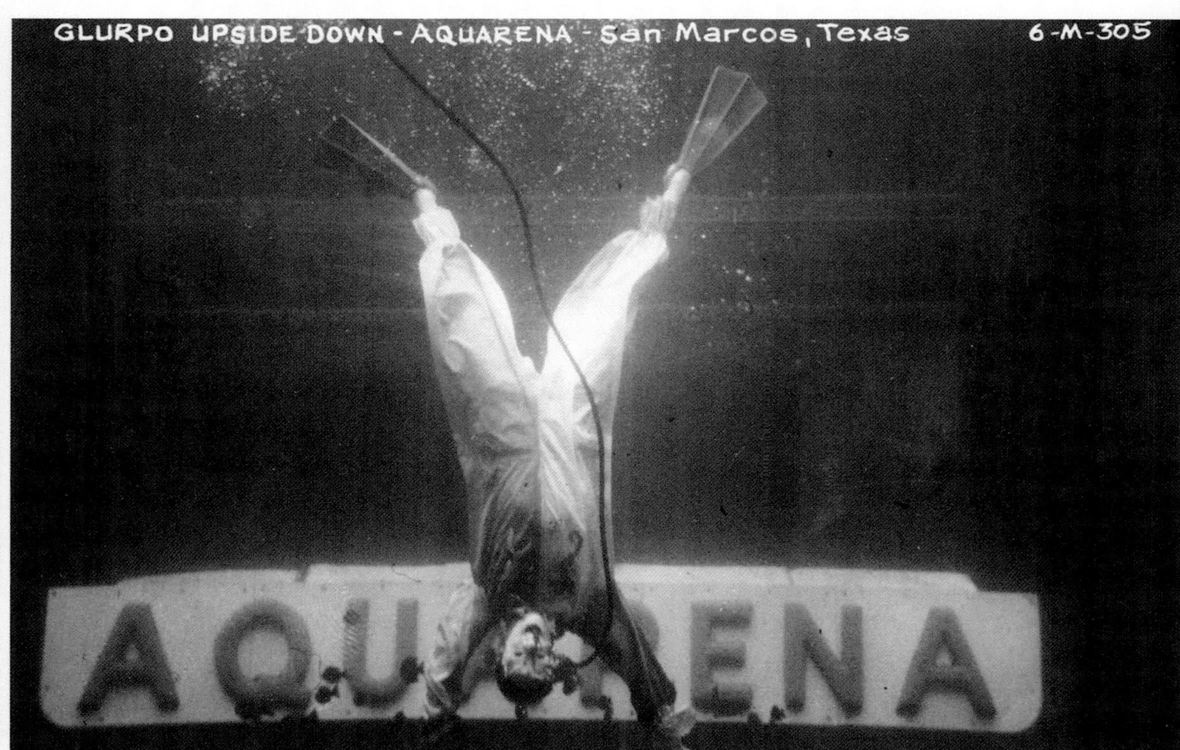

In this postcard, Glurpo the clown, always an audience favorite, poses upside down in front of the underwater stage. Supported by concealed pontoons, the stage was built of steel, glass, and wood. Thirty feet from the theater, it served as an underwater breathing station for performers. Air pressure supplied by two compressors forced the water level downward within a special compartment where performers could wait between acts without having to ascend to the surface. Once performers were in the underwater arena, they breathed compressed air carried by long rubber hoses as necessary during their routines. However, they were trained to perform for at least two minutes without having to take a "sip" of air. Glurpo's air hose can clearly be seen in the photograph, as can a school of the numerous fish that were welcome participants in every performance, awaiting handfuls of fish food courtesy of the Aquamaids during the underwater picnic portion of the show.

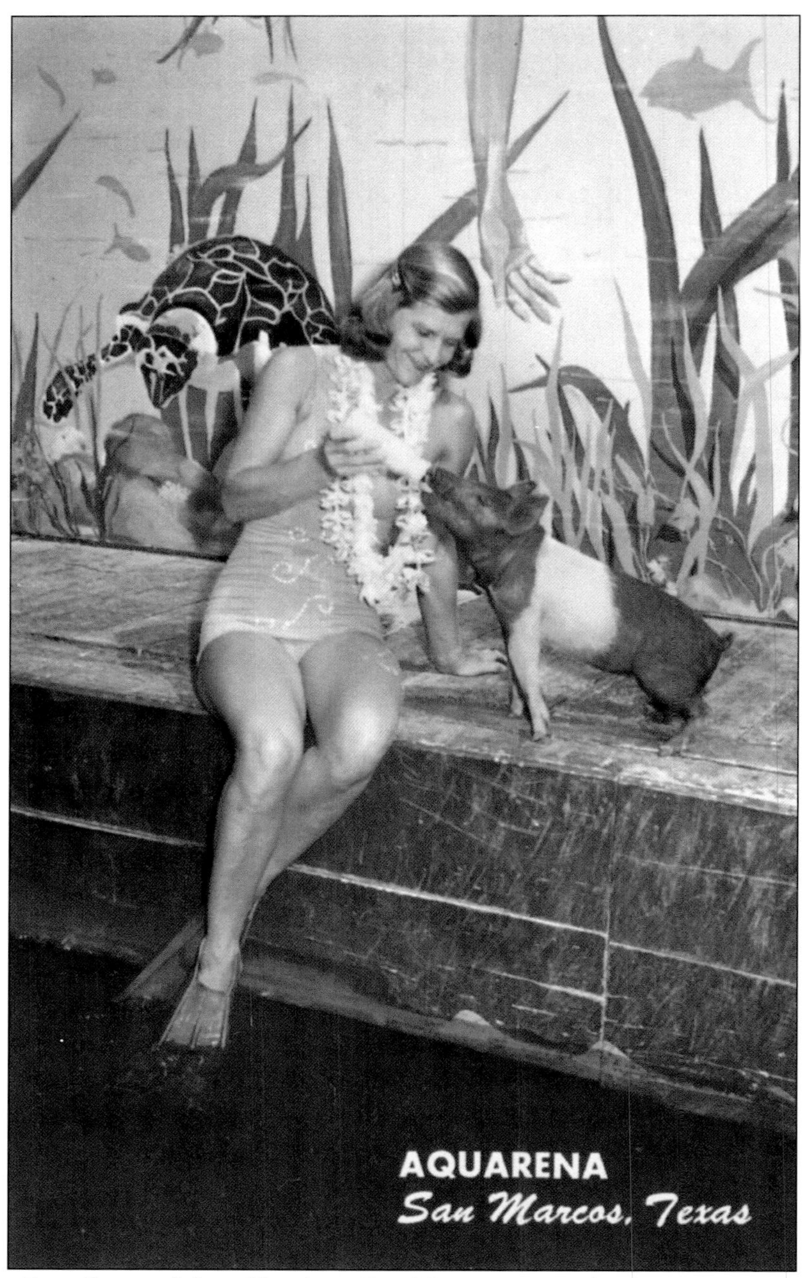

When Don Russell moved from Florida to San Marcos to join the Aquarena team as general manager, his talented wife, Margaret, accompanied him. Margaret Russell had been an instructor and performer at Weeki Wachee Springs and had served as the underwater double for actress Ann Blyth in her role as a mermaid in the 1948 film *Mr. Peabody and the Mermaid*, which was filmed there. Russell's talents were invaluable to Aquarena. She created the submarine theater show, training performers in underwater ballet and in the art of breathing, eating, and drinking under water. Russell once speculated that between her tenure at Weeki Wachee Springs and her career at Aquarena, she had spent at least three years of her life under water. In this photograph, Russell trains Missy the Pig for her role in the submarine theater show. Aquarena's swimming pigs became widely known for their unusual performances.

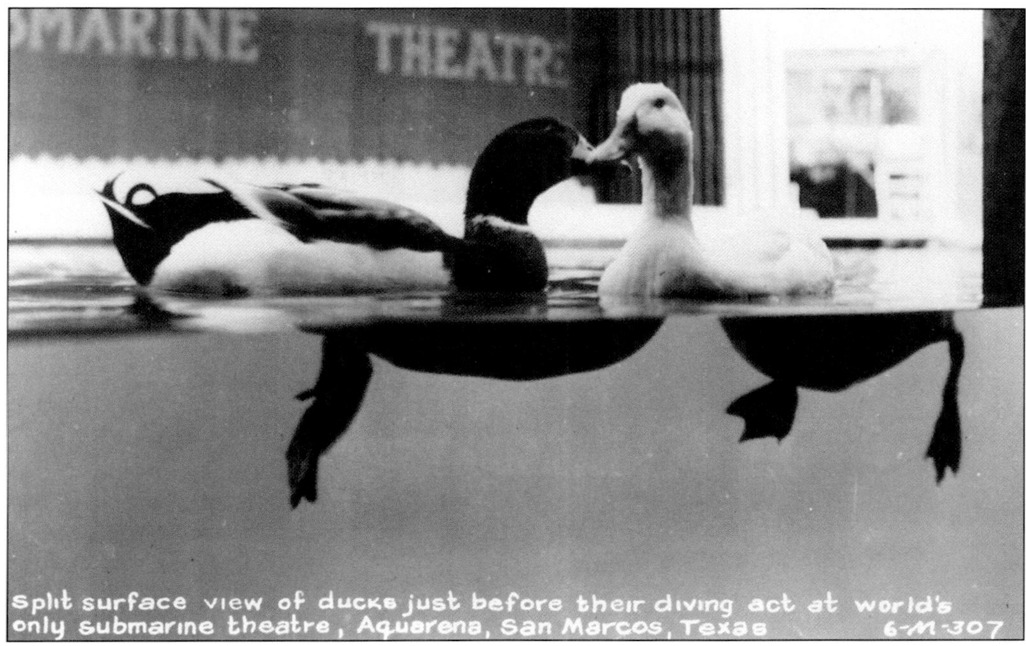

As audience members took their seats in the theater, the windows were above the water, and the outdoor stage was visible. To entertain viewers as the submarine slowly submerged, two or three Aquamaids performed a synchronized surface ballet routine. This was also the portion of the show in which the swimming pigs made their appearance. As the water level rose on the windows, audiences were treated to a split surface view, as seen in the above photograph. The mallard ducks that inhabited the theater area could be seen from both above and below the water's surface, and the effect was of top and bottom halves that did not quite match up. When a performer began throwing corn into the water, the ducks appeared to compete to see which one could dive the deepest in search of a snack.

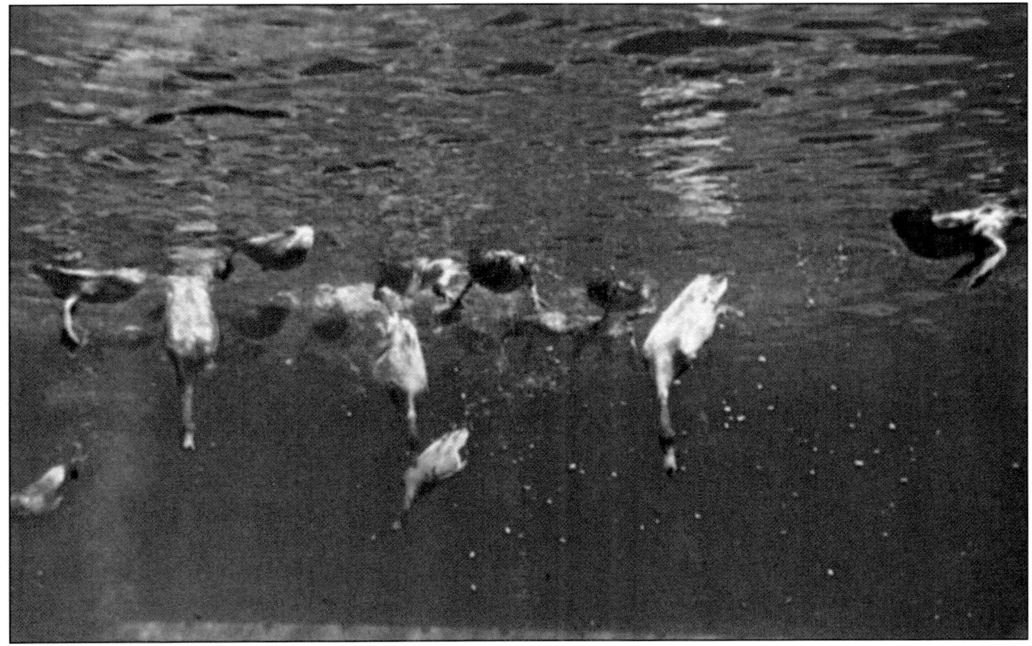

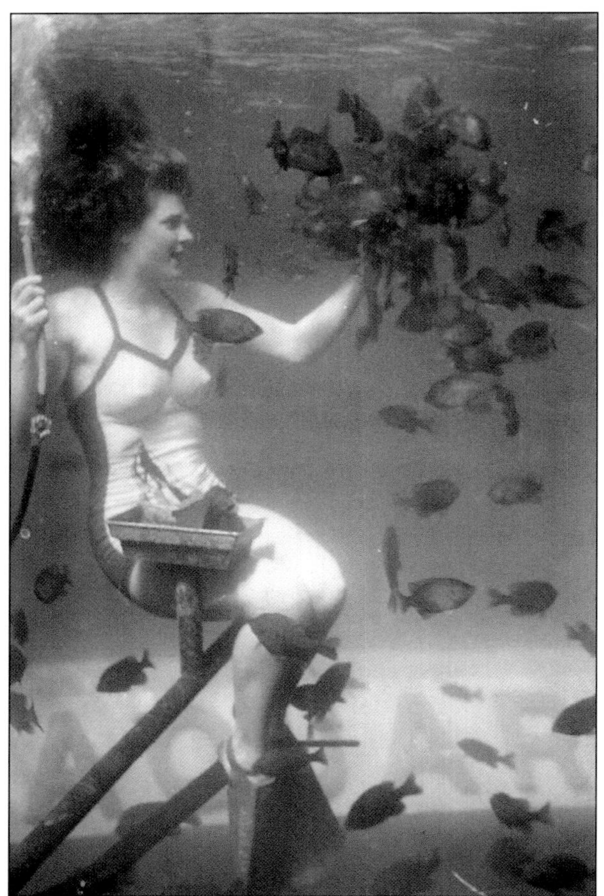

Picnics invariably attract pests, and the underwater picnic in the photograph at left of Aquamaid Margaret Russell is no exception. Underwater picnics were a highlight of the submarine theater performances. At the beginning of each picnic, Aquamaids generously fed the aquatic intruders a handful of fish food before shooing them away with a friendly burst of air from their hoses. Then the Aquamaids entertained viewers by eating celery (first sprinkling it with salt) and drinking soft drinks. In the photograph below, an Aquamaid enjoys a refreshing soda while perched at a picnic table surrounded by a crowd of fascinated underwater friends. (Left, courtesy SMHCC-San Marcos Public Library.)

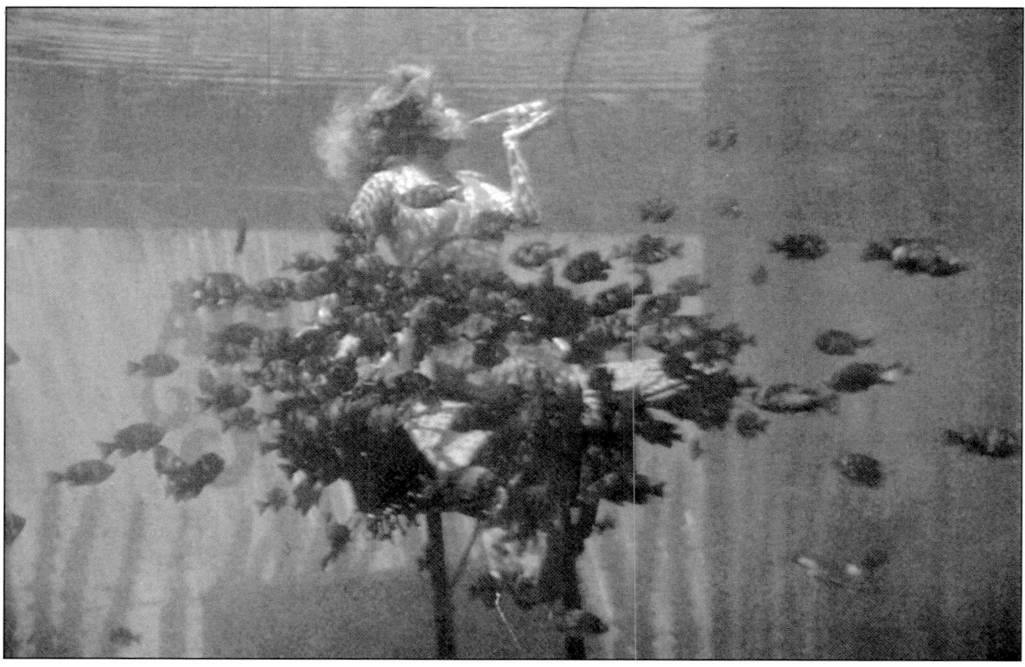

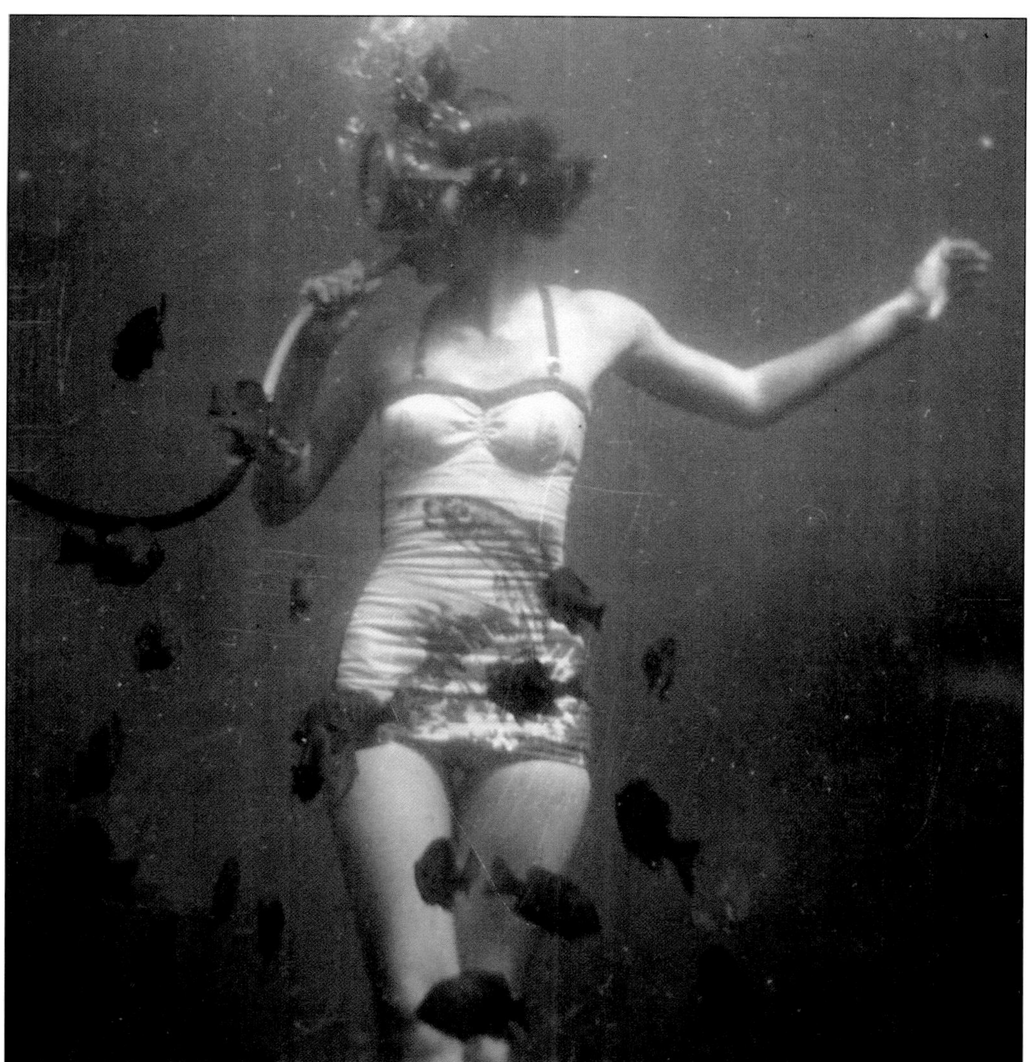

Although Aquamaids performed graceful dance routines with no apparent effort, it took eight weeks of training in breath control to learn how to remain at a given depth without rising or sinking. Buoyancy demonstrations were a regular feature of the shows, with performers showing the audience how they maintained a constant underwater position simply by controlling their breathing. Aquamaid Shirley Rogers, pictured here during a 1950s demonstration, remembers finally convincing her father, Paul Rogers, to allow his two daughters to swim together. "During one of the shows in which Jean and I swam together," she recalls, "we got the giggles for some reason and totally lost control. When you laugh underwater, you expel all your air, which causes you to sink to the bottom. The announcer was desperately trying to explain to the audience how we maintained a level position in the water, and there we were laughing uncontrollably at the bottom of the show area. We finally managed to regain our composure and finish the show, but needless to say, we were never allowed to perform together again."

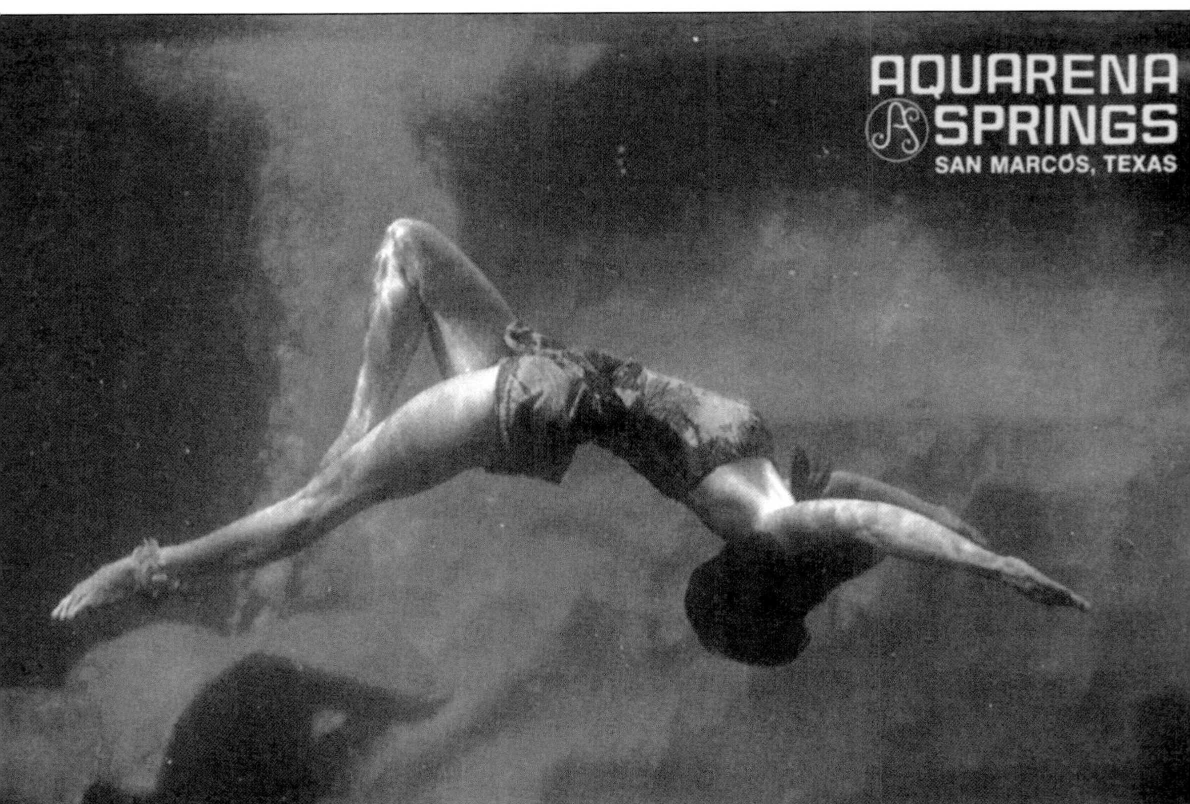

This Aquamaid's pose represents one of the signature images of Aquarena Springs. The focal point of every submarine theater performance was the graceful synchronized underwater ballet performed by two or three Aquamaids. Almost all the Aquamaids were students from the nearby Southwest Texas State Teachers College (rechristened Southwest Texas State College in 1959, Southwest Texas State University in 1969, and Texas State University in 2003). Aquamaids, and their male clown counterparts, spent as much as three hours a day under water. The 45-minute shows were presented every day of the year except for Christmas day. The constant year-round water temperature of approximately 70 degrees allowed performers to transition between heated dressing rooms and the water without discomfort from low temperatures outside. Among requirements for a professional mermaid were good looks, character references, and the ability to hold her breath for at least two minutes.

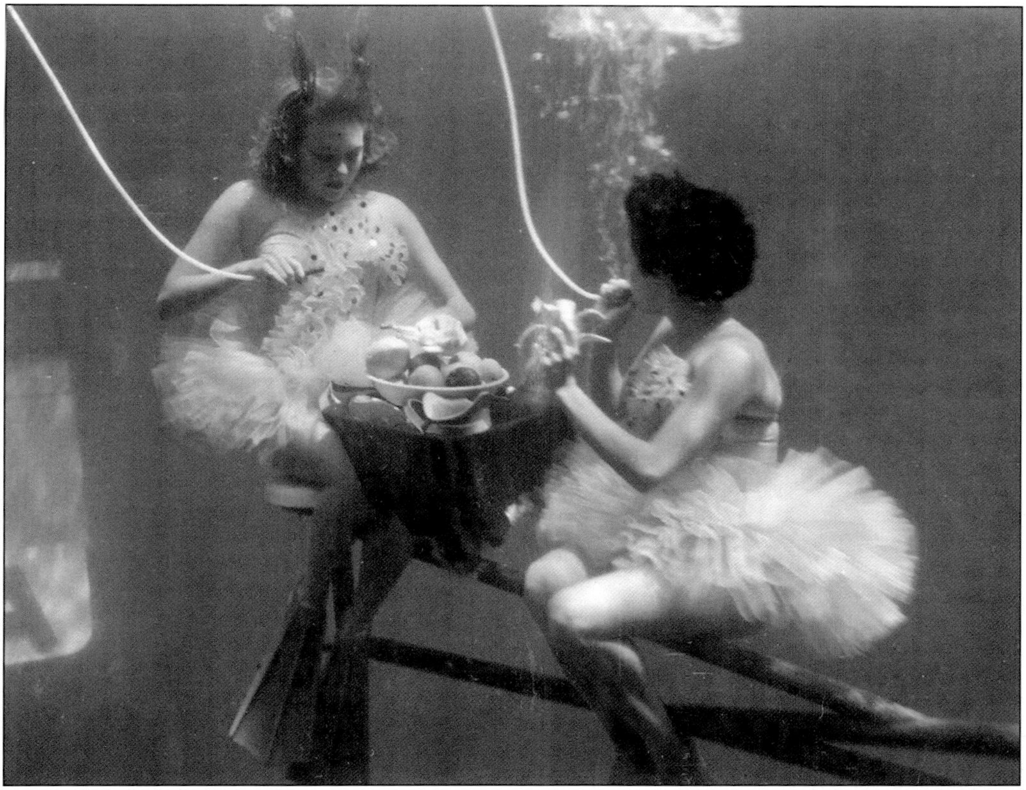

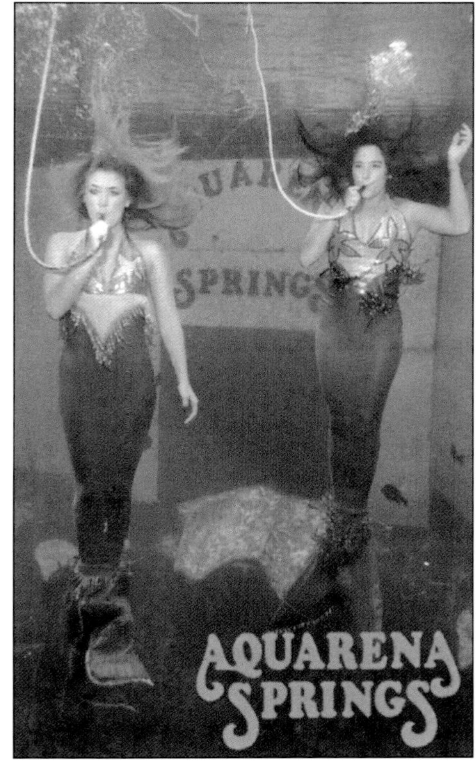

These two photographs show the metamorphosis of the Aquamaids' costumes over four decades. There were many variations between the costumes in the 1955 photograph (above) and the postcard from the early 1990s. Nevertheless, there were constants that kept audiences returning to the submarine theater. The underwater picnics remained largely the same, although the bowl of fruit in the above photograph would give way to a more modest stalk of celery in later years. Aquamaids continued to rely on their breathing hoses. In the unlikely event that an air hose were to fail, performers could simply surface or make a graceful underwater exit and come up in the air-filled dressing room. One proud Aquamaid declared that she would "rather die" than go to the surface during a show and would make her way to the dressing room if it became necessary. (Above, courtesy TxDOT; right, photograph by Don Anders.)

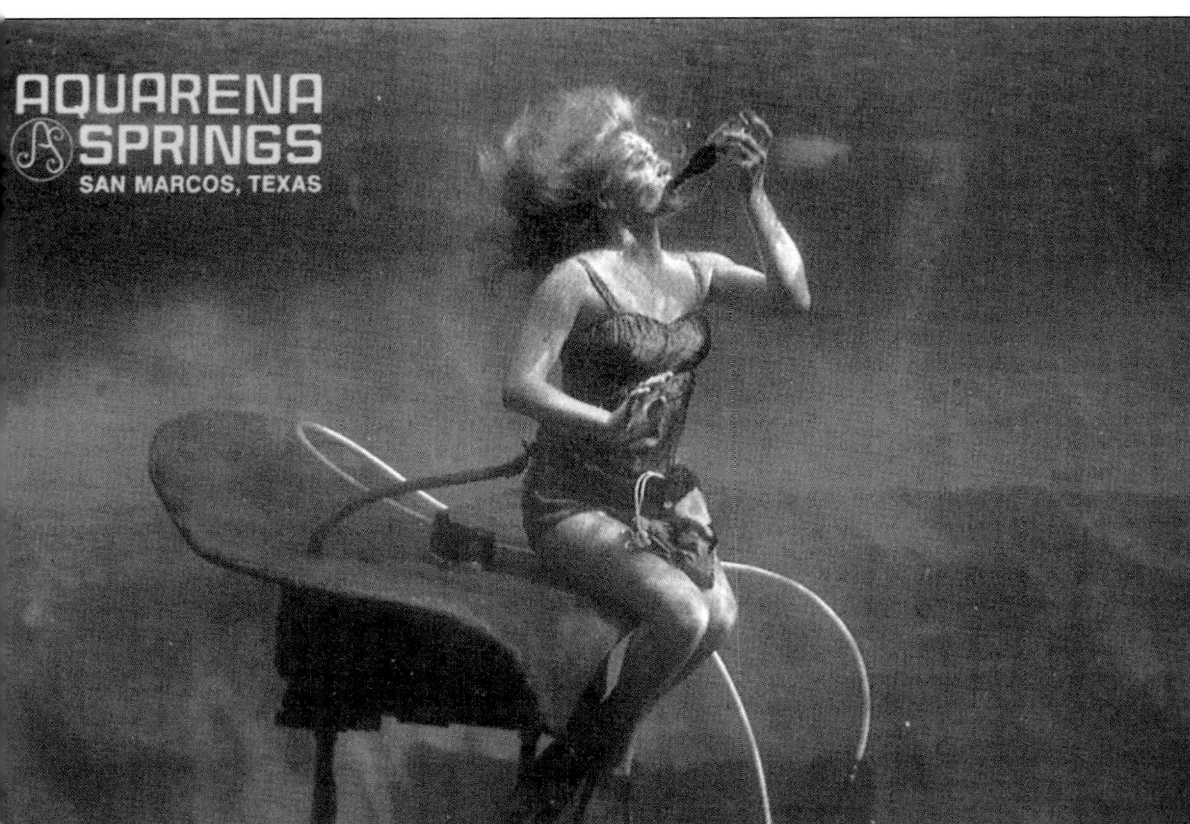

Every part of the underwater picnic was impressive, from the Aquamaids' interaction with the fish to their daintily folding their napkins in their laps and dabbing "crumbs" from their mouths. Eating celery or a piece of fruit under water took some practice, but by far the most challenging part of the subsurface picnic was drinking the soda. Trainer Margaret Russell explained that drinking was the "tricky part" and that performers always swallowed a part of the river during the process of learning. To accomplish this challenging feat, the Aquamaids removed their diving masks and took a breath from the air hose. They then exhaled into the soda bottles, which displaced the liquid into their mouths. Sometimes swimmers performed in multiple shows over the course of a day. In such cases, the "soda" in the bottles might be replaced with colored water. Underwater drinking took talent, and audiences never tired of watching this part of the show.

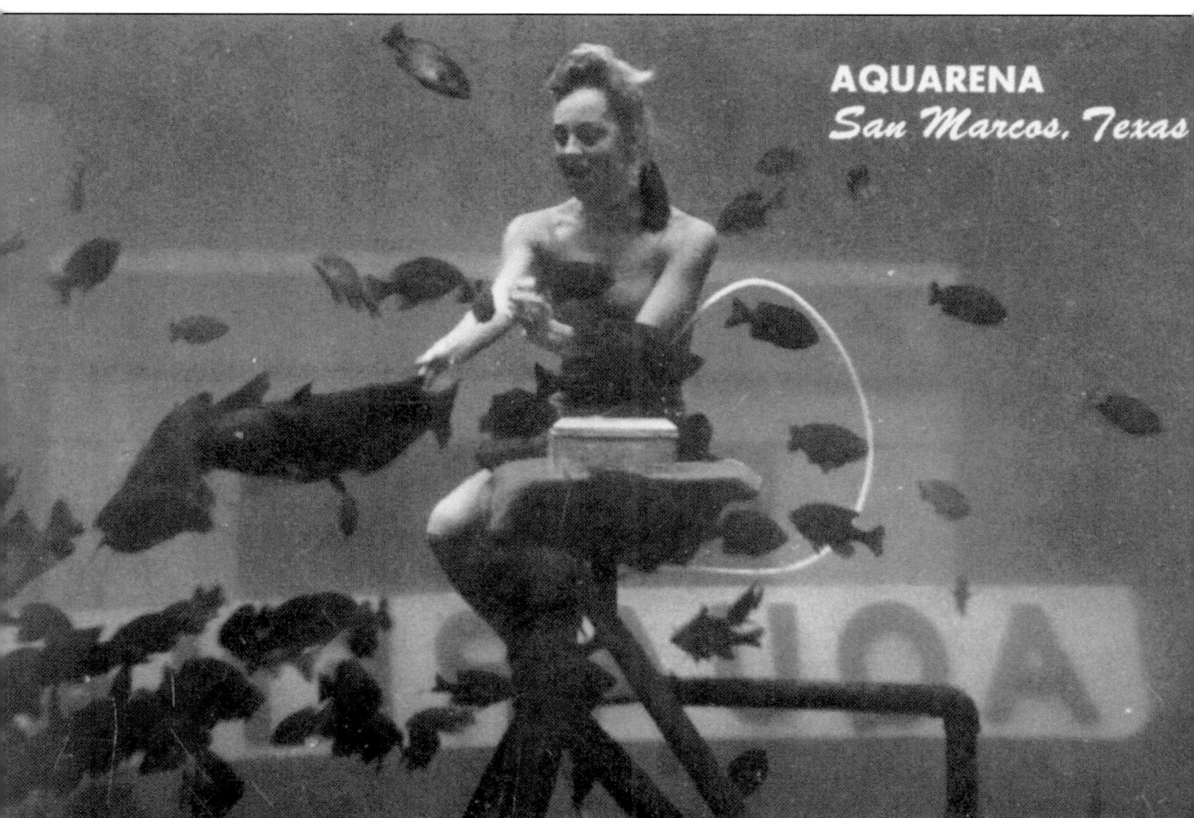

A former Aquamaid remembers the underwater picnic process: "We swam out from the underwater stage carrying our picnic basket. The first thing we did was pull out the picnic table from alongside the submarine theater so that we could sit facing the audience. The table consisted of a long pole on which was attached a stool and a little picnic table. The first thing we did after sitting on our 'perch' was to remove our face plate, take out our napkin, and spread it on our lap. Remember, we had excellent manners and made sure to wipe our mouth after taking several bites of food. Next, we took out the fish food to feed the fish. Immediately, swarms of them came out of nowhere. These fish were mostly small blue gill perch, but occasionally one or two of the large catfish would appear, giving the audience a thrill."

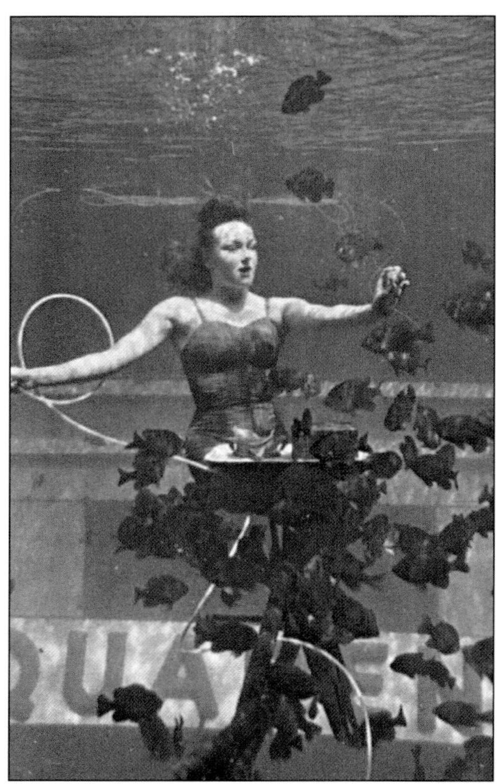

The picnic snacks changed over time. An Aquamaid recalls: "We ate everything from plums, peaches, and bananas to Hershey bars. In the case of the candy bars, we would peel the paper off the bars and then neatly store the wrapper inside our picnic basket. The cold water kept the Hershey bars nice and firm. In the long run, celery became the preferred and most practical food to eat under water. After eating our snack, we took out our bottle opener and opened our soda, making sure that we kept our thumb on top of the bottle to keep the water out and the soda in. After each sip, the thumb had to be immediately replaced atop the bottle so the drink would not be diluted." (Left, photograph by Gene Aiken.)

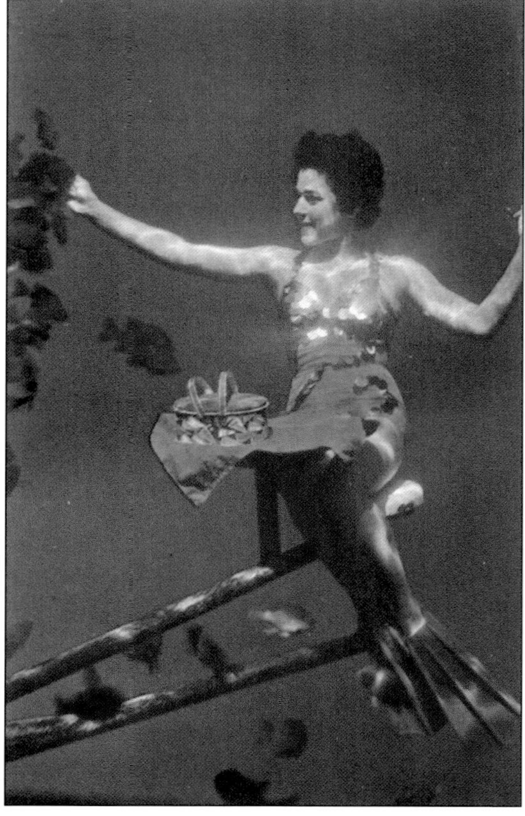

Along with the glass bottom boats, the submarine theater was the centerpiece of Aquarena Springs, and the Aquamaids were the centerpiece of the underwater shows. The mermaid became an iconic symbol of Aquarena, adorning billboards and brochures. The postcard at right shows an image of a mermaid intended to typify "the welcome spirit of Aquarena, where friendliness is the emphasis." The artwork on the brochure reflects the modern design of the 1970s. Mermaids could be found flanking the entrance to the submarine theater, and of course visitors were enticed by mermaid-themed items in the gift shop, from key chains to coin purses and snow globes representing the bubbly, underwater world.

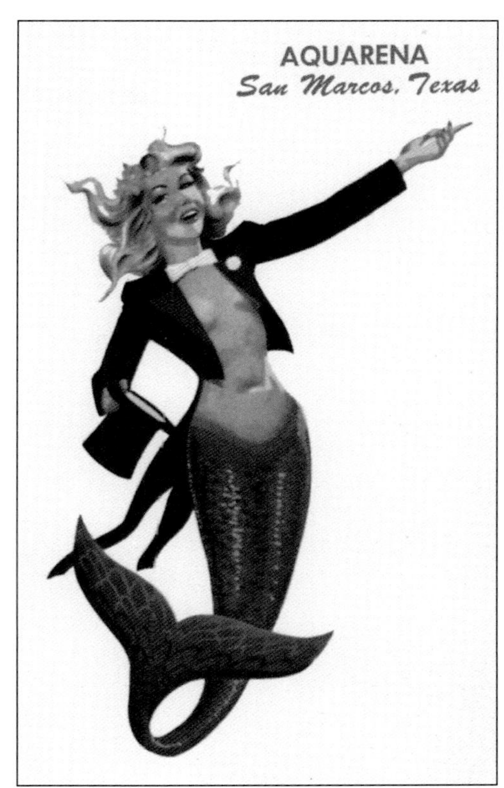

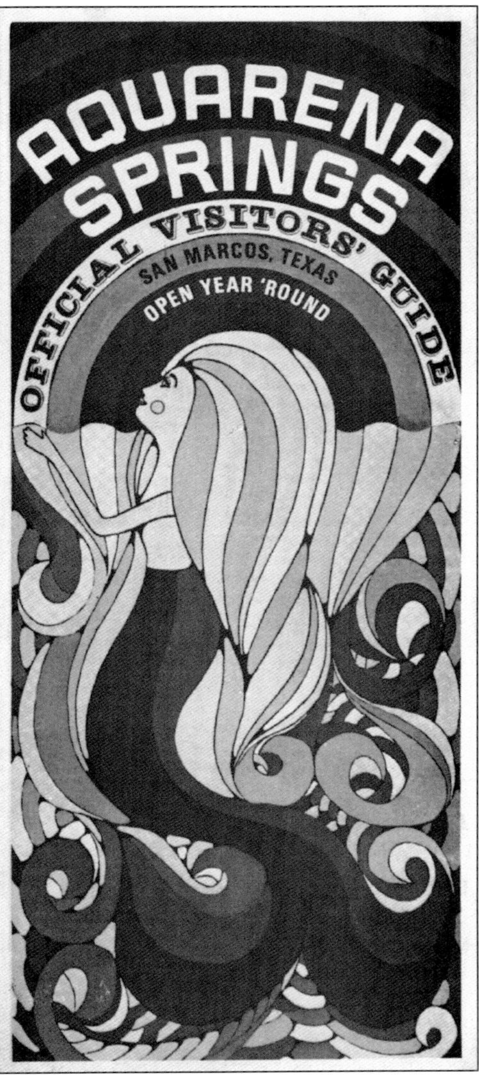

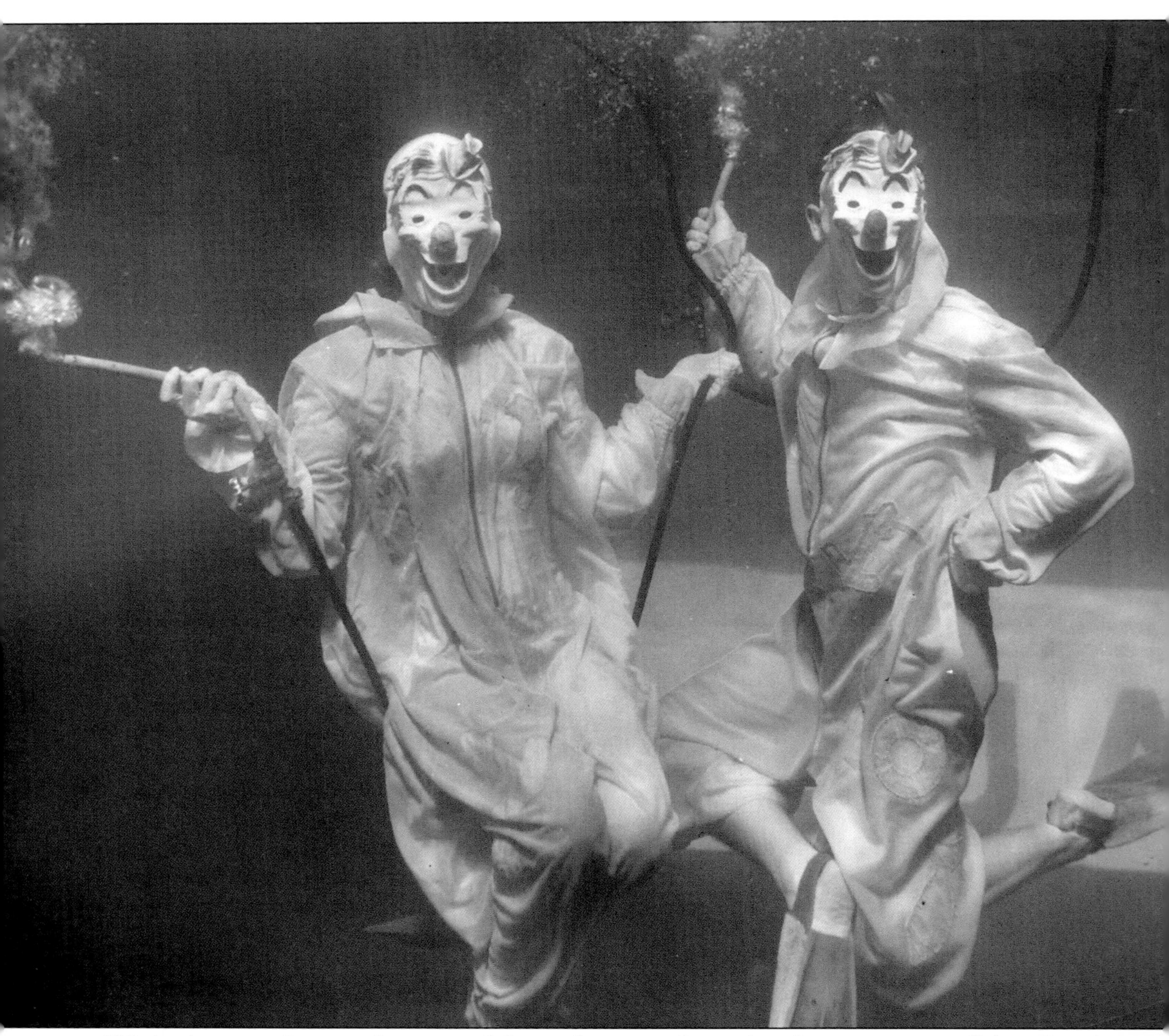

While Aquamaids were the stars of the underwater show, the clowns were a well-loved and indispensable component. From the earliest days, Glurpo the clown (sometimes accompanied by a female, Glurpette) entertained audience members of all ages. Performing as a clown required great athleticism from the swimmers, who had to maintain the same breath control required of the Aquamaids even as they made their underwater antics look effortless. Through the decades, Glurpo evolved from a traditional clown to a hapless witch doctor to a prankster from the lost island of Atlantis. One endearing quality of all the clowns was their enthusiastic interaction with audience members, from flirting with pretty women in the crowd to playing jokes on young spectators. Mugging for the audience, posing for pictures, and using their air hoses as swings or jump ropes were favorite pastimes of the underwater clowns. (Courtesy SMHCC-San Marcos Public Library.)

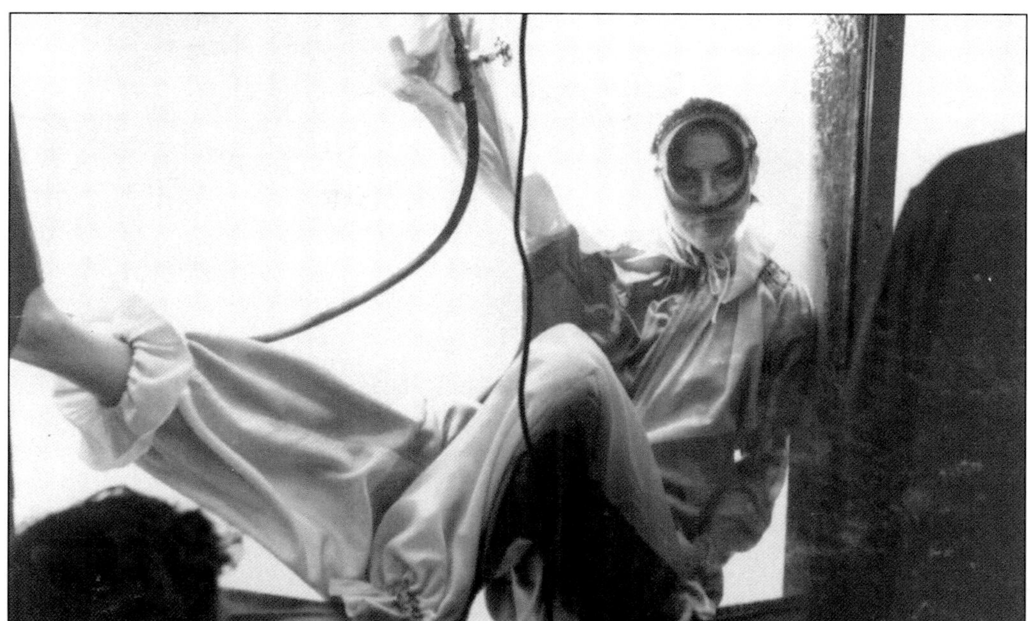

These photographs demonstrate how the clowns, in this case Glurpette, as portrayed by Shirley Rogers, liked to get "up close and personal" with the spectators. Perched just outside the submarine theater window, Glurpette is no doubt signaling her intention to amuse the audience with a display of one of her unique clown "talents," such as underwater singing, or perhaps to invite an unwitting audience member's participation in one of her practical jokes. The show's announcer acts as "translator," speaking to Glurpette through his microphone and relaying her gurgled messages to the spectators. Children of all ages enjoyed the portion of the show in which the clowns approached the windows and invited audience participation.

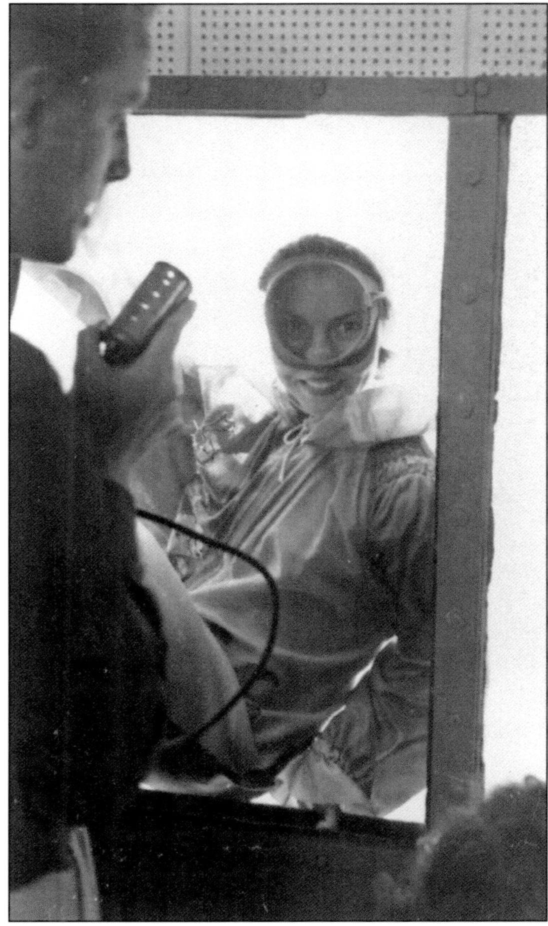

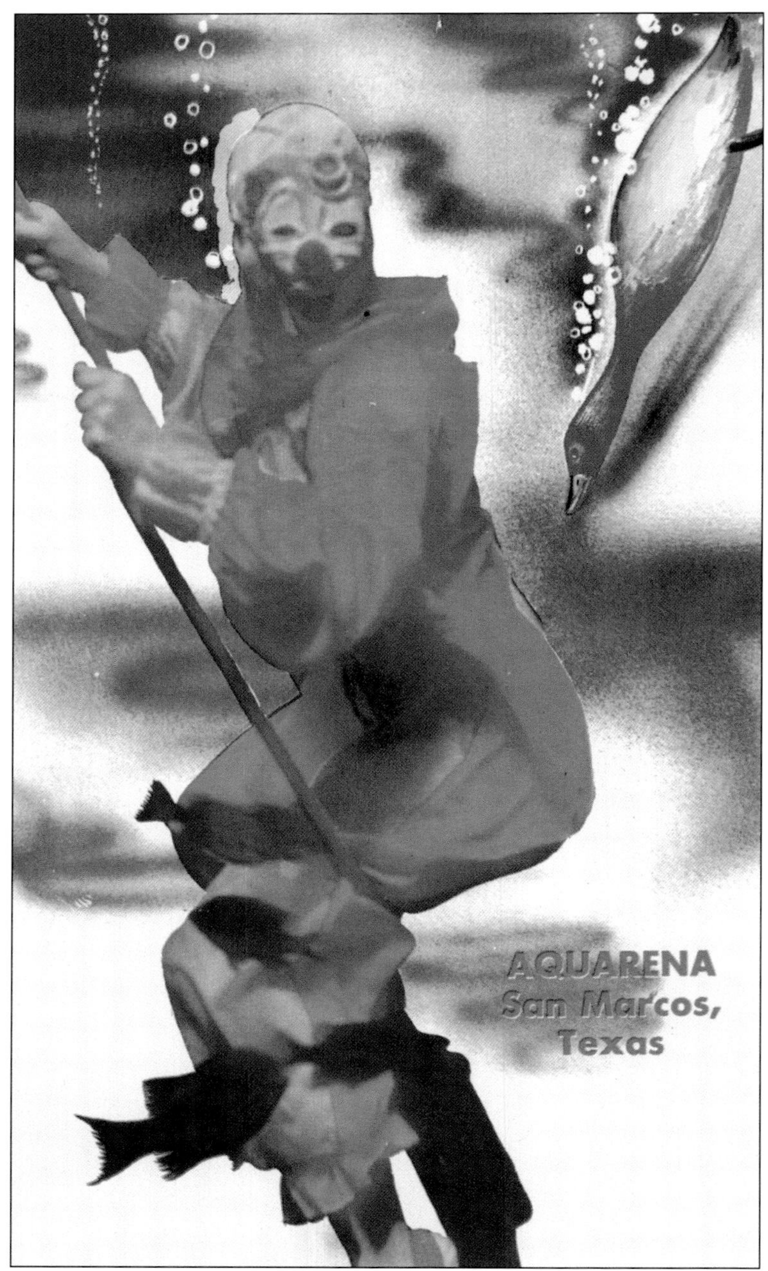

A 1960 article in *South Texan* magazine describes the submarine theater as the "center attraction and focal point for the eyes of visitors who wheel in at a rate of as many as 2,000 a day during busy seasons." The article gives most of the credit for the underwater show's success to manager Don Russell and his wife, Margaret, crediting Margaret Russell with designing the show and her husband with promoting the attraction with various publicity stunts such as an underwater wedding. The article goes on to say that Don Russell himself considered the best advertising to be the roadside billboards touting the unusual show. The billboards, featuring images such as this picture of "Glurpo, Aquarena's Famous Aquatic Clown" and one of Aquarena's famous diving ducks, lured visitors from the highway. "Children seem to find them irresistible," the article notes, "and vacationing parents quickly fall into line."

Theatrical masks worn by the clowns in the early 1950s required the swimmers to rely on physical gestures to amuse the audience. Later the clowns simply wore swimming masks that allowed them to make eye contact with the audience and to perform one of the most popular clown stunts—blowing underwater "smoke rings." Approaching the theater windows, the clowns inhaled from their air hoses and then turned face upward, exhaling ring-shaped bubbles that floated toward the surface. Usually, two clowns were blowing the rings simultaneously, each entertaining one side of the theater. Invariably, the audience members thought "their" clown was the best ring-blower. The clowns often followed this demonstration by singing a tune the audience could recognize as "I'm Forever Blowing Bubbles." Another trick was to appear to smoke under water by blowing white "smoke" from a milk-filled smoking pipe. (Below, photograph by Jack Lewis; courtesy TxDOT.)

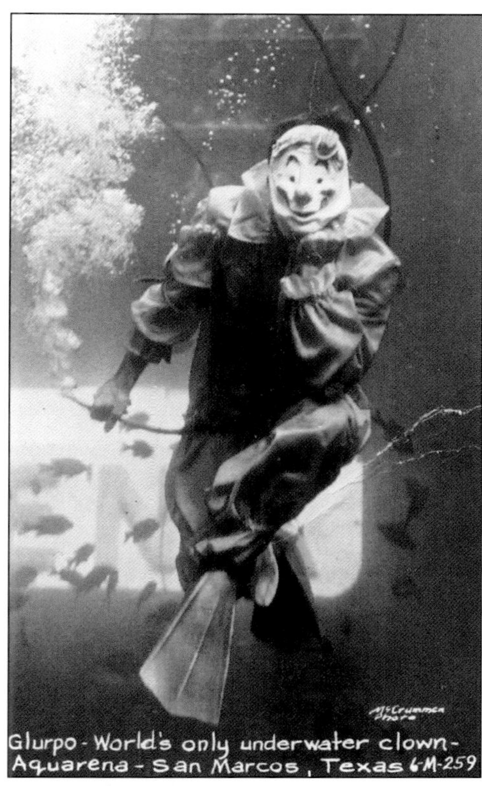

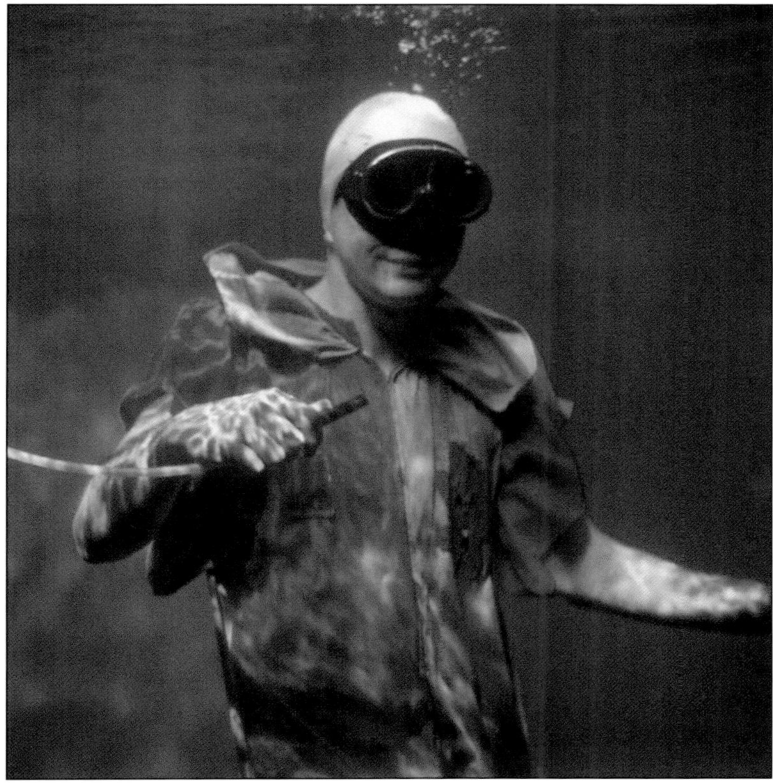

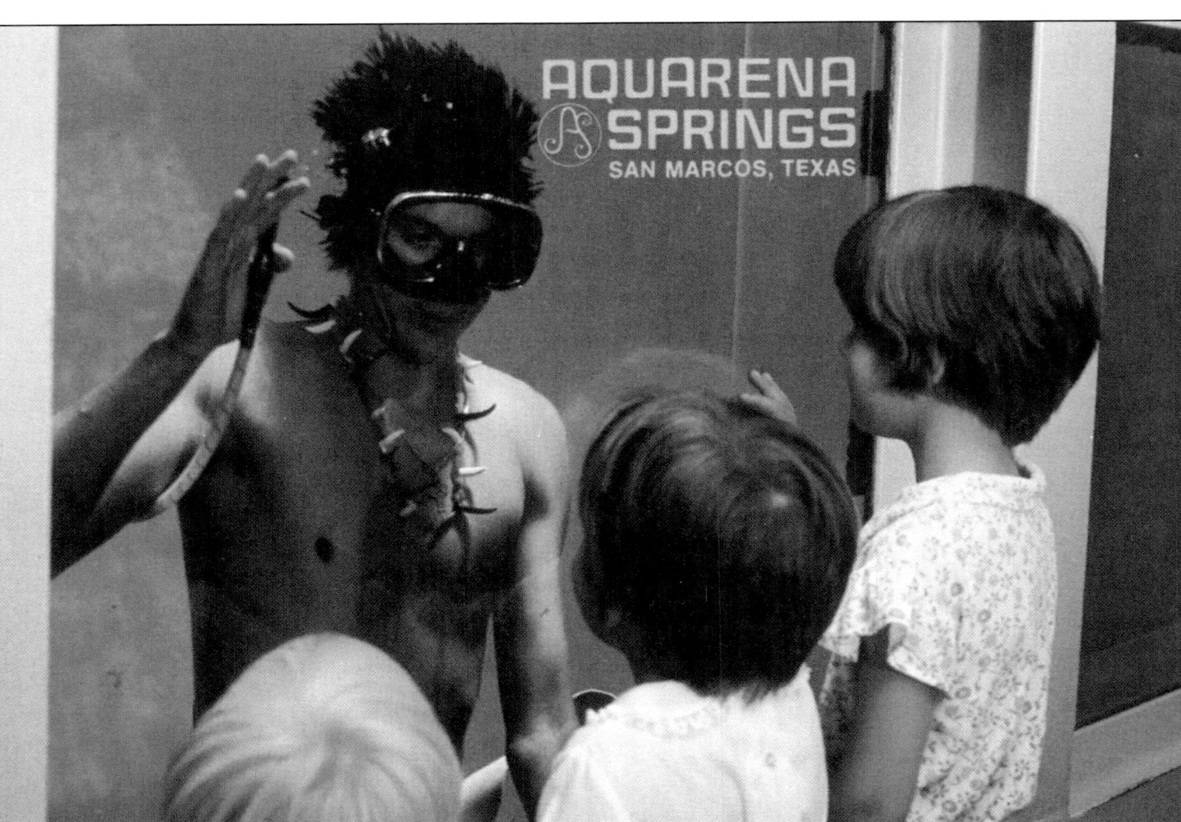

These children interact with Glurpo the inept witch doctor, an incarnation the clowns assumed in the late 1960s when the show adopted a Polynesian theme in keeping with the large fiberglass "volcano" that was added to the stage in 1967. Glurpo, whatever the costume, was always happy to wave to children and to allow them to take his picture, flexing his muscles manfully as he hammed it up for the young photographers. After posing for pictures, Glurpo would often ask permission, with the announcer translating, to take a picture of the children. Permission granted, Glurpo produced an "underwater camera" and clicked as the children smiled. The announcer would inform the children that Glurpo would develop their picture in his underwater workshop, at which point Glurpo descended, and the children heard banging from underneath the theater. Emerging with a framed "photograph" of the children, Glurpo proudly held a mirror to the theater window, and the children saw their own grinning reflections.

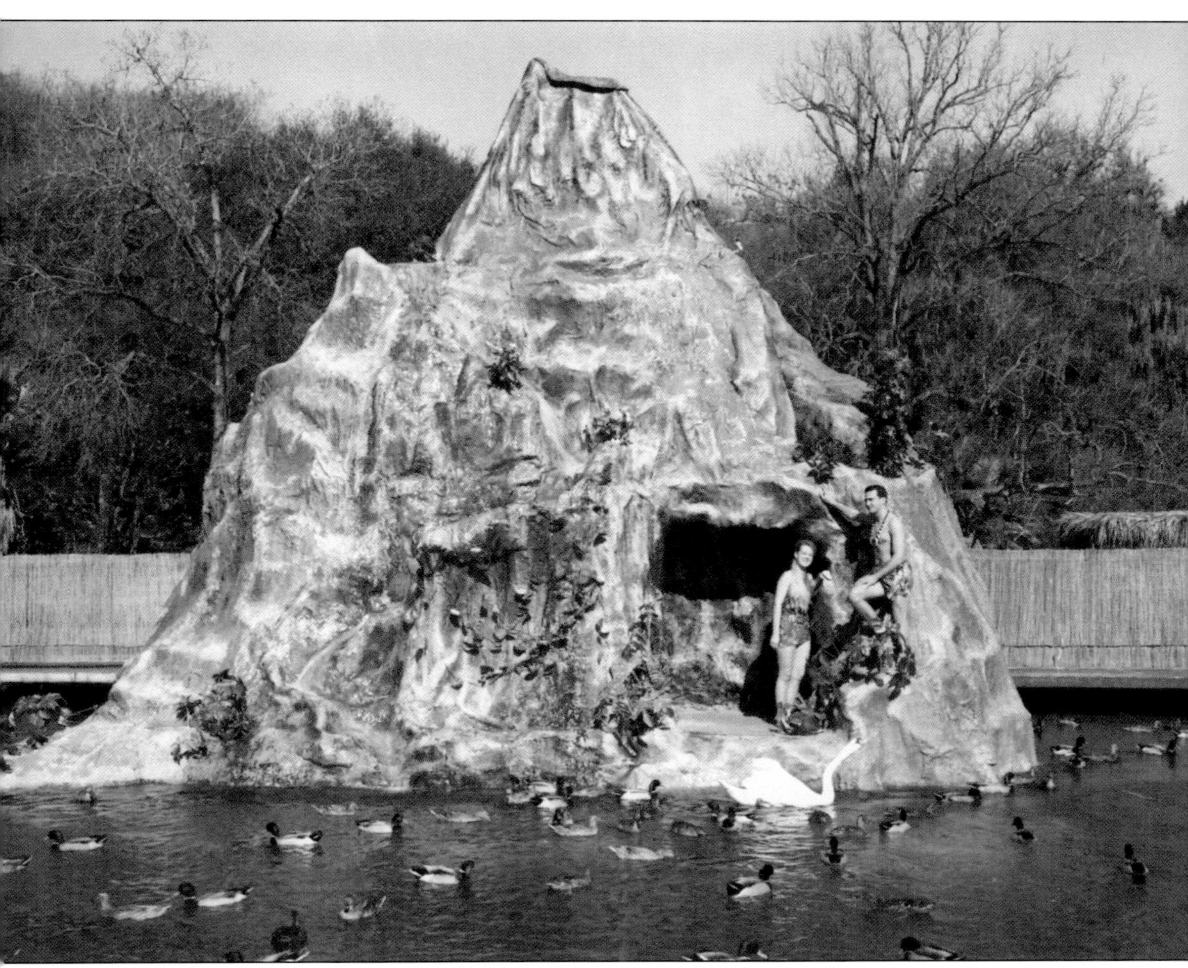

Big changes were in store for the submarine theater in 1967. Fire and sparks, a volcanic roar, and a belch of smoke now began the show after new scenery in the form of a huge volcano was added to the stage. The facade of the volcano was a piece of fiberglass that gave the appearance of pitted limestone, with a hole near the bottom that resembled a cave opening. At the time, the volcano was the largest single-pour piece of fiberglass in the world, according to Aquarena Springs general manager Don Russell. Russell remarked that every piece of the construction project was a challenge "since it's never been done before." Ducks floating on the river's surface at the show's opening now encountered native Polynesian men and women, but the ducks did not seem to mind since the "newcomers" were happy to throw them corn, just as their predecessors had done. (Photograph by Jack Lewis; courtesy TxDOT.)

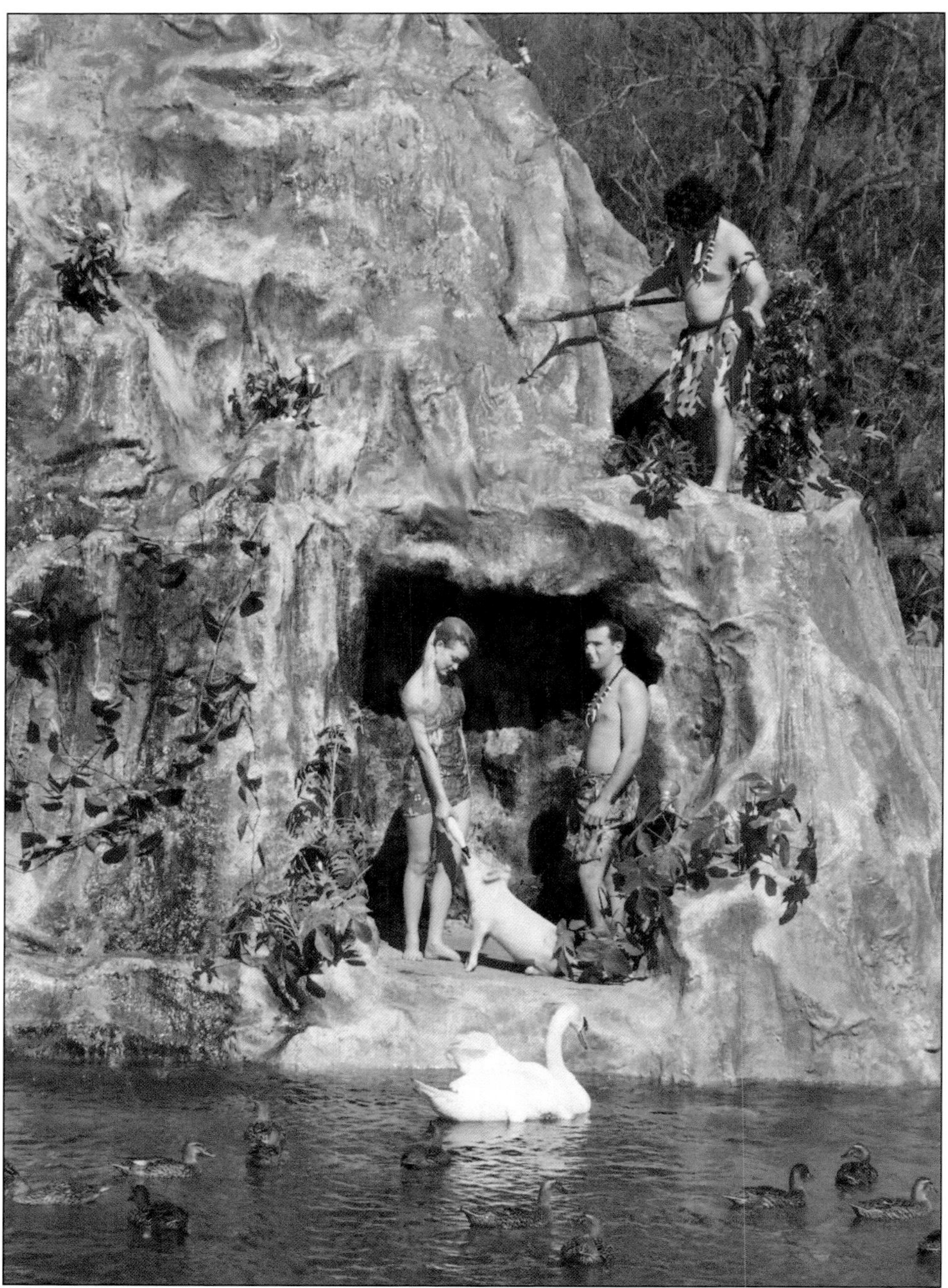

Here actors prepare to begin the Polynesian-themed underwater show. The Aquamaid feeds Ralph the swimming pig from a milk bottle. Soon she will coax Ralph into the water, where he will follow her along the surface, enticed by the bottle. The audience, still above the surface in the submarine theater, would be introduced to the story they were about to witness. According to the new script, the volcano is angry and has threatened to erupt, endangering the peaceful native village if he is not appeased. Unfortunately, the witch doctor, Glurpo, is rather bumbling, and the suspense builds as the audience wonders if the calamity can be averted. In this photograph, Glurpo stands above the cave, spear at the ready, to try to work his magic. The costumes of all the performers have been redesigned to reflect the new script. (Photograph by Jack Lewis; courtesy TxDOT.)

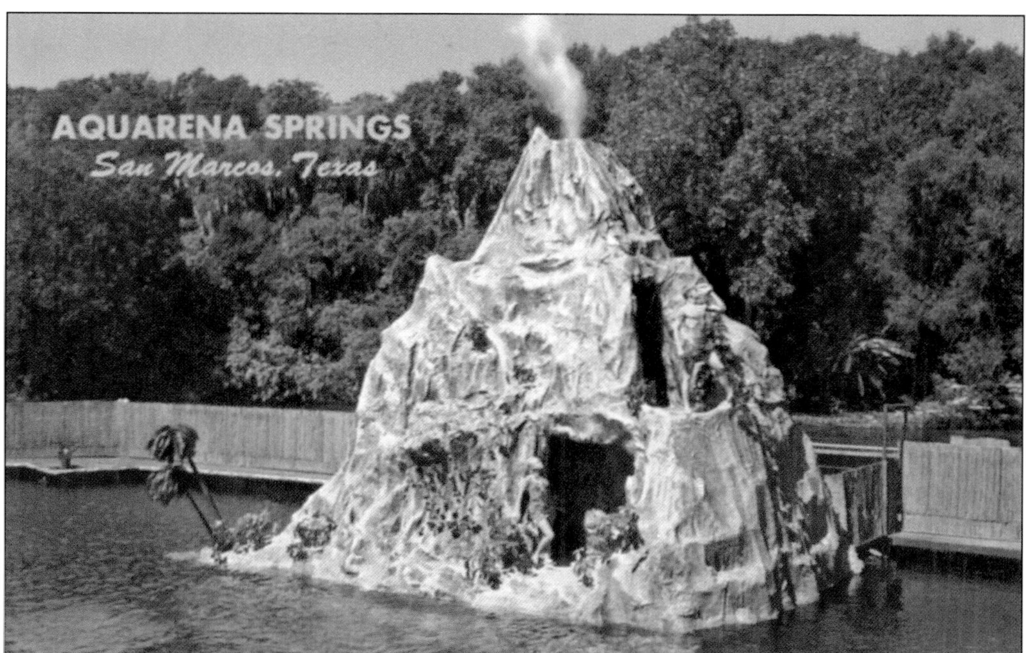

As the show opens, an ominous puff of smoke emerges from the volcano's top, and the romantic tones of the conch shell announce the beginning of another performance. Glurpo the witch doctor is poised to bring help to the native village. Artificial plants were used liberally both on the volcano structure and beneath the water. Each night, the underwater plants were raised to the surface and cleaned to prevent mold. Unique lighting effects, tape recordings, and fire and smoke flares furnished excitement on the surface before the theater began its descent. During its submersion, audiences were treated to the perennial diving ducks and to Ralph's swim across the show area. (Above, photograph by Bill Kobert.)

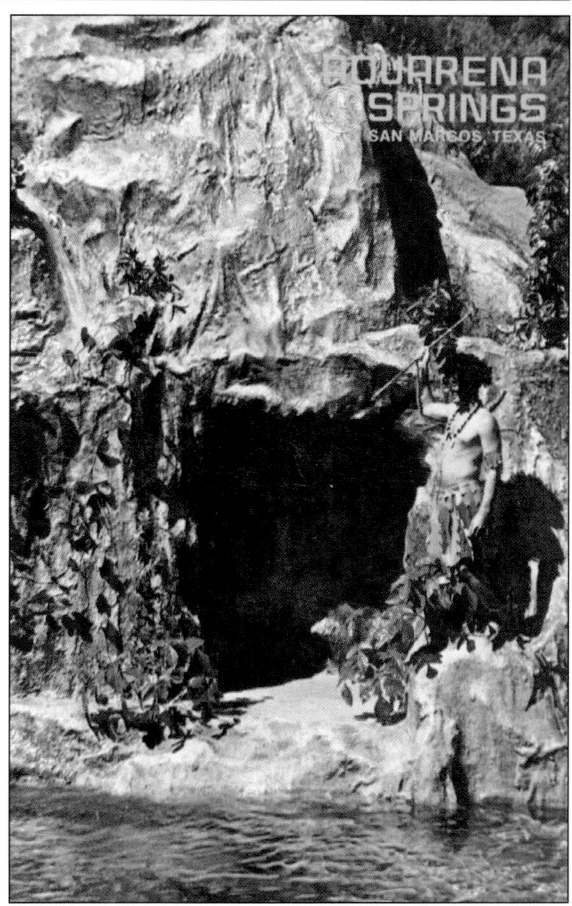

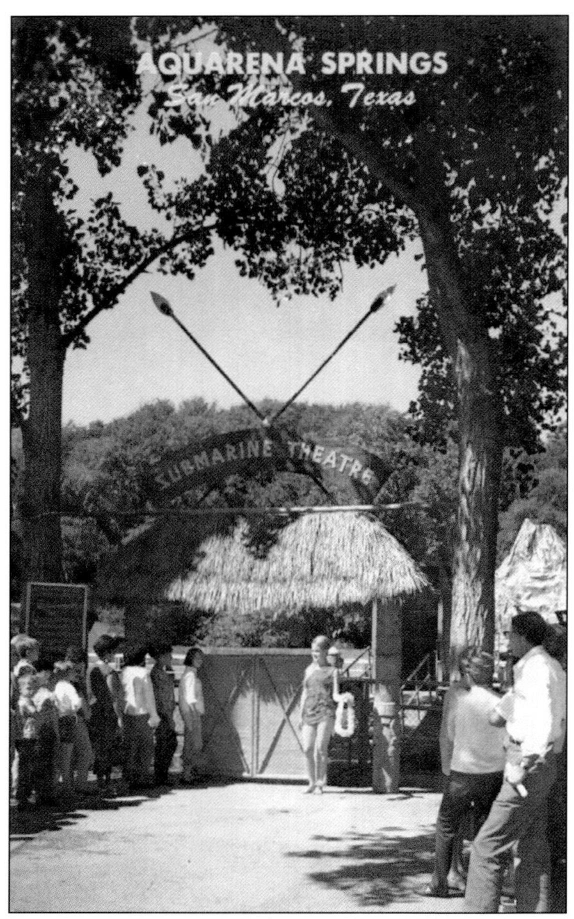

The Aquamaids were now Polynesian maidens, and the entrance that was formerly flanked by the iconic Aquarena mermaids now featured a thatched roof and crossed spears. In the photograph at left, one of the native girls greets guests as they await entrance to the theater. The volcano can be seen rising in the background. The only noticeable difference in the picnic portion of the show, pictured below, is that colorful, flowered sarongs have replaced the more traditional ballerina-inspired swimsuits, and the picnic basket now consists of brightly colored drawstring bags. No doubt the hungry fish were oblivious to the changes in costume. (Left, photograph by Bill Kobert.)

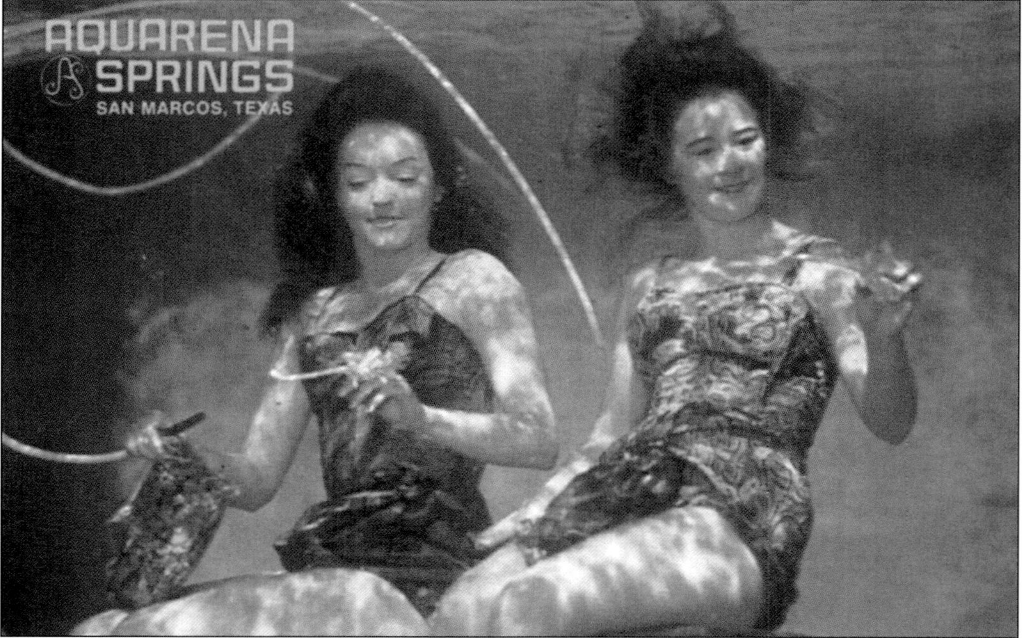

Once the theater had submerged, spectators were treated to a new underwater set that included thatched huts, underwater vegetation, and a giant clam. Dramatically, in a cloud of bubbles, a beautiful native girl erupted from the clamshell as it slowly opened and began to entertain the audience with her underwater ballet. She was soon joined by yet a second maiden for synchronized ballet. After their routines, and some good-natured taunting from Glurpo, the girls sat down for their picnic. In keeping with the Polynesian theme, the picnic became a luau and included bananas and grapes along with the traditional celery. The crowd-pleasing sodas would of course remain part of the show. By this time in its history, Aquarena Springs was drawing over half a million visitors each year. (Both photographs by Jack Lewis; courtesy TxDOT.)

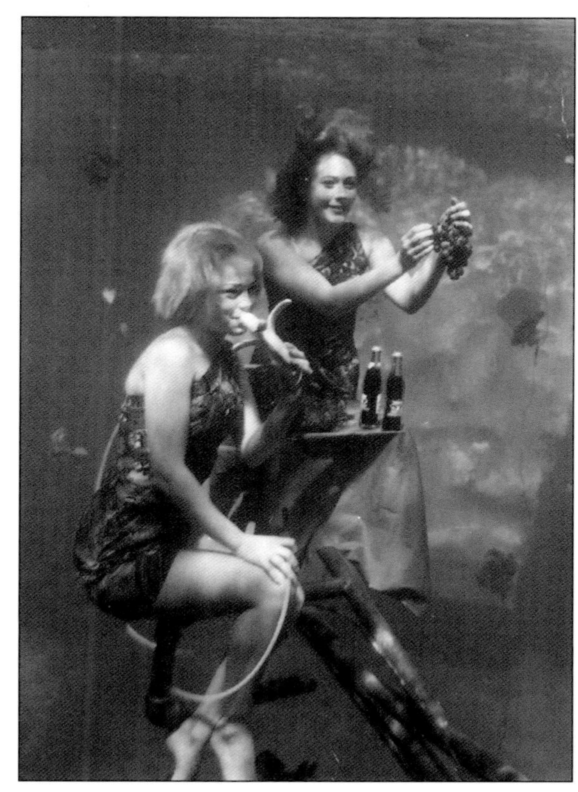

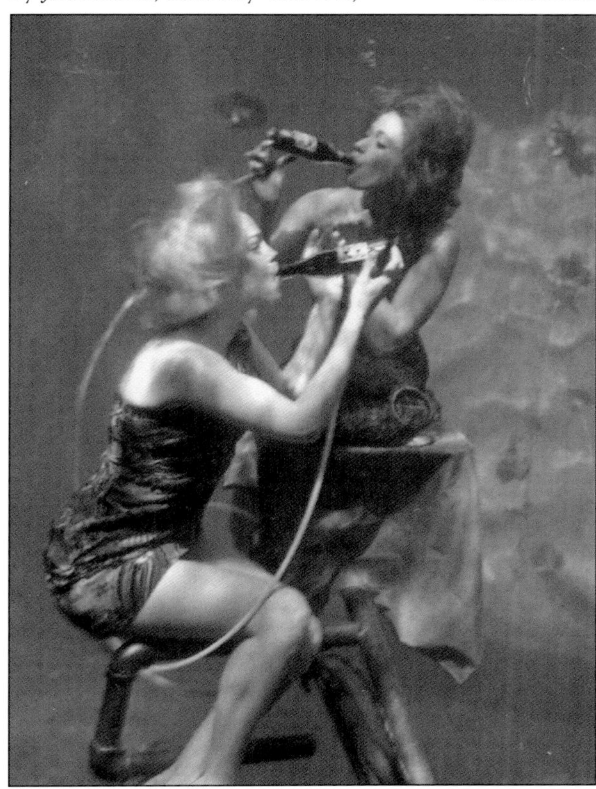

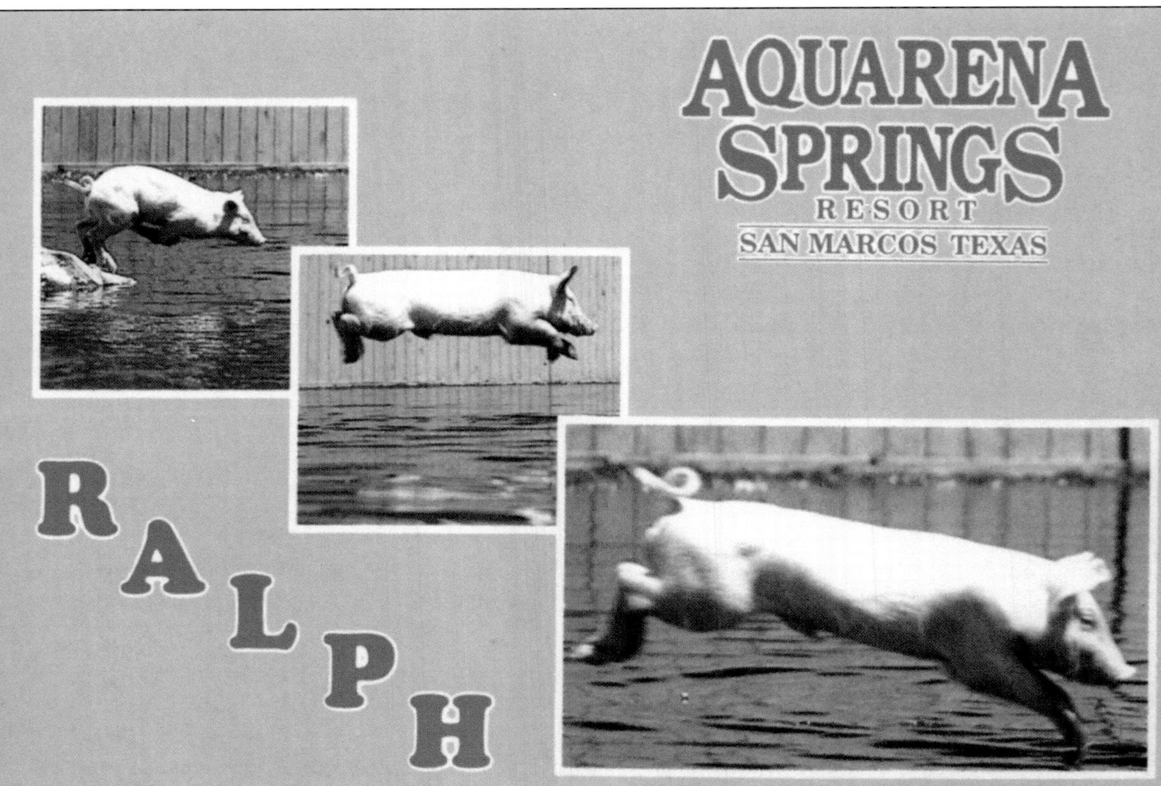

If all the visitors to Aquarena Springs throughout the decades were asked to list their favorite memories of the park, it is safe to say that almost no one's list would fail to mention Ralph the Swimming Pig. As the show evolved, swimming pigs with various names were featured, including Missy, Magnolia, and Little Mister, but Ralph was the hammiest and the most popular by far. Manager Don Russell noted that "Ralphie" was a favorite with everyone. As the submarine began to submerge, Ralph would perform his famous "swine dive" into the water and, enticed by a bottle of milk, enthusiastically paddle across the river's surface with one of his trainers. Of course there were numerous "Ralphs" throughout the years. The swimming pigs began training when they were only a few weeks of age and were performing by the time they were two to three months old. They retired when they became too large for the trainers to handle in the water.

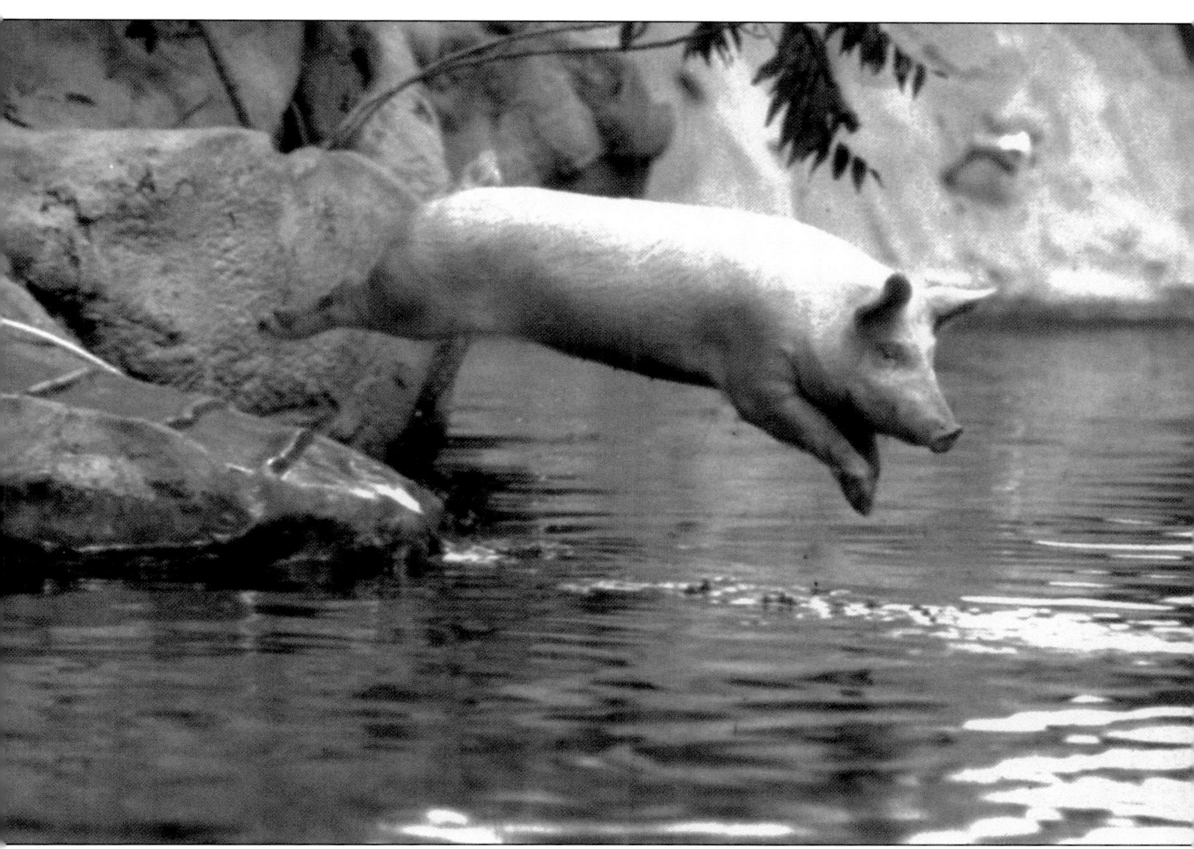

Over the years, Ralph the Swimming Pig became somewhat of a celebrity. Perhaps the height of his fame occurred in 1967, when he was featured in Charles Kuralt's segment on Walter Cronkite's CBS news program. In the early 1980s, Ralph was featured in the television show *That's Incredible*, performing his famous swine dive, pictured above. In 1984, he stole the show in his first appearance at the Aquacade at the World's Fair in New Orleans, during a celebration of Texas Week. In a 1996 newspaper survey conducted in Sonora, California, respondents were asked if they had any famous people among their ancestors or family. Joice Swadell of Sonora responded, "My cousin Barbara used to swim with a pig at the Aquarena in San Marcos, Texas. She made good money, too. Her sister took over when she left. She appeared on *What's My Line?* and they didn't guess what she did." (Courtesy Carole McCarley.)

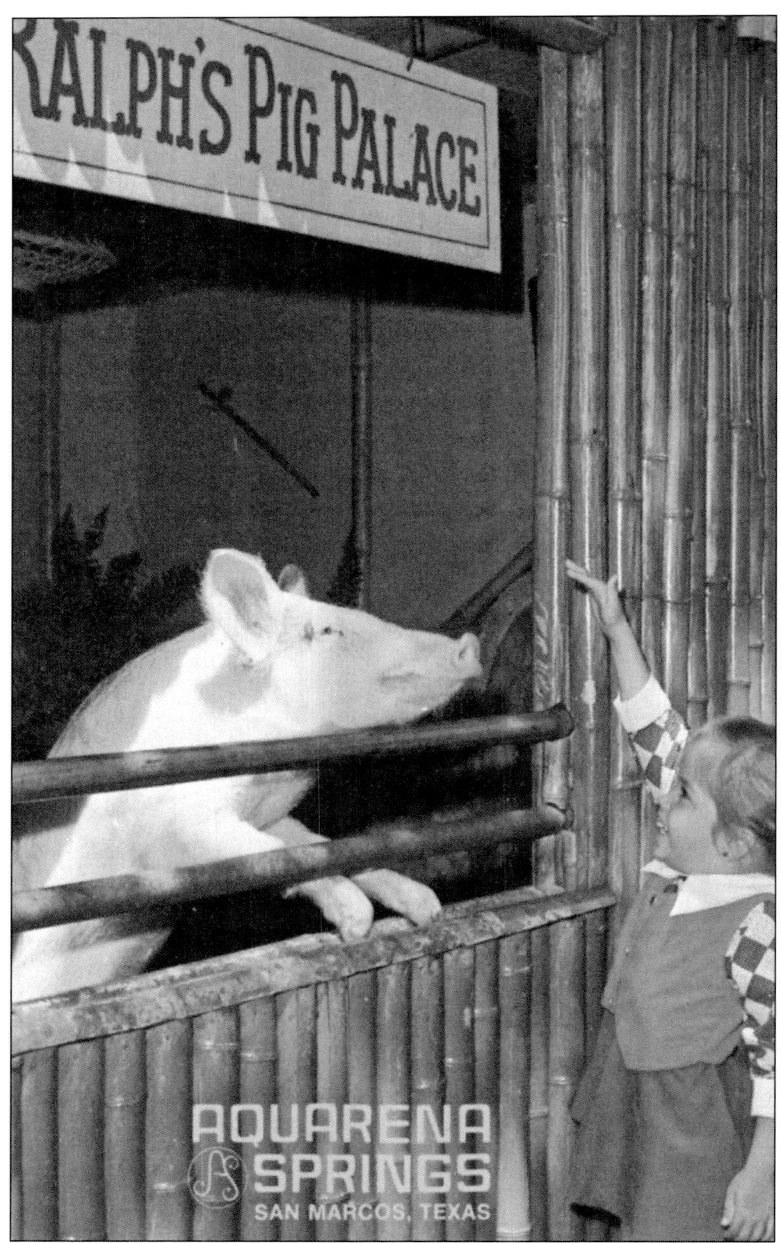

Although his national fame was impressive, Ralph was particularly beloved by the people of San Marcos. Visitors, especially children, delighted in visiting Ralph "back stage" in his own "Pig Palace." Local residents, who could visit Aquarena frequently and need not even spend any money if they simply wanted to enjoy the grounds and the river, were charmed by the young Ralphs-in-training. A regular visitor remembers, as a child, watching the tiny pigs toddling around on the grass and being fed from bottles. In the minds of many outsiders, the mention of San Marcos immediately brings Ralph to mind, and San Marcans do not seem to mind this. Dancer LeAnne Smith, who performs regularly with repertory dance companies nationwide, speaks of how pretentious some of the performers' biographies in the programs can sound. She says, "I decided to proudly end my biography with this sentence: 'LeAnne hails from San Marcos, Texas, home of Ralph the Swimming Pig.'"

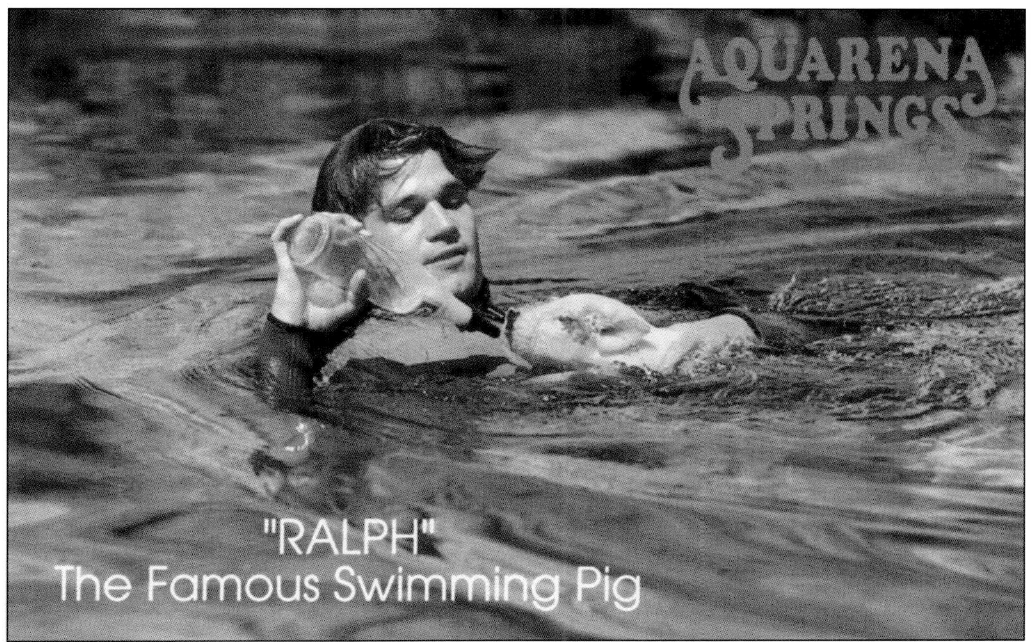

The myth that there was only one "Ralph" was enticing, but practicalities dictated that there was a series of swimming pigs, all of whom debunked the notion that it was impossible for a pig to swim. The trainers invariably fell in love with their charges, working with them just weeks after birth until they outgrew their trainers' capacity to handle them in the water. Visitors to Aquarena today miss the submarine theater performances, but by far the most poignant memories are of the swimming pig that stole everyone's heart. To this day, collectors search out memorabilia with Ralph's image on them, from T-shirts to souvenir mugs to "floatie pens" and other inexpensive items that were offered in the Aquarena gift shop during Ralph's performing days. (Above, photograph by Don Anders; below, photograph by Greg White; courtesy TxDOT.)

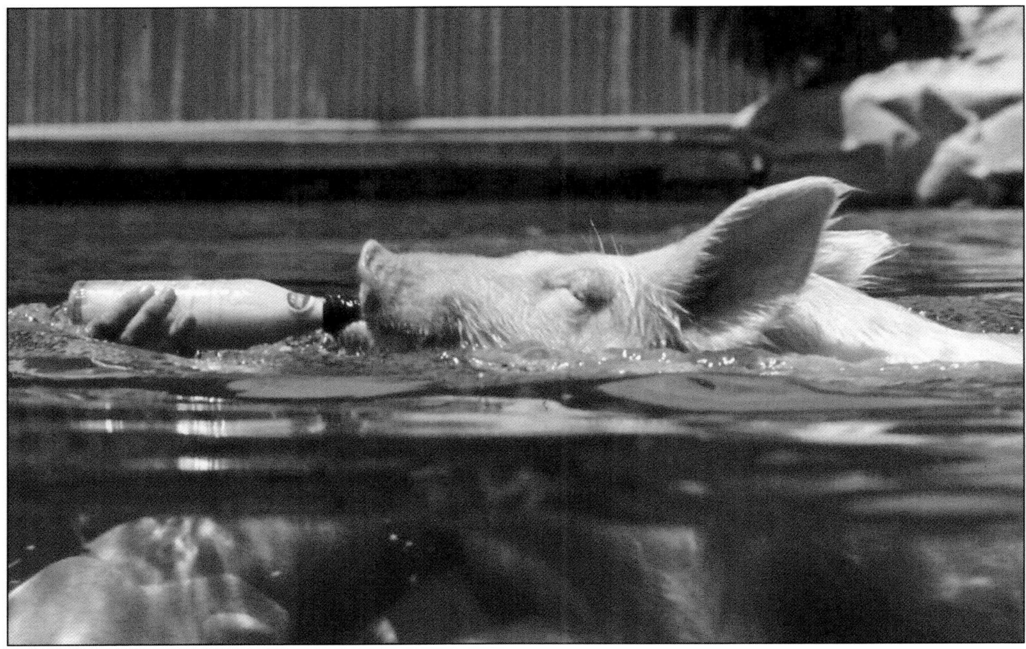

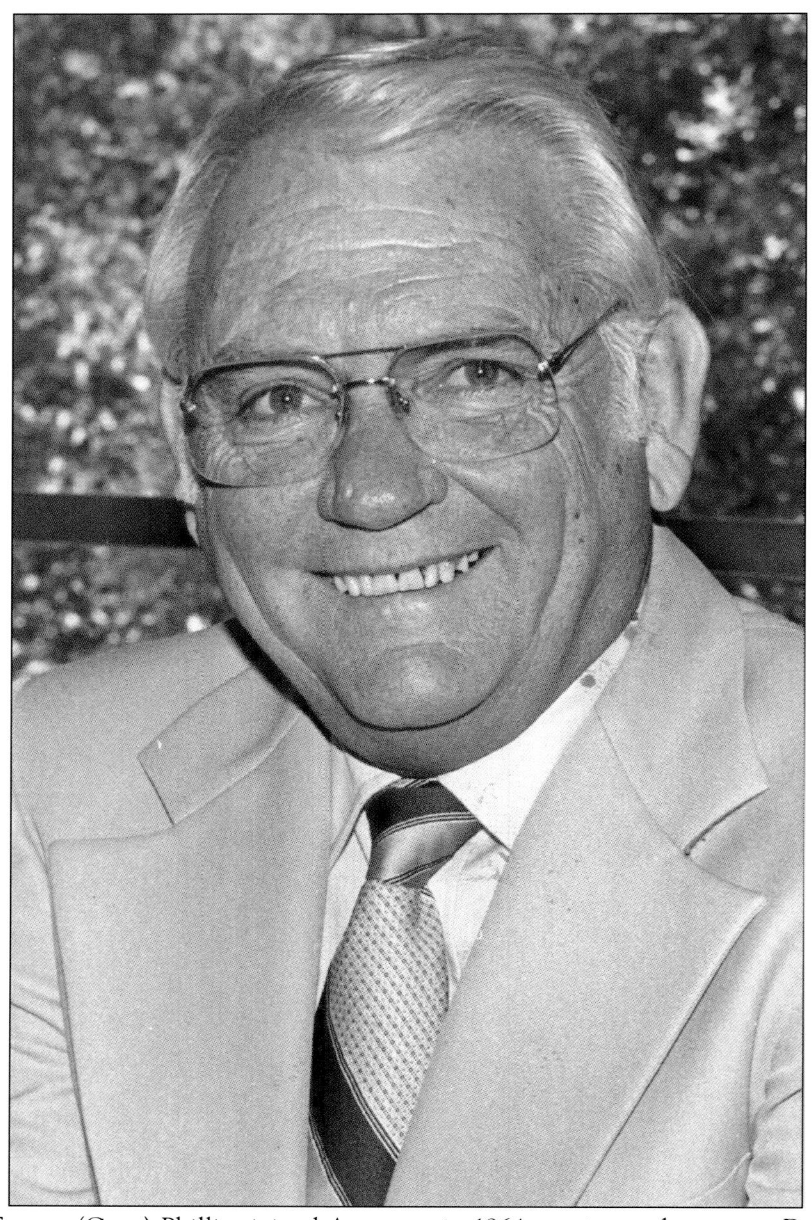

Richard Eugene (Gene) Phillips joined Aquarena in 1964, serving under mentor Don Russell until 1971, when Phillips became president and general manager, positions he held until the attraction was sold by the Rogers family in 1985. Phillips, known as "Mr. Hospitality," was a widely respected and well-loved leader in Texas tourism, earning the Texas Travel Industry Association's prestigious Lifetime Achievement Award for his service. He served on the TTIA board for many years, including one term as chairman. After his death in 1988, his colleagues in the tourism industry established the Gene Phillips Scholarship Award through Texas A&M University. This award is given annually to three deserving students in the field of tourism. Under his direction, Aquarena Springs enjoyed its most prosperous years. In 1972, early in his tenure as Aquarena president, Phillips announced construction of a new submarine theater, explaining that the original structure could not accommodate the increasing number of yearly visitors. (Courtesy SMHCC-San Marcos Public Library.)

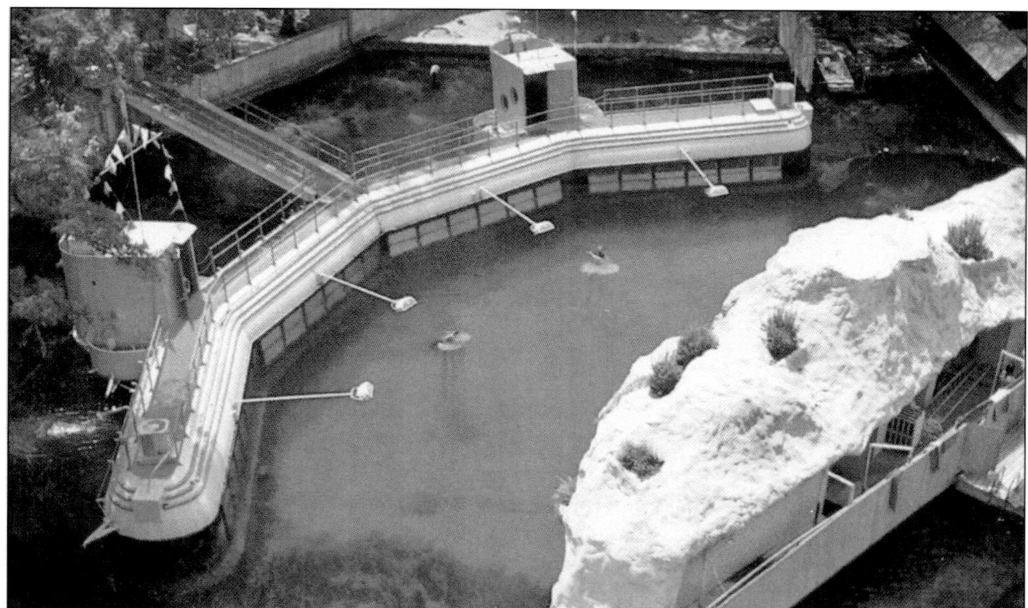

The new submarine theater planned by Gene Phillips was to include an improved overall design, being curved like an amphitheater and seating approximately 300 instead of 125 spectators. It would submerge 6 feet instead of 42 inches, as the original theater did, and audiences would be afforded better views through 24 six-foot-tall windows. The photograph below shows spectators in 1985 enjoying the underwater show in the considerably more spacious theater. In the early 1980s, the show was changed from the Polynesian-themed script to a performance centered around the mythical Greek island of Atlantis. Producer-director John Brooks said, "We wanted to create something that would take people on a fantasy trip." The show offered numerous variety acts and was expected to attract over 700,000 visitors yearly. (Below, photograph by Richard Reynolds; courtesy TxDOT.)

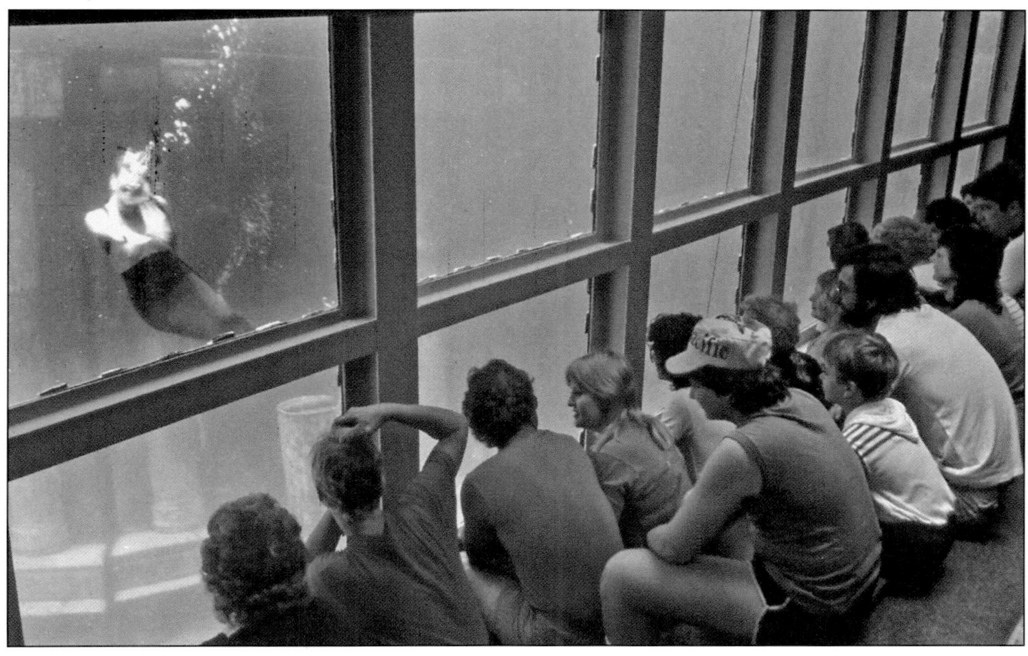

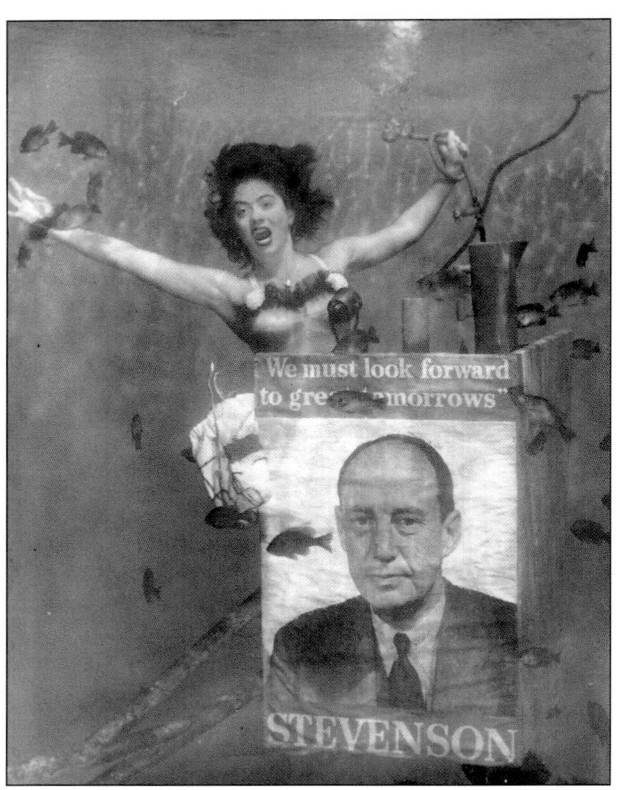

During the 1950s, Aquarena manager Don Russell was always thinking of ways to promote Aquarena. In 1952, during the presidential campaigns of Adlai Stevenson and Dwight David Eisenhower, Russell directed a little underwater political skit for the benefit of newsreel and television reporters. Photographers from several publications, including *Life* magazine, were also in attendance. Russell and the Aquamaids dreamed up and staged a unique show in which the girls gave political speeches for the candidates and passed out favors to "voters," in this case a crowd of hungry fish. Russell explained that the event was all in good fun. It was a stunt to attract publicity, he said, and no partisanship was shown. (Both courtesy SMHCC-San Marcos Public Library.)

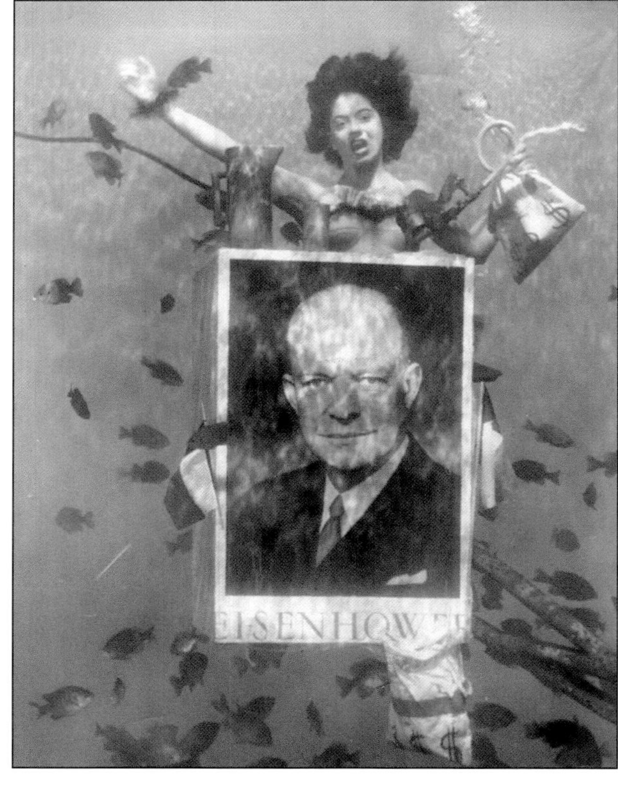

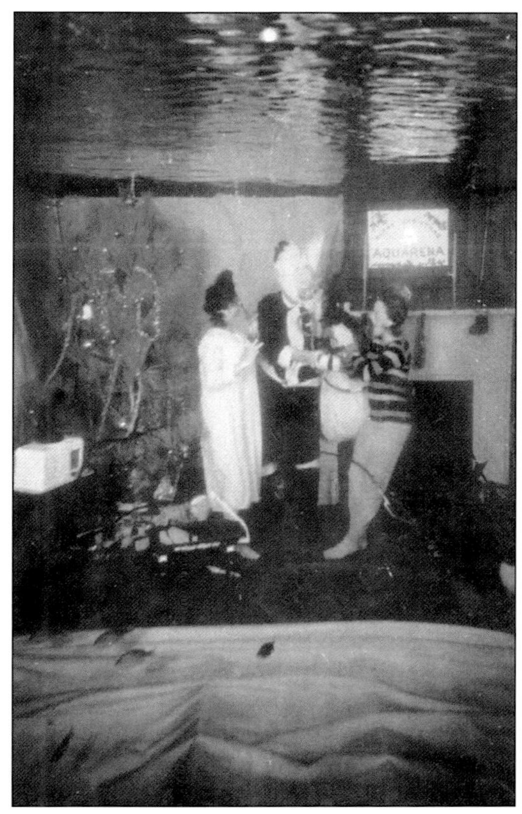

The submarine theater provided another publicity opportunity in late 1952, when Don Russell arranged for a promotional photo shoot and underwater Christmas party. Russell, along with Bush Ewing and several other assistants, conceived the set. With air hoses nearby, and weights strapped around their middles, three nightgown-clad Aquamaids eagerly awaited Santa's appearance in the "Underwater Living Room," complete with Christmas tree, furniture, and stockings hung with care from the fireplace mantel. The Aquamaids loitered around the tree until Santa dropped through the chimney and emerged from the fireplace. The actor who played Santa almost lost his trousers and padding shortly after clambering through the chimney, but he kept his head while Russell, clad in swim trunks, snorkel, and fins, leaped in to adjust matters.

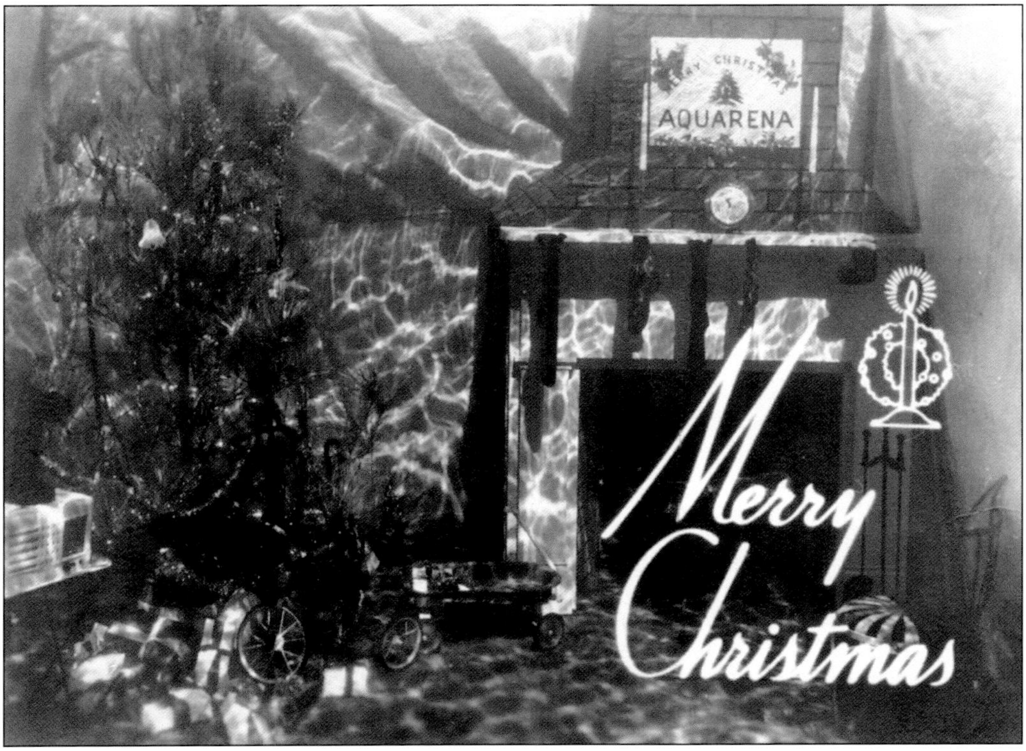

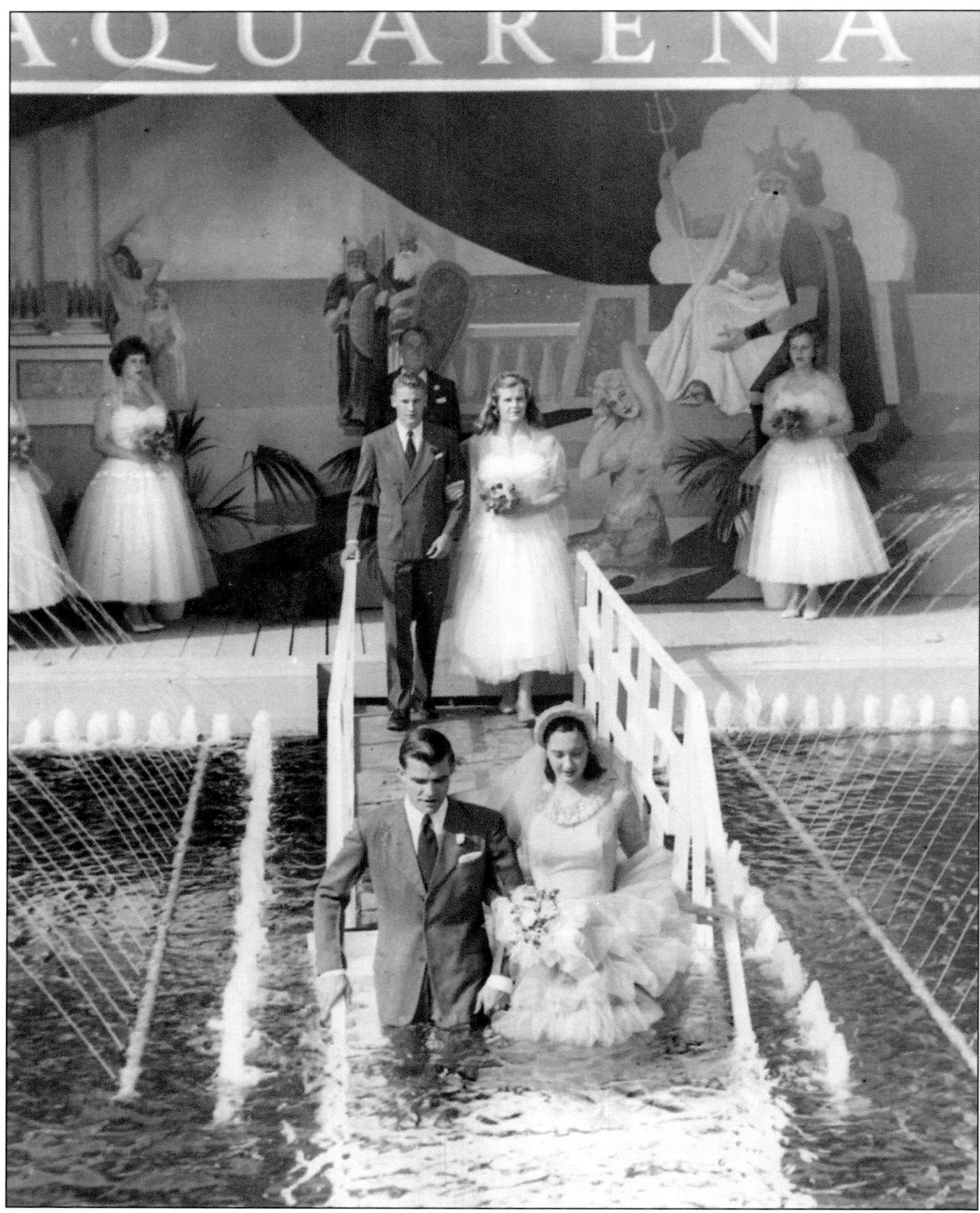

Arguably the most well-publicized event in Aquarena's history was the 1954 wedding in which former underwater clown Bob Smith and former Aquamaid Mary Beth Sanger exchanged vows under water in the submarine theater arena. The ceremony was prominently featured in *Life* magazine, in a pictorial article that described both the rehearsal and the actual wedding. Although the bride found the water chilly during the rehearsal, the couple remained enthusiastic about exchanging vows under water. The ceremony got underway when the couple and their undaunted attendants descended a stairway from the Aquarena stage to an underwater altar in front of the submarine theater, in which their guests were able to view the exchange of vows, rings, and kiss in dry comfort. The event garnered publicity for Aquarena when the March 8, 1954, issue of *Life* devoted several pages to this unusual wedding. (Courtesy SMHCC-San Marcos Public Library.)

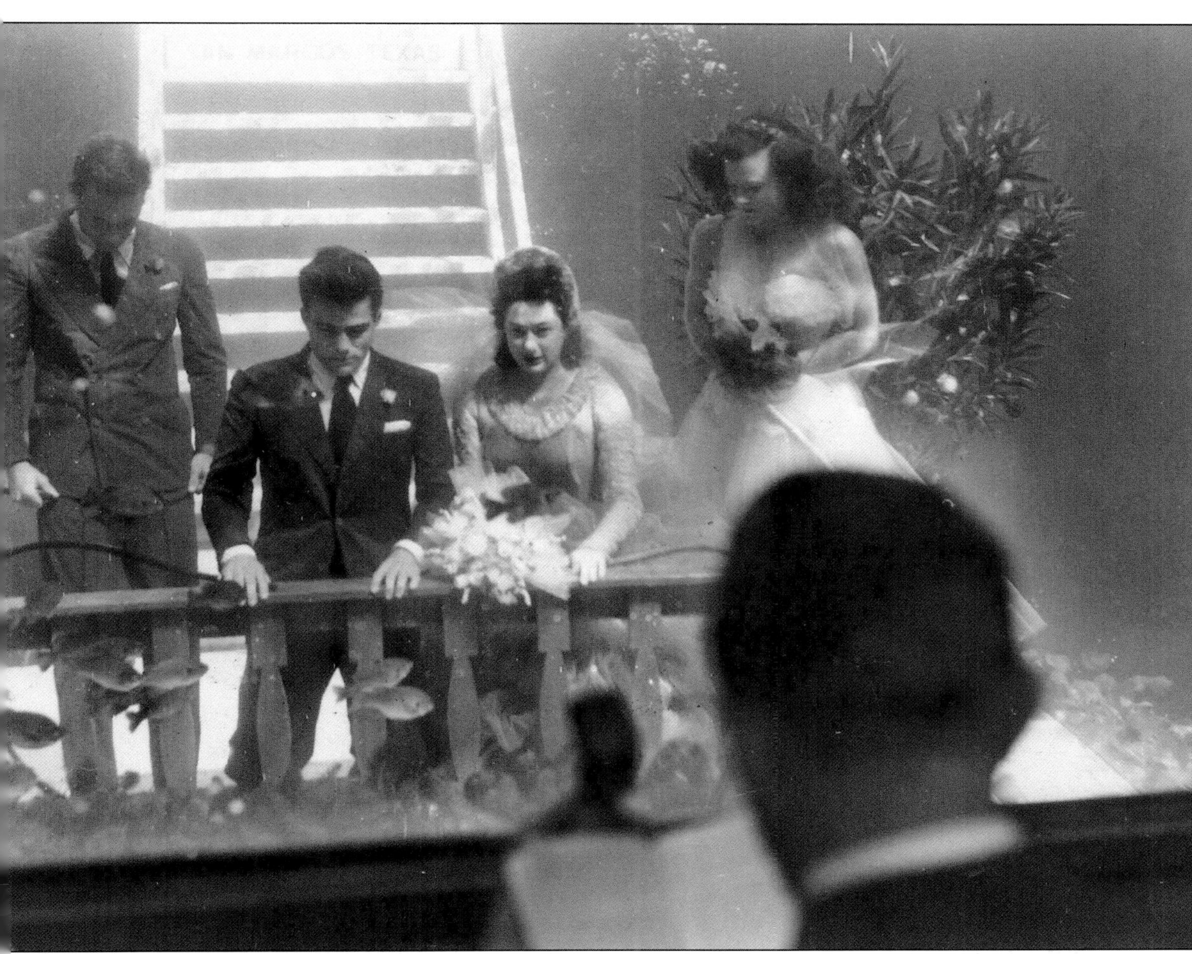

The underwater bride and groom wore lead weights under their clothing. In addition, bride Mary Beth Sanger's skirt hoops were weighted with lead to prevent billowing, and a weight was wrapped around her knee to allow her to kneel under water. Groom Bob Smith's arms were covered with waxed cardboard to keep his coat arms stiff, and his shoes were weighted with 12 pounds of lead, enabling him to remain steady while standing. Accompanied by attendants, including numerous fish, bride and groom bubbled their vows, taking gulps from their air hoses as necessary. From inside the submarine theater, the Reverend Curtis Ellison, a Baptist minister, officiated. After exchanging vows and kisses, the happy, dripping couple emerged from the water to be showered with rice. The couple returned to Aquarena, with their two young daughters, to celebrate their seventh wedding anniversary under water, complete with a cake made of plaster of Paris. (Courtesy SMHCC-San Marcos Public Library.)

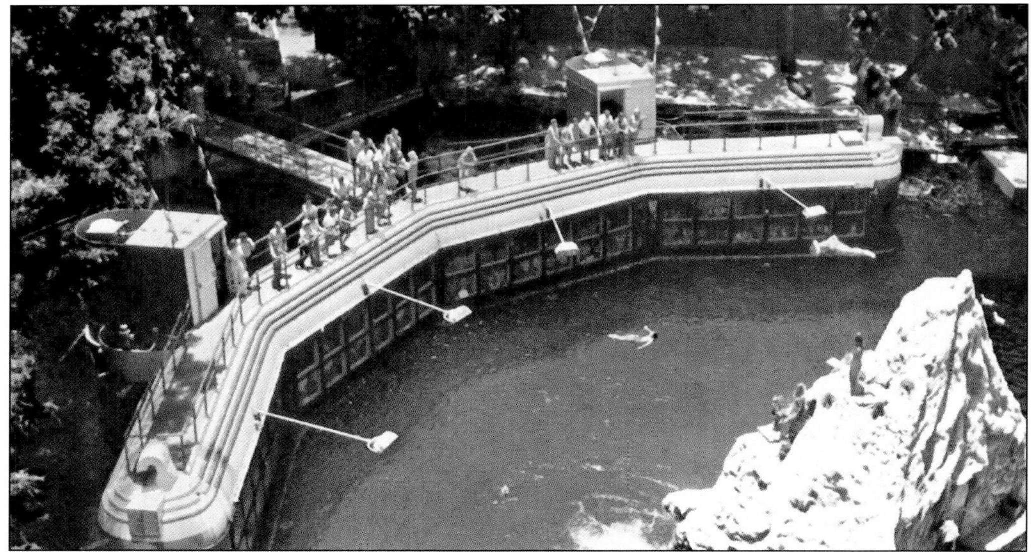

These two photographs provide a sense of the submarine theater's place at the center of Aquarena Springs. In the above aerial view, shot from the sky ride, all the submarine's windows are above the surface, and performers on the volcano begin the performance as guests are being seated. The photograph below, which shows the theater as it submerges, emphasizes the coexistence of the theater and the glass bottom boats, two very different ways for Aquarena's visitors to enjoy the San Marcos River. The walkway that stretches behind the volcano is the route performers took to access the stage. In the background, Old Main maintains the prominent spot it has held above the river since 1903. (Below, courtesy SMHCC-San Marcos Public Library.)

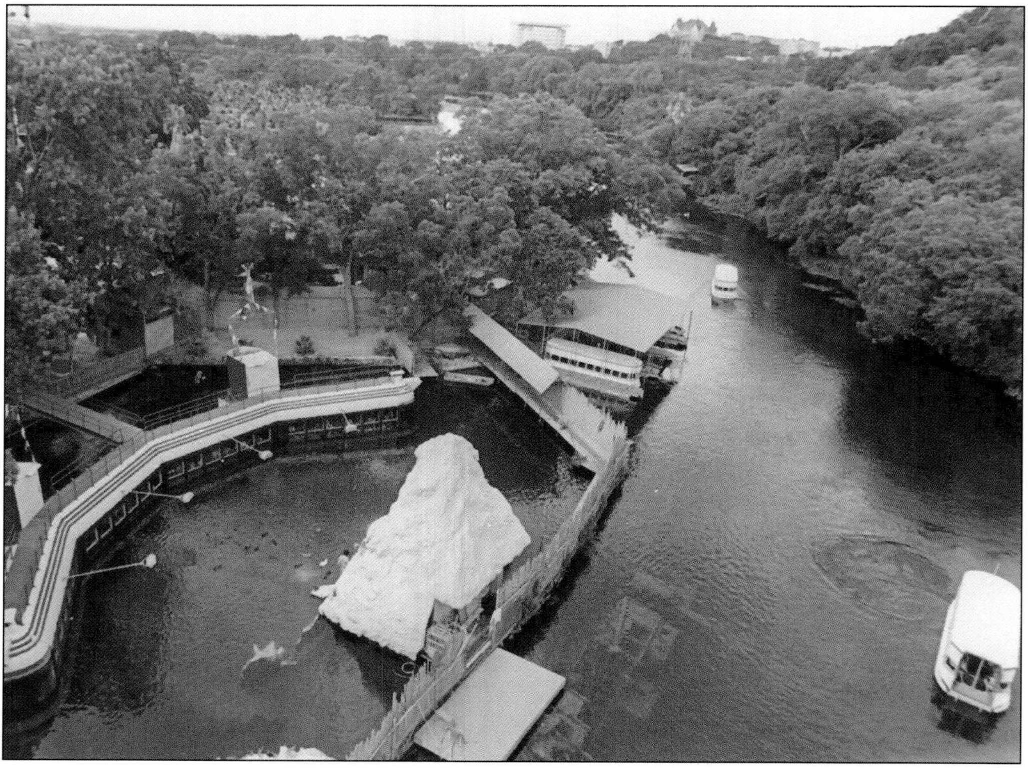

Four

The Sky Ride

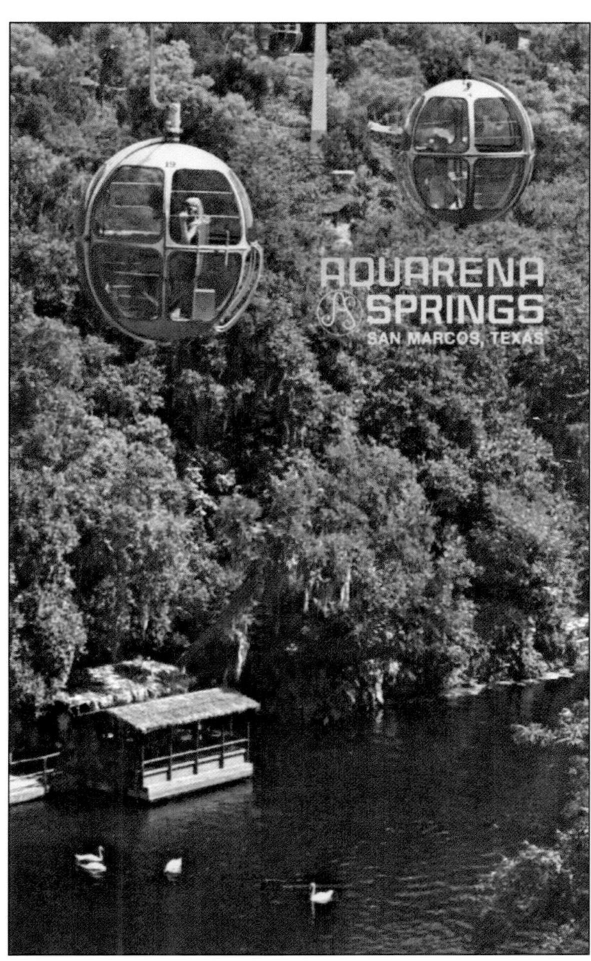

In 1963, the Swiss sky ride made its maiden voyage from the liftoff platform at Aquarena. Gondolas rose to a maximum altitude of 110 feet above the river, giving visitors a bird's-eye view of the submarine theater, the glass bottom boats, and the Hanging Gardens across the river from the rest of the park.

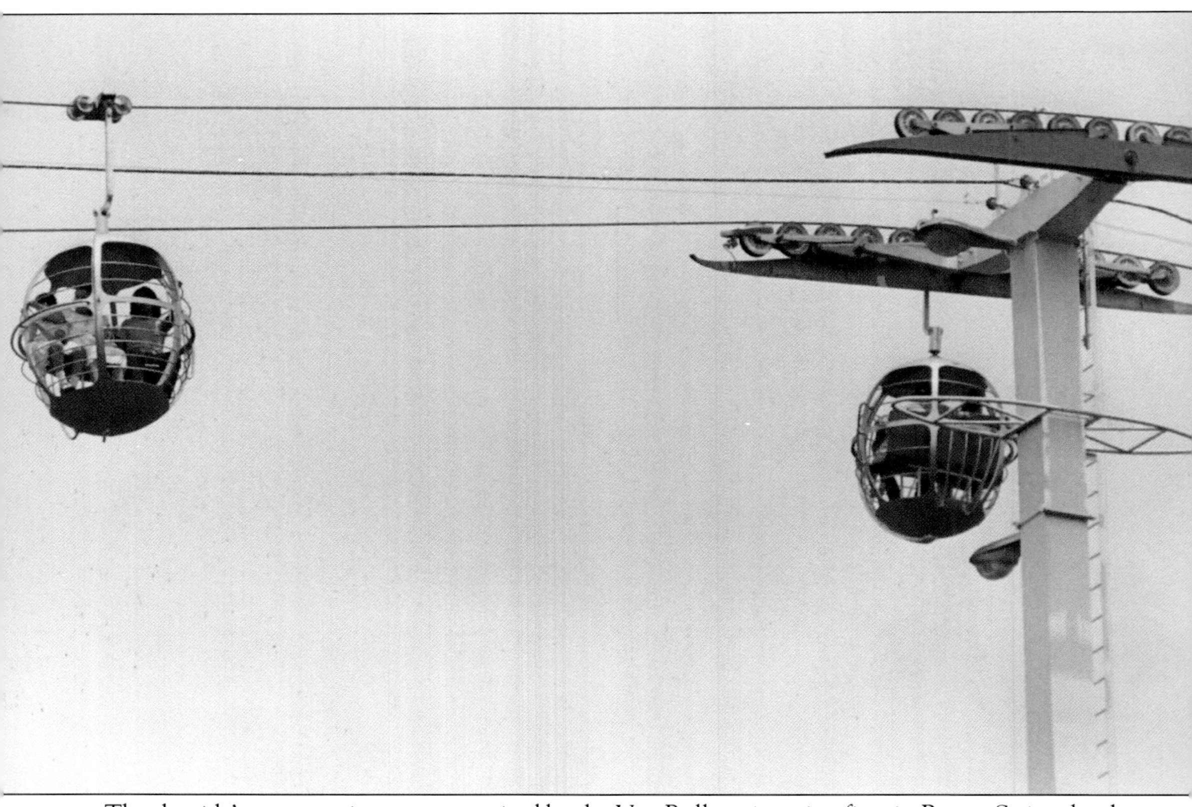

The sky ride's construction was supervised by the Von Roll engineering firm in Berne, Switzerland. The sky ride equipment traveled by ship from Hamburg, Germany, to Houston, where it was loaded onto transport trucks for the journey to San Marcos. Frank Bryant of Austin engineered the foundation work, and Stokes Construction Company built the foundations. Other local contractors working on the job included Ted Breihan Electric and Hamilton Glass Company. Fred Biegler, the engineer in charge, said that along with the Aqua-Lift at Six Flags Over Texas, the Aquarena sky ride was the most enjoyable project he had ever worked on. Biegler described the sky ride's cable as 1 inch in diameter and made up of six strands, each of which was formed from 19 separate steel wires. The cable's total length was 2,160 feet, and it had a breaking point seven times the maximum stress that it would bear with 15 fully loaded gondolas—more than 47 tons of safe-carrying capacity. (Courtesy SMHCC-San Marcos Public Library.)

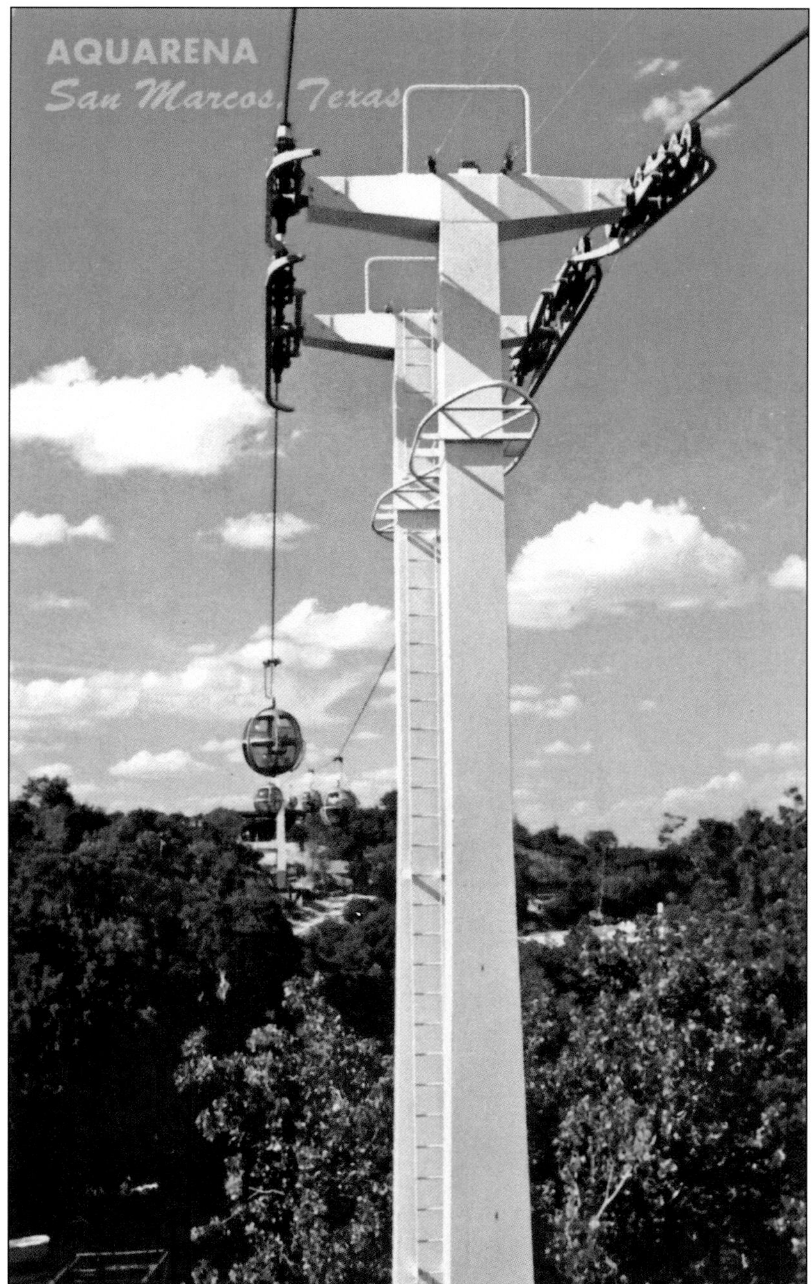

A week before the sky ride's maiden voyage, James Bagby flew to San Marcos from Los Angeles to finish splicing the steel cable that would carry the gondolas. Bagby, who had started splicing lines in the navy, later used his talents to do all the rigging at Disneyland and at many other places where his unusual expertise was required. He spent two days making the complicated splice in the 1-inch, endless stainless steel cable. The splicing was so expertly done that it was almost impossible to see the splice, even upon close inspection. Bagby took just enough time away from his work to enjoy an evening with Aquarena president Don Russell and his family before leaving for New York and another splicing job. Meanwhile, workers put the finishing touches on the ride to prepare for its highly anticipated opening the following week.

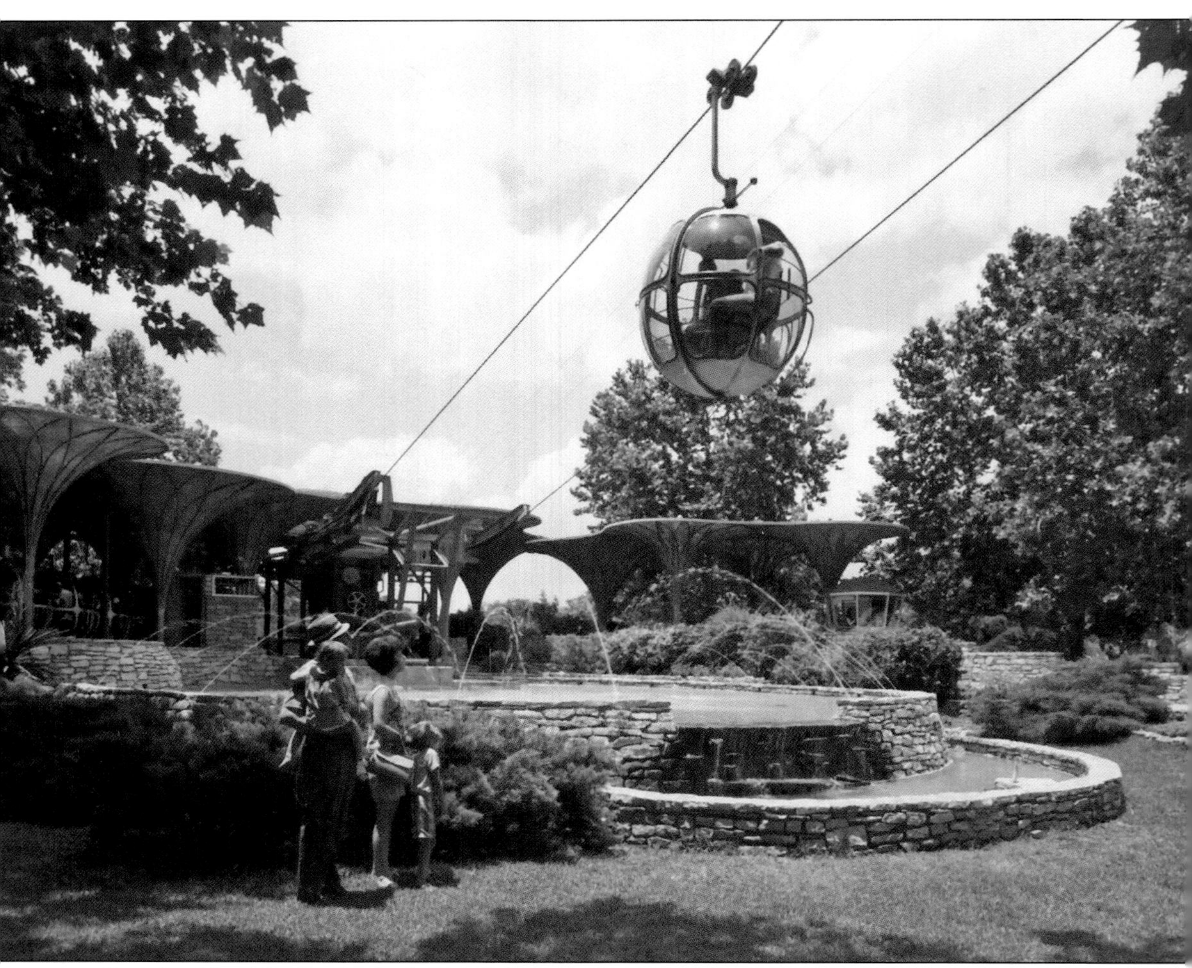

On May 28, 1963, the Swiss sky ride was ready for its debut. The first passengers were Paul Rogers and Don Russell, who were followed in the second gondola by reporters who described the journey as "silk-smooth." One reporter, Walter Buckner, elaborated, "The ride itself was thrilling and gave one a fine, bird's-eye view of the Aquarena area and especially of the beautifully clear San Marcos River springs." He speculated that the sky ride would be "the most beautiful and spectacular such ride in America when it is fully developed and landscaped." In its report on the opening, the *San Marcos Record* noted that the sky ride was one of the three highest in the western hemisphere and was "completely unique in its own right, with fifteen completely enclosed oval gondolas with tinted plastic panels." All of those involved in the maiden voyage praised the new attraction enthusiastically. (Photograph by John Suhrstedt; courtesy TxDOT.)

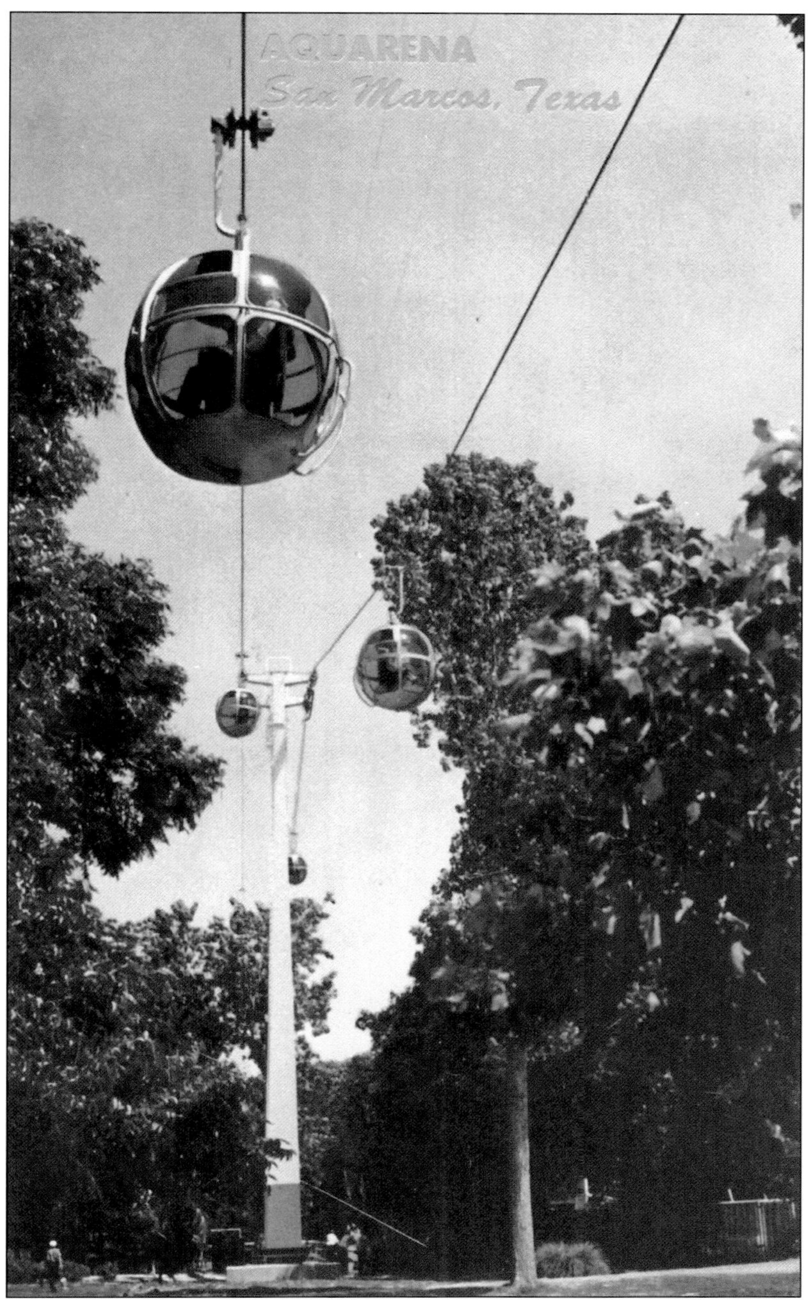

Immediately after Paul Rogers and Don Russell took the first trip on the sky ride, the attraction was opened to the public at 75¢ per ride. Each gondola could carry three passengers at a time, and the daily capacity was approximately 2,500 visitors. Jim Collins, Aquarena's operations supervisor, said that the new ride had operated without a hitch during its first hours. "It's amazingly smooth compared to other rides," he added. "It's no trouble at all." Soon after the sky ride's premier, 120 large billboards were erected across Texas, enticing visitors to come to the park and experience the ride that was touted as "taller and longer than the famed ride at Disneyland." A local reporter noted, "The Aquarena sky ride will far outshine the ones at Disneyland and at Six Flags, according to those who have ridden all three."

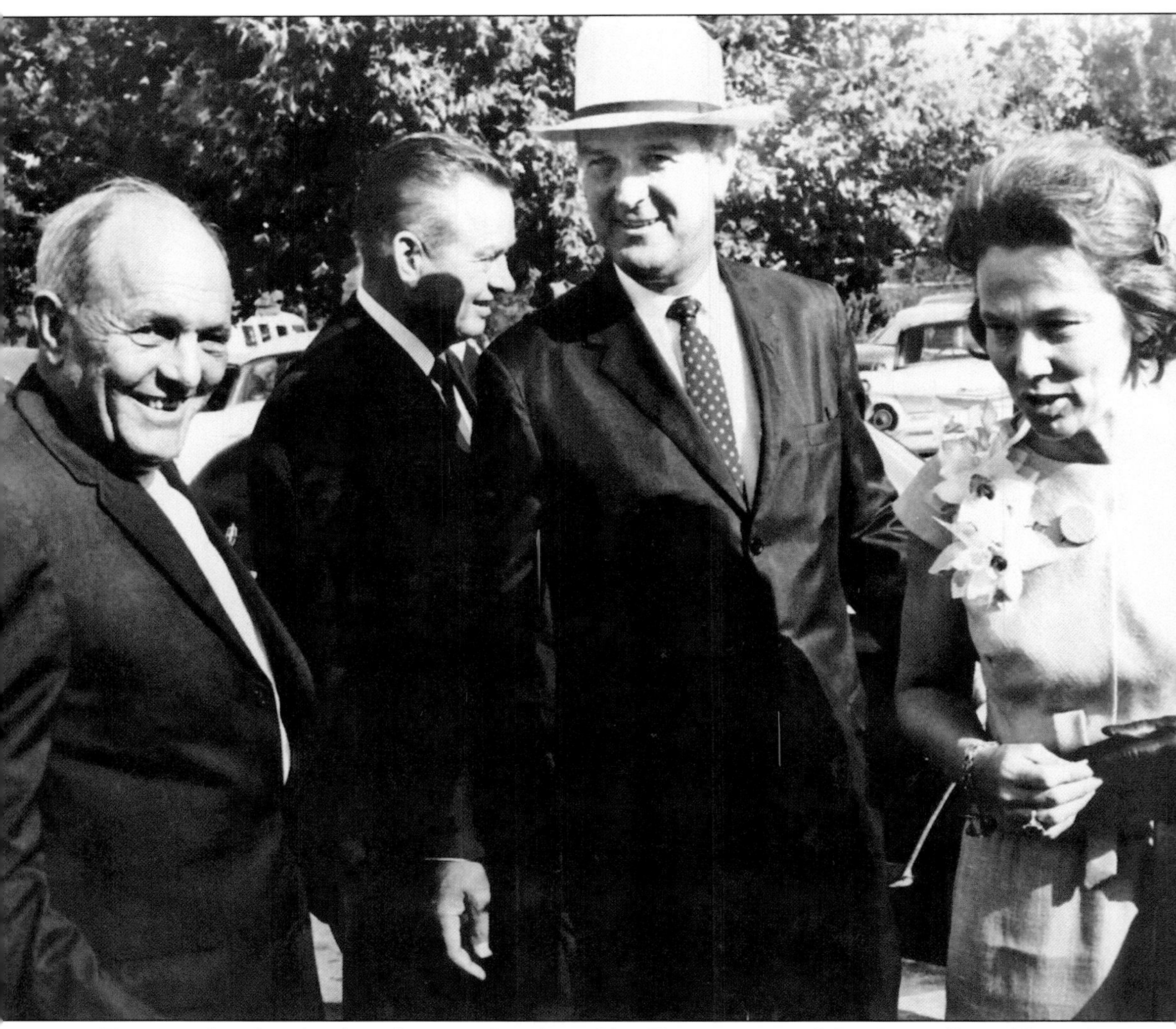

Two months after the sky ride opened to the public, Texas governor John Connally and his wife, Nellie, accepted Aquarena's invitation to preside at the official dedication of the ride during Tourist Attraction Week. The culmination of the weeklong celebration occurred on Friday, July 26. The dedication ceremony began with skydivers from the 149th Air National Guard from San Antonio executing a series of parachute jumps. A concert by the army band from Fort Hood followed. At the climax of the ceremony, the governor and his wife cut the ribbon, marking the official opening of the sky ride. Governor Connally told a crowd of 2,000 gathered at Aquarena, "You in San Marcos have led the way in building the tourist and vacation business, and this development at Aquarena is the greatest thing you have ever done with the exception of locating that great institution on the hill" (referring to Southwest Texas State College). Pictured are, from left to right, Paul Rogers, unidentified, Gov. John Connally, and First Lady Nellie Connally.

PAUL J. ROGERS AND ROY GULLEDGE

AND

THE STATE FAIR OF TEXAS

CORDIALLY INVITE YOU AND YOUR FAMILY

TO TAKE A PREVIEW RIDE ON

THE FABULOUS NEW

SWISS SKYRIDE

AT STATE FAIR PARK

(The Nation's Longest Amusement Park Aerial Ride)

5 TO 8 P.M.
FRIDAY, OCTOBER 2
— OR —
1 TO 6 P.M.
SATURDAY, OCTOBER 3

PRESENT THIS INVITATION AT
SWISS SKYRIDE TERMINAL
OPPOSITE STATE FAIR MUSIC HALL
FOR YOUR COMPLIMENTARY RIDE TICKETS

Encouraged by the popularity of the sky ride at Aquarena Springs, Paul Rogers, along with Roy Gulledge, developed plans to build the nation's longest sky ride at the Texas State Fair in Dallas. The new ride would have 62 four-passenger gondolas that could accommodate about 2,400 passengers per hour. Like the San Marcos attraction, the new sky ride was manufactured by Von Roll, Limited, of Berne, Switzerland. As planned, the ride opened in October 1964, just in time to debut at the giant "Texposition." At a cost of $500,000, the 2,800-foot aerial path was supported by eight towers, ranging from 49 to 85 feet in height. The six-minute one-way trip, running from near the front gate of the fairgrounds to a point near the roller coaster on the midway, afforded riders a new and different view of the entire state fair.

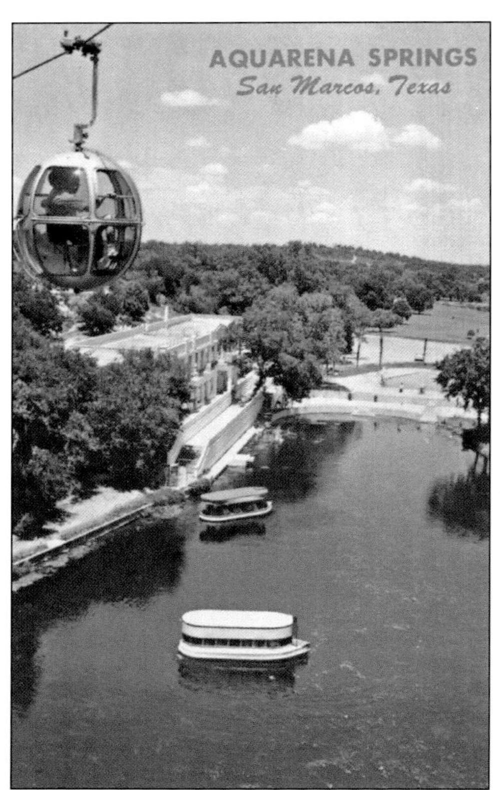

A trip on the Aquarena sky ride began with a liftoff from the platform near the restaurant and carried visitors over the submarine theater and across Spring Lake to the landing terminus above the hotel. Visitors could stay in the gondola and complete the seven-minute round-trip, or they could disembark and tour the Hanging Gardens on the northern side of the river before catching another gondola and completing their trip. The aerial journey offered spectacular views not only of the park and its many attractions but also of the entire city of San Marcos and the surrounding countryside. (Below, courtesy SMHCC-San Marcos Public Library.)

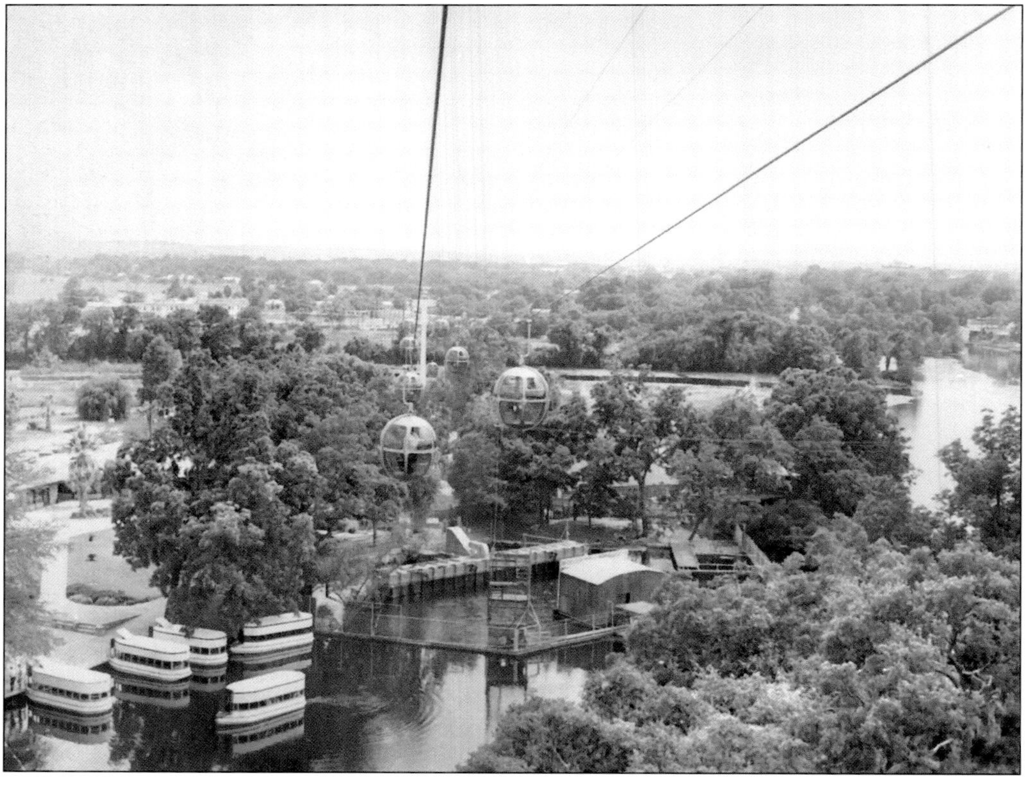

Visitors of all ages enthusiastically boarded the sky ride gondolas at the liftoff platform. The sky ride drew even more tourists to the already popular park, enhancing the role San Marcos played in the development of the Texas tourist industry. At the official dedication of the sky ride, Gov. John Connally commented on tourism in Florida, adding, "But with all their development, they have nothing that can compare with what you have here." He went on to say, "The towns and small cities of Texas must develop tourist attractions or small industries or both to survive. Otherwise, the trend will be toward the cities, and the small towns will wither on the vine and die. San Marcos has shown the way for other towns in Texas." (Right, courtesy Carole McCarley.)

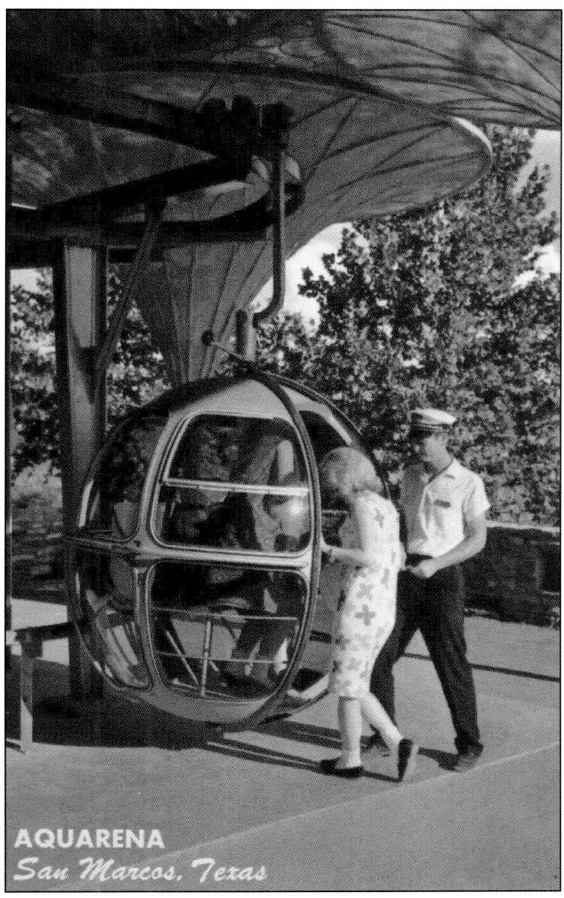

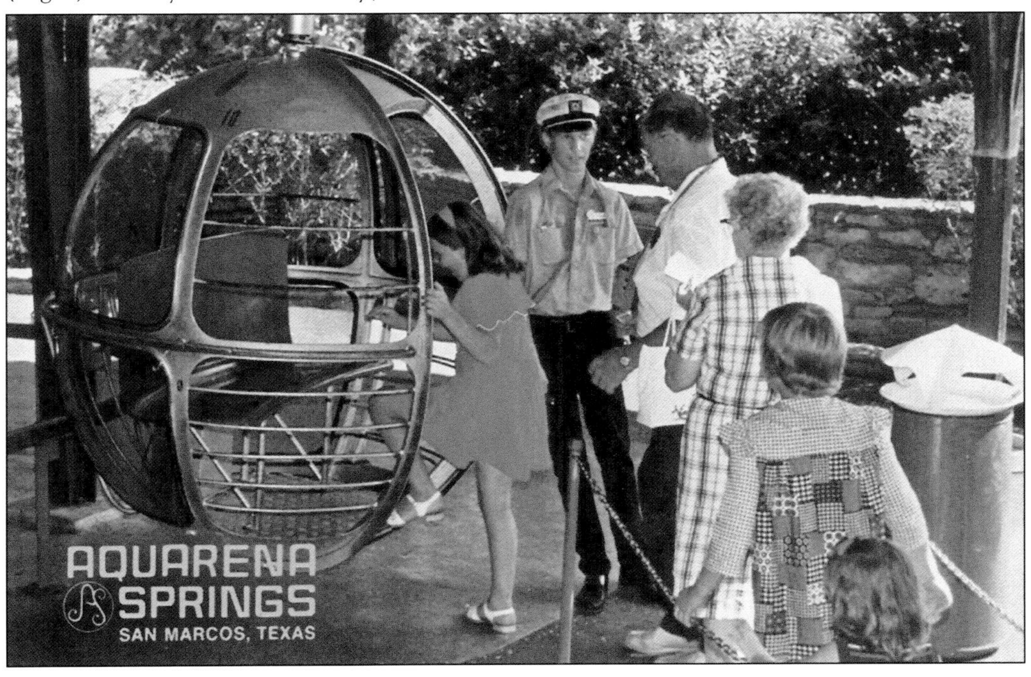

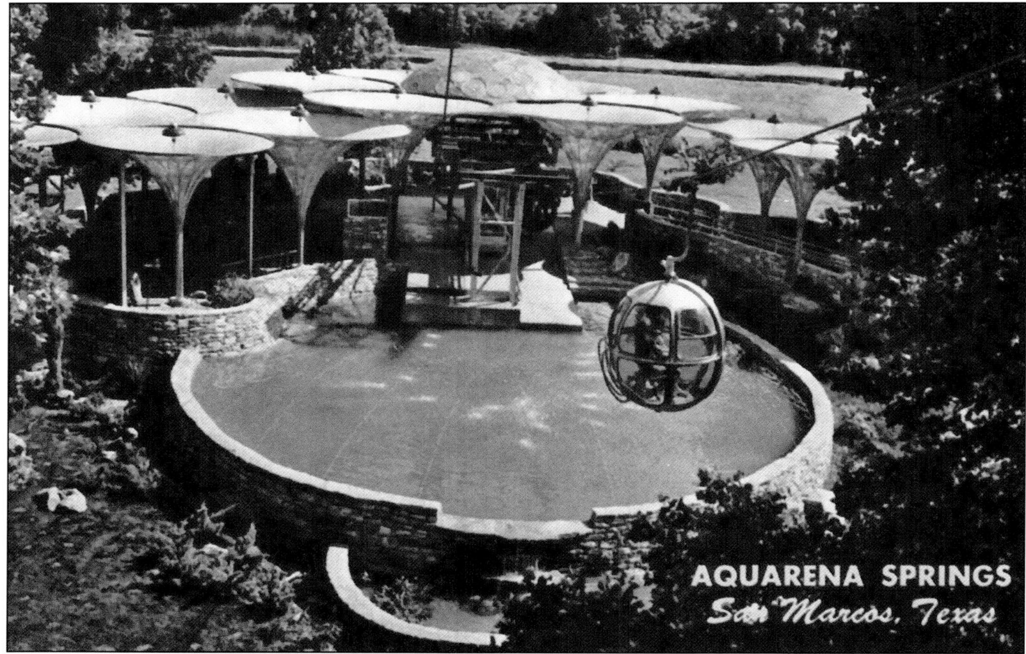

The $300,000 sky ride remained a popular part of the Aquarena Springs experience as long as the park was operated as a tourist attraction. Any initial worries about safety were assuaged by Fred Biegler, engineer for Von Roll, Limited, which manufactured 90 percent of all amusement park rides of this type in the world. He noted, "There have been more than four hundred million people travel on Von Roll rides without one serious injury or accident." The photograph below shows a gondola beginning its journey over the pool at the launching pad on a sunny day with Old Main just visible in the background. However, the ride continued to operate after dark, especially on weekends. Lights installed within the park enhanced the beauty of the night rides, which offered an entirely different perspective from the daytime trips. (Above, courtesy Carole McCarley.)

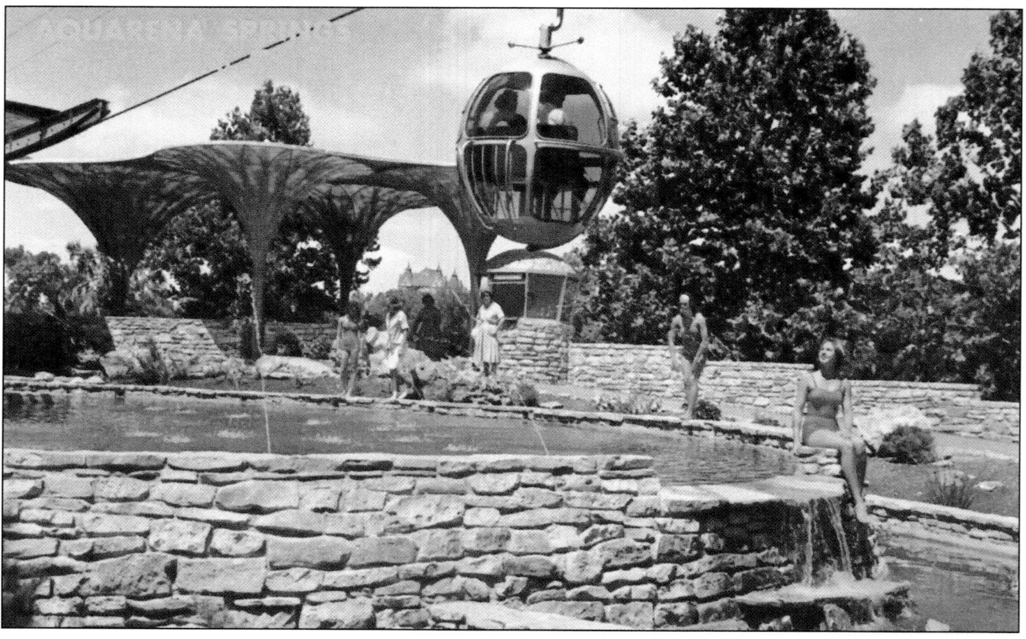

Five

The Park

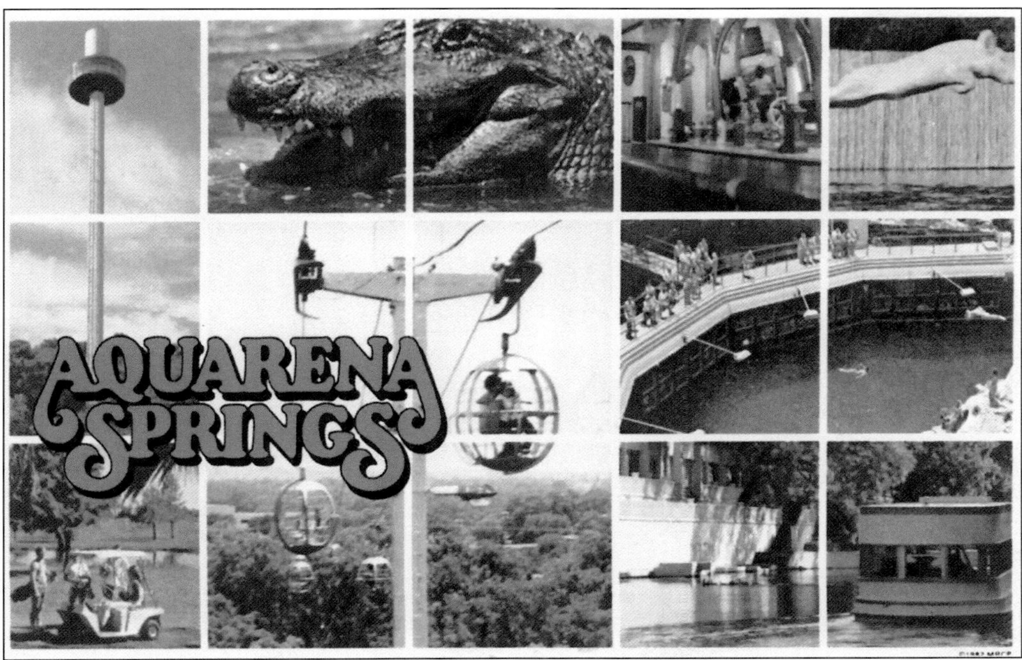

The glass bottom boats, submarine theater, and sky ride were the three primary features of Aquarena Springs. However, as this postcard shows, they were not the park's only attractions. Visitors could spend an entire day exploring Aquarena Springs on both sides of the river, or they could simply play golf and relax at the restored hotel.

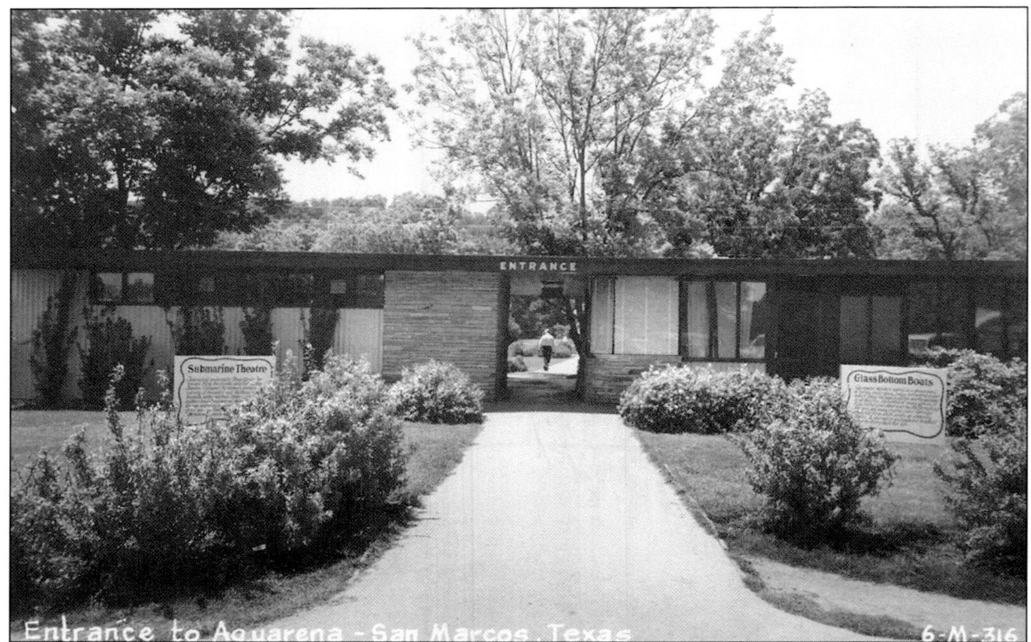

Visitors to Aquarena Springs entered the park through the breezeway pictured above. Immediately to the left of the entryway was the Aquarena restaurant. To the right was the gift shop, where souvenirs and tickets to the park's attractions could be purchased. Upon emerging from the gift shop, visitors were greeted with their first sight of the sparkling river and only had to choose which attraction to enjoy first.

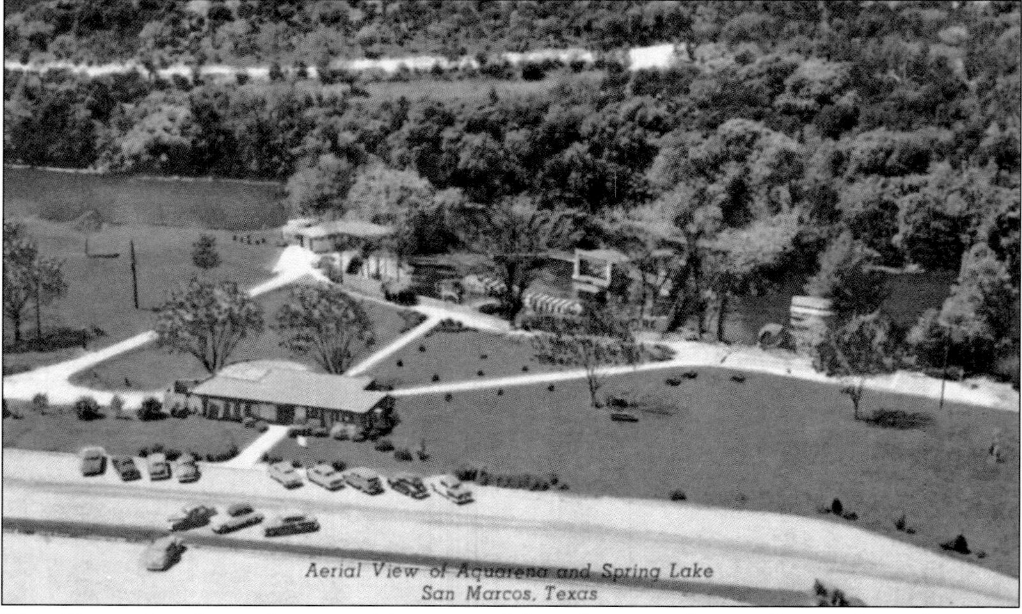

This illustration shows the central location of the submarine theater. Just to the right of the area depicted were the glass bottom boat docks. The parking lot was usually full of cars, except when it was closed to hold the first four Chilympiads, 1970 to 1973, at which an emerging central Texas talent named Willie Nelson performed. This annual Olympics of chili cooking continued in Texas until 2003.

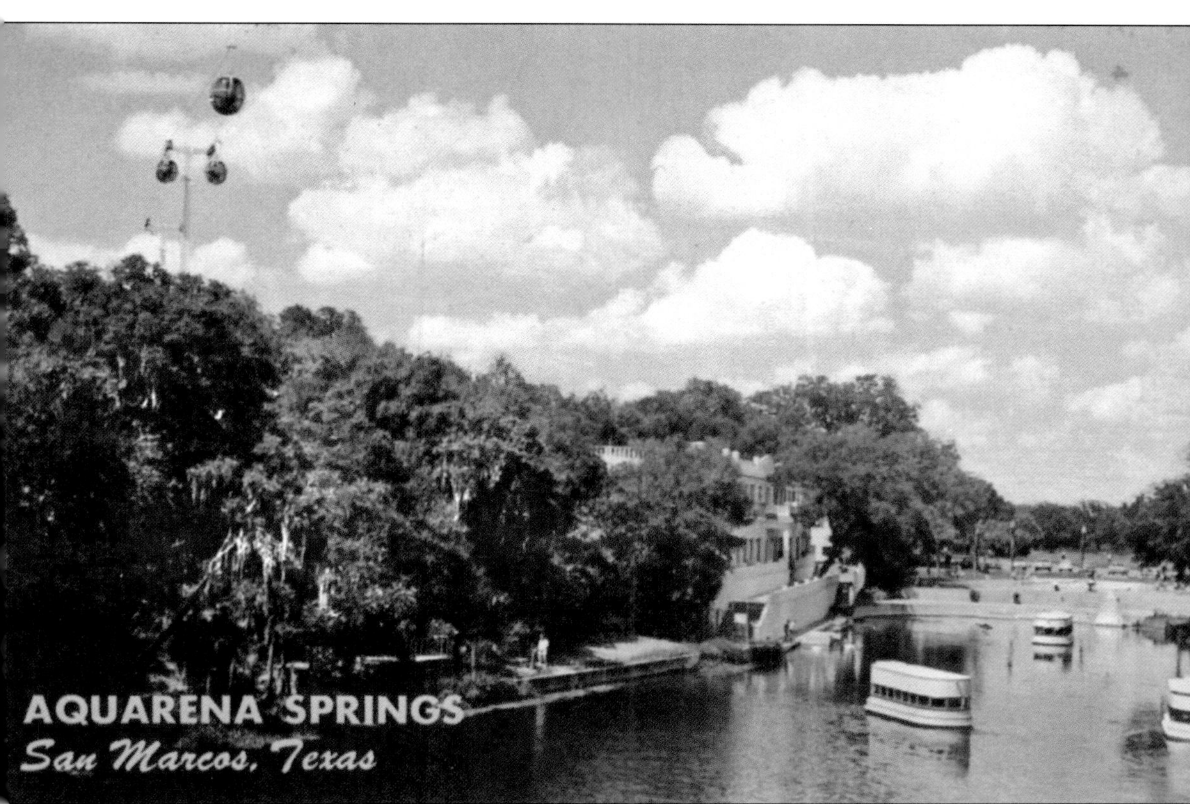

The Spring Lake Park Hotel that A. B. Rogers opened in 1929 served as a hotel for only seven years before being pressed into service as a hospital and then a school. In 1960, Paul Rogers decided to restore the hotel to its earlier grandeur as a resort hotel with numerous innovations in each room, including wall-to-wall carpeting, individually controlled air-conditioning, coffee machines, television, radio, and private telephones complete with signal lights alerting guests to messages. All rooms on the front side of the hotel would have balconies overlooking the river. At the rear of the hotel, built against a rock bluff, Rogers planned an aviary, complete with a waterfall, that would house several hundred exotic birds, including parakeets and parrots. Room service would be provided via electrical carts traveling between the Aquarena restaurant and the hotel. On June 10, 1961, the general public was welcomed to an open house, and a group of San Marcos residents was invited to spend the first official night in the Aquarena Springs Motor Hotel's 26 guest rooms.

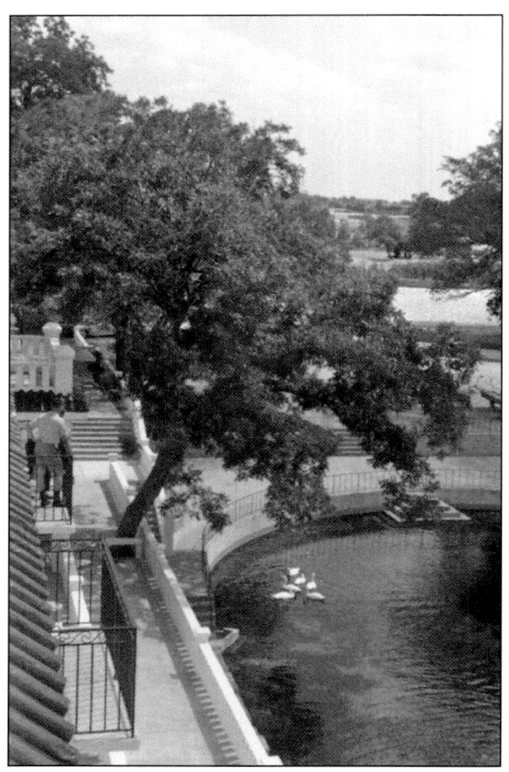

From their balconies, hotel guests could enjoy a view of swans gliding on the San Marcos River headwaters, which, according to a hotel brochure, flowed "from the very foundation of the motor hotel itself." In addition to enjoying the attractions of Aquarena Springs, guests could swim in the hotel's Olympic-size pool, play golf on the Aquarena course, or even take a scenic hill country tour in the hotel's limousine. Use of the heated pool was limited to guests at the hotel and a special 150-family swimming club opened to local residents. Today many San Marcos residents fondly recall the "pool club," which provided a place for local families to gather.

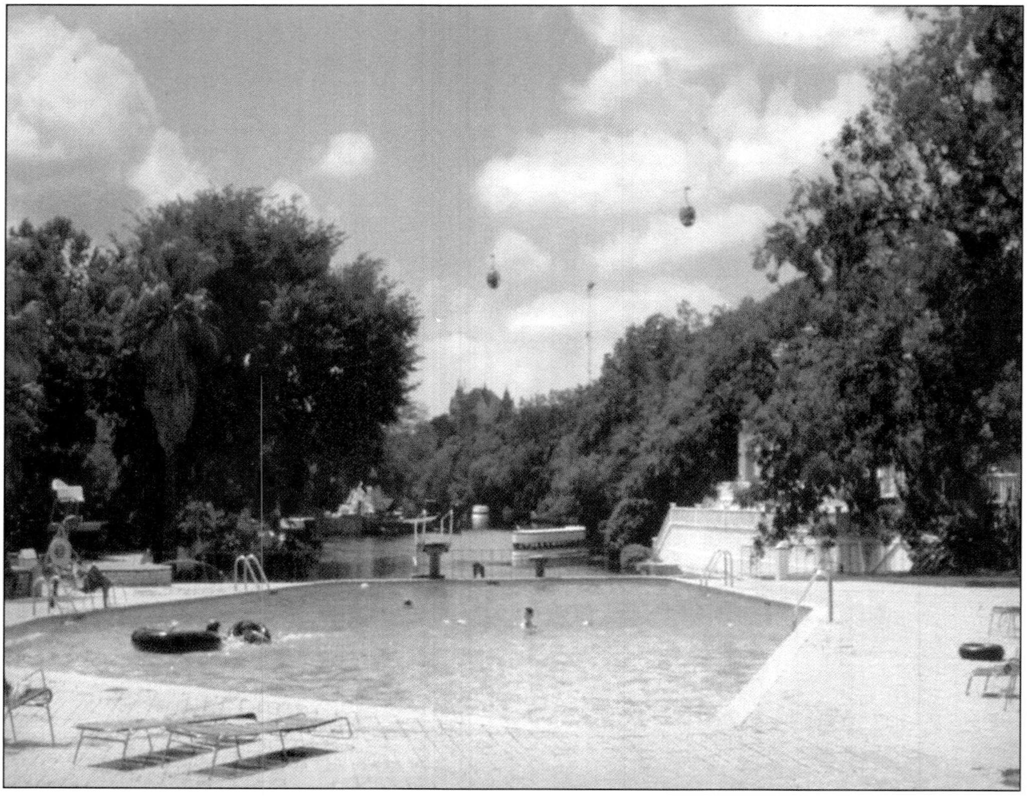

As the sky ride debuted in 1963, workers were putting the finishing touches on the Hanging Gardens located on a cliff overlooking the springs. Visitors could access the gardens by taking the sky ride to its terminus, and the price of admission was included in the sky ride ticket. In the gardens, guests could take a leisurely stroll on more than a mile and a half of nature trails that wound through native flowering trees and shrubs. Colorful bedding plants added additional interest along the sun-dappled path. All of the trails ultimately led to a 100-year-old working gristmill. Along the way, visitors could see a re-created Spanish mission, view the river from a wooden viewing platform, or stop by the historic Burleson house to see a glassblower practicing his craft. (Right, photograph by Greg White; courtesy TxDOT.)

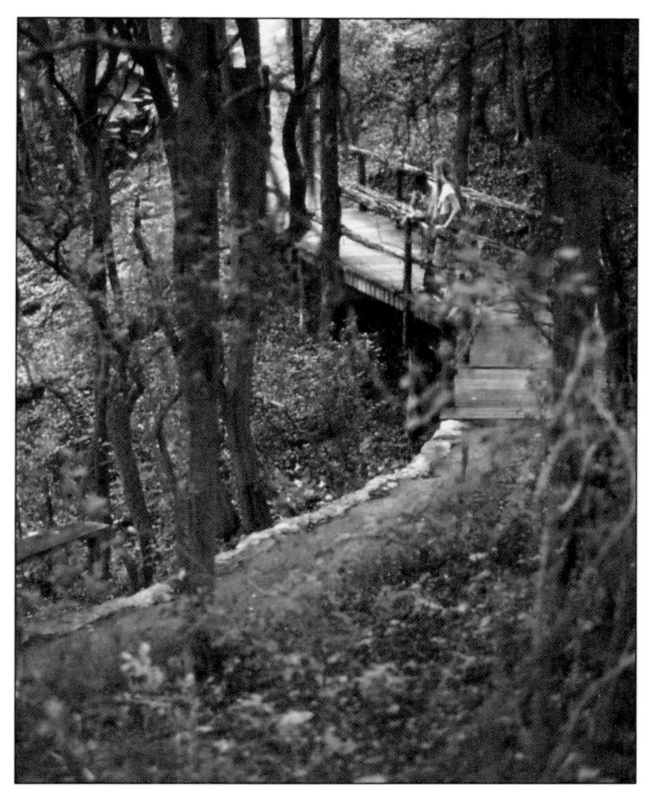

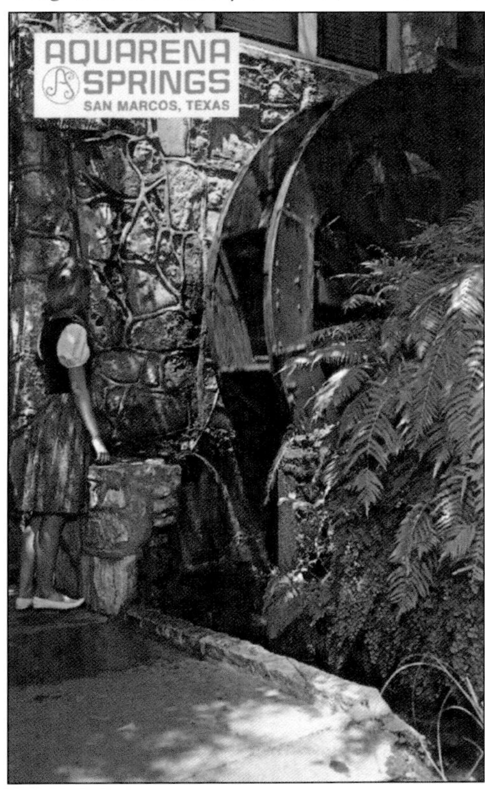

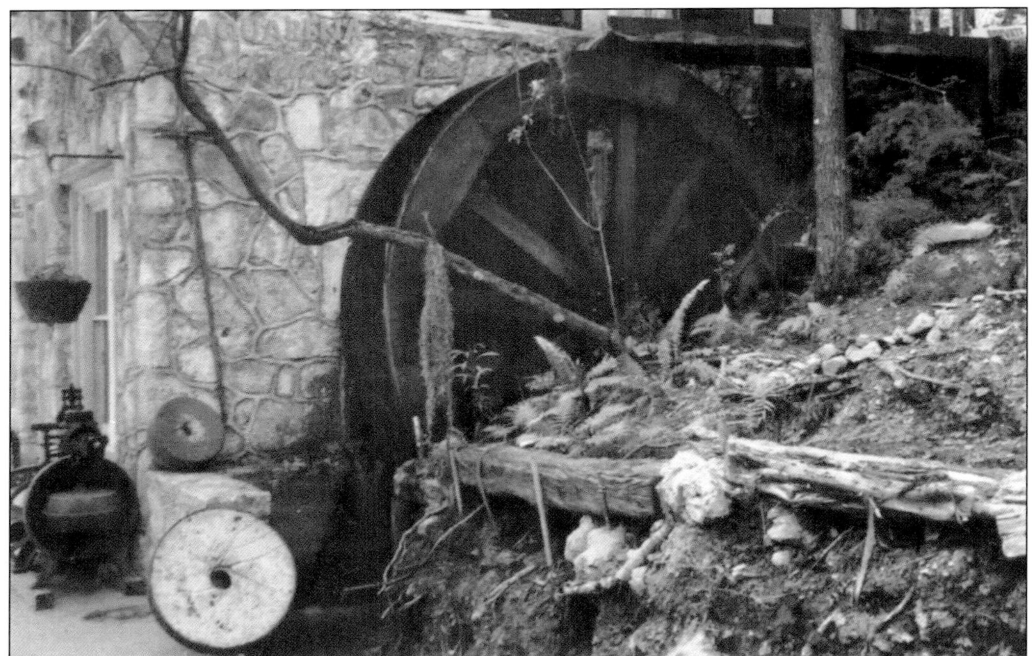

Tucked at the end of a shady walk was a gristmill turned by powerful springs. Early settlers came to a mill at the head of the San Marcos River to have their corn ground into meal. While the stones in the gristmill were originally part of an early San Marcos mill, the machinery was brought from France in the 1800s to the small Texas town of Galle, 15 miles south of San Marcos. Unlike the mill in Galle, which was turned by six mules, the Aquarena mill was powered by a clear brook of spring water. The water dropped into a balanced scoop, which lowered when it was full, emptying the water into a brook that flowed into the river. Paul Rogers modeled the scoop after one he had seen in Hawaii.

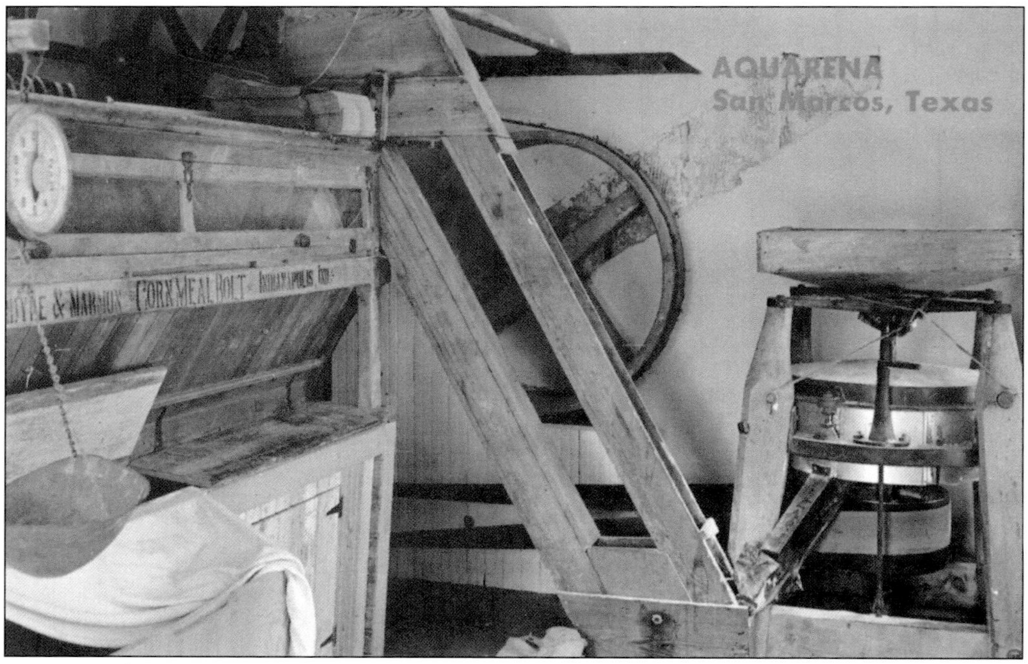

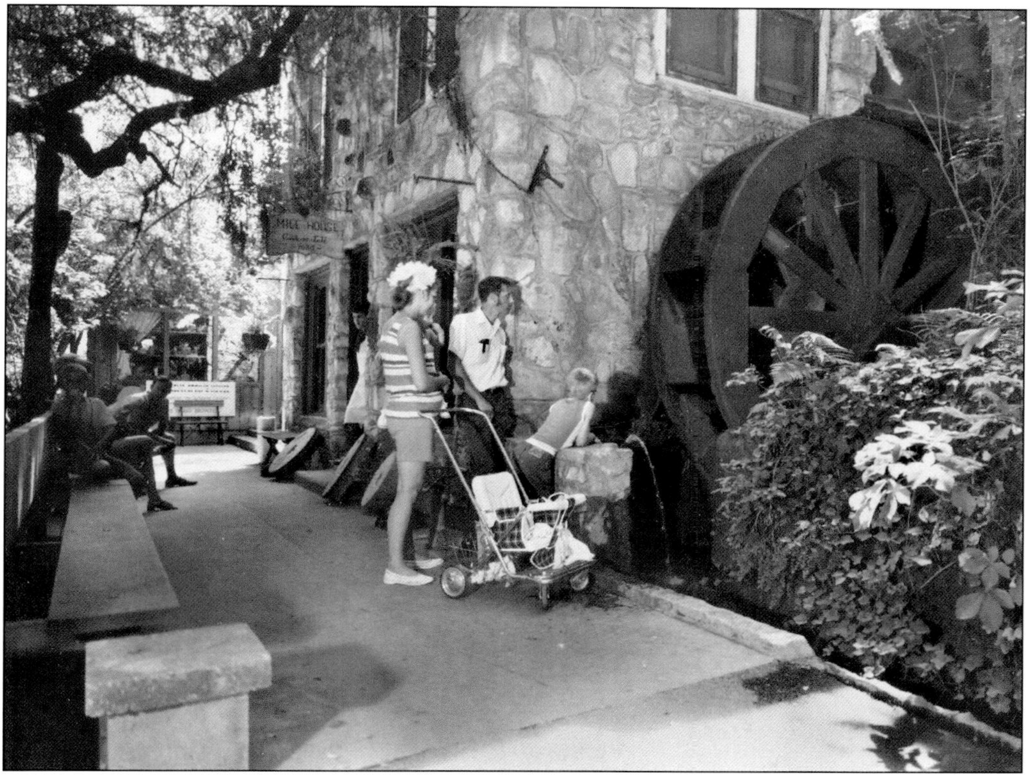

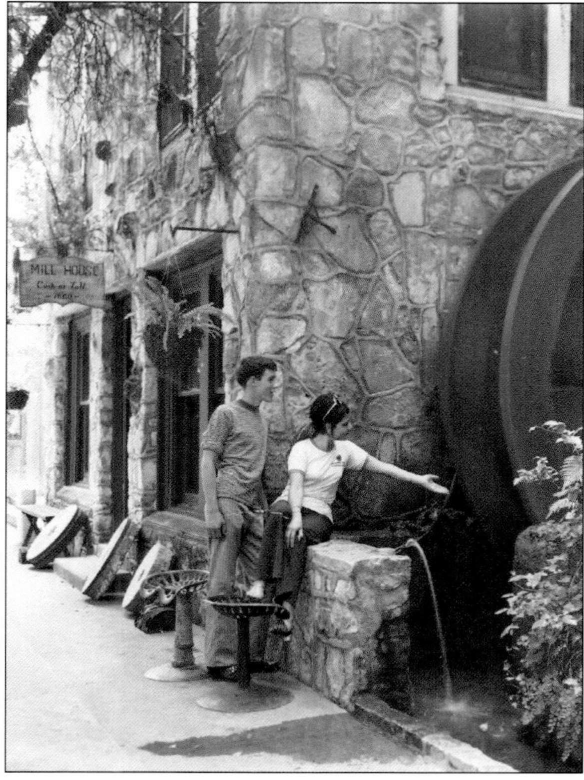

The gristmill was operated by C. W. Wimberley, the fourth generation of Wimberley millers to produce corn meal in this manner. In 1874, Wimberley's great-grandfather, Pleasant Wimberley, established the first mill in the nearby town of Wimberley, Texas, which bears his name. C. W. Wimberley enjoyed entertaining Aquarena visitors with hill country philosophy and folklore. He proudly produced "the best whole grain corn meal and wheat flour available anywhere," according to the Aquarena brochure. Wimberley noted that, during the tourist season, he could hardly grind corn fast enough to keep visitors supplied with 25¢ sample bags. Visitors from across the country and around the world flocked to see the mill in operation. Whenever visitors from a new state or country came to the mill, Wimberley had them write their names on the old corn meal sifter. (Both photographs by John Suhrstedt; courtesy TxDOT.)

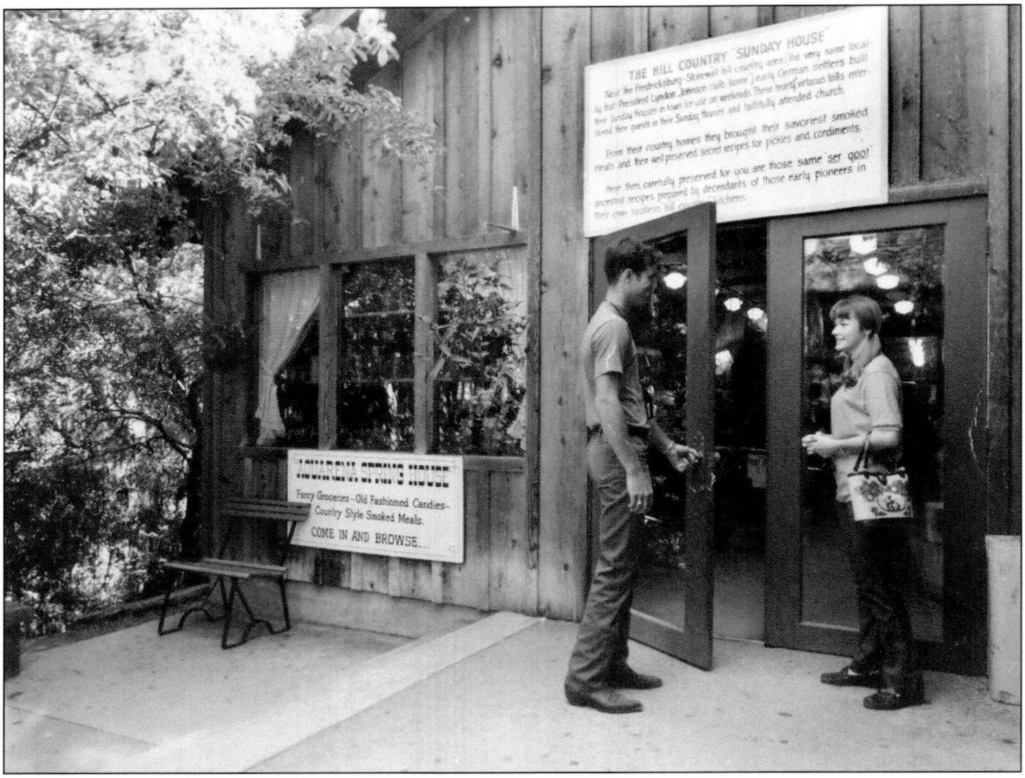

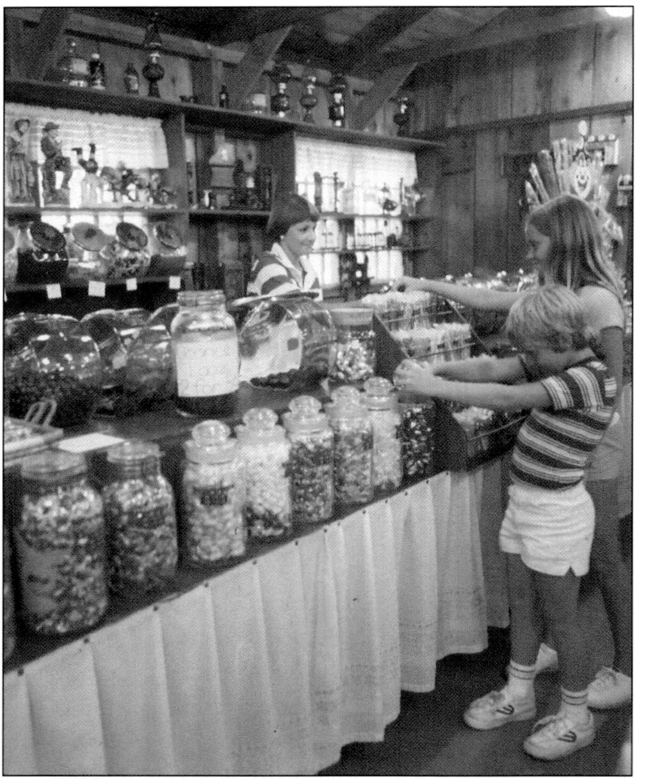

Adjacent to the gristmill was the Aquarena Spring House, an old-fashioned hill country general store where choice local home-prepared foods were available. Docia Baldridge, the proprietress, was always happy to show visitors around. Smoked sausage and other German hill country foods were offered, and a cracker barrel sat near the cheese block. Guests could also purchase bags of the fresh corn meal milled at the gristmill. For children, however, it was the rows of jars filled with colored hard candy or clear, sugary rock candy that held the greatest appeal. Old-fashioned taffy was another popular draw. In the photograph at left, Jay and Melissa Busby try to make a difficult choice among all the delicious options available. (Above, photograph by John Suhrstedt; left, photograph by Greg White; courtesy TxDOT.)

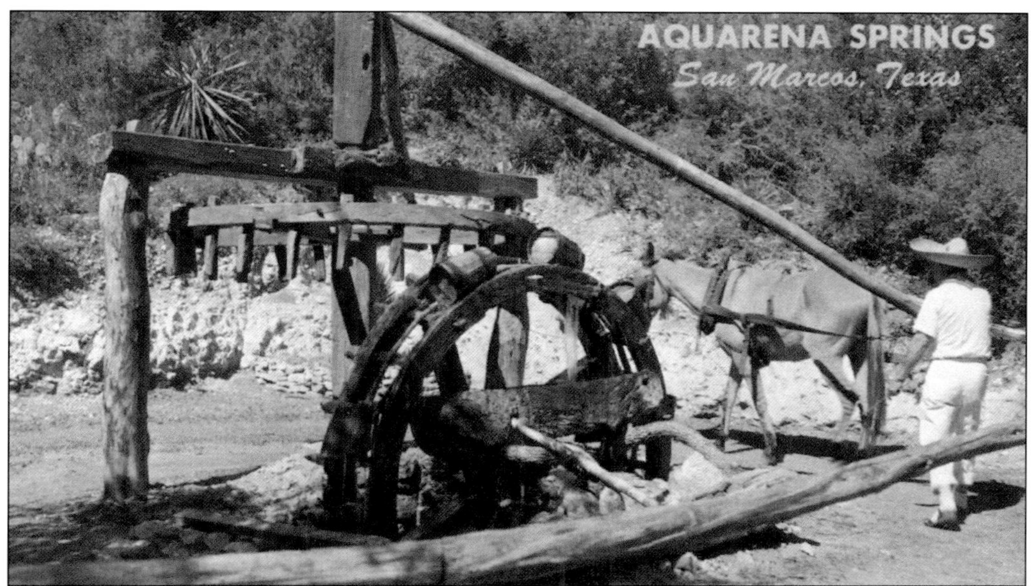

Visitors wandering down the path from the gristmill were often puzzled by a strange contraption installed in the middle of a field. What they were seeing was a 300-year-old *noria*, or water lift, imported from San Luis Potosi, Mexico. Until 1967, when Aquarena acquired it, the *noria* was still in operation. The long pole extending from the top of the base was turned by either man power or mule power, causing the horizontal wheel to turn. Like meshing gears, the upper wheel turned the vertical lower wheel, which pumped water from under ground. At times, a mule was employed, along with a trainer who could explain the ancient water-well device to visitors. Usually, though, the *noria* was unattended, and visitors were left to speculate about the unusual mechanism. (Below, photograph by John Suhrstedt; courtesy TxDOT.)

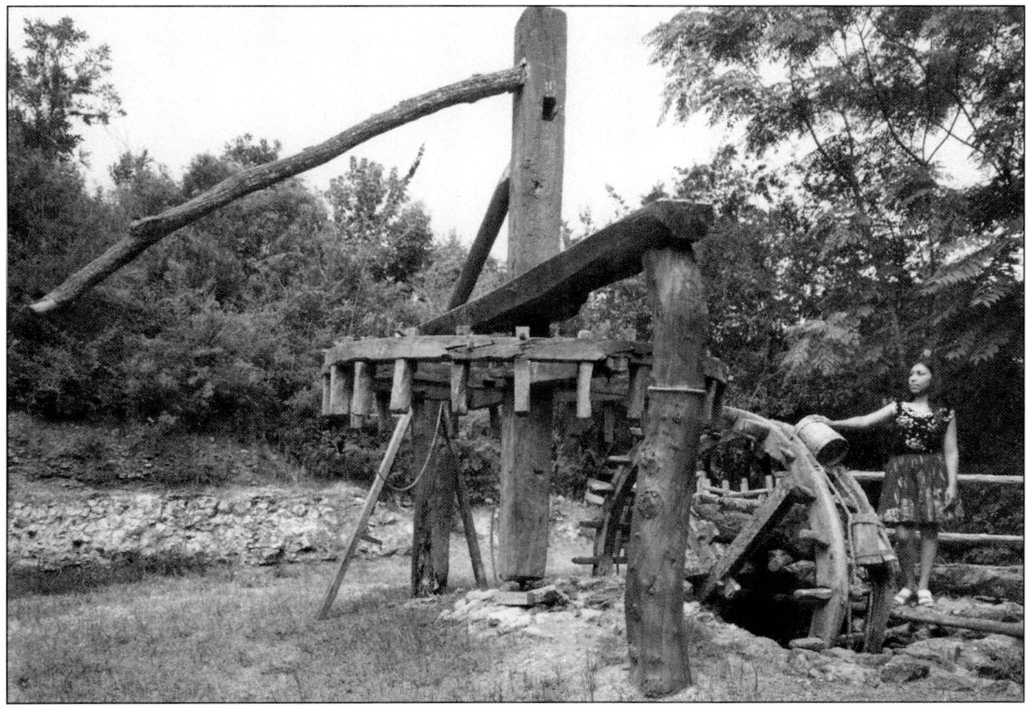

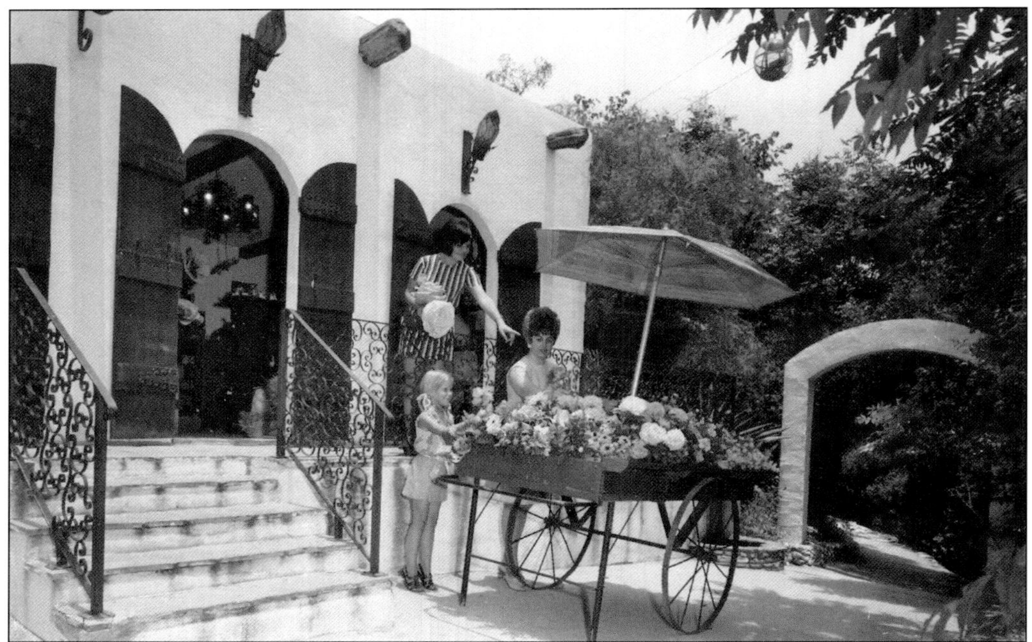

Not far from the *noria*, and in keeping with the Mexican theme, was Casa de Papel (House of Paper), a market that offered visitors an authentic bit of old Mexico with handcrafted artifacts and gifts from south of the border. Adjacent to the structure was an open-air Mexican market. When Casa de Papel opened, an artisan was brought in from Mexico to make beautiful, handcrafted paper flowers that were truly works of art. In the above photograph, employee Vivian Hamadeh helps guests Lolly Balzer and her daughter Lisa select actual flowers from a shaded cart. After serving as a Mexican market for several years, the building was later occupied by craftsman John Medford, who created and sold stained-glass works of art in the space. (Above, photograph by John Suhrstedt; courtesy TxDOT.)

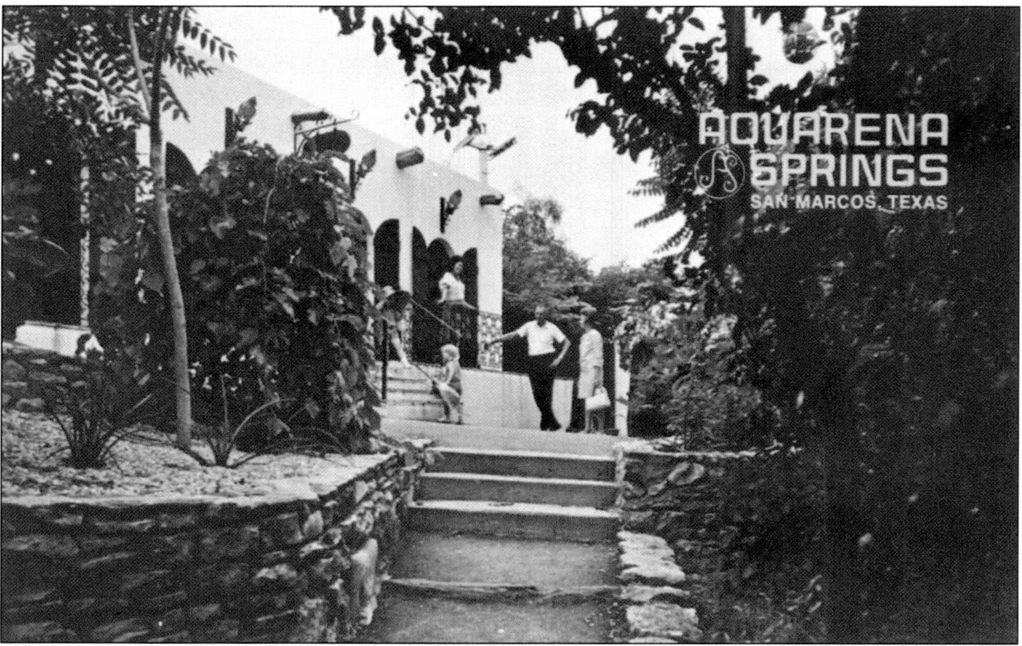

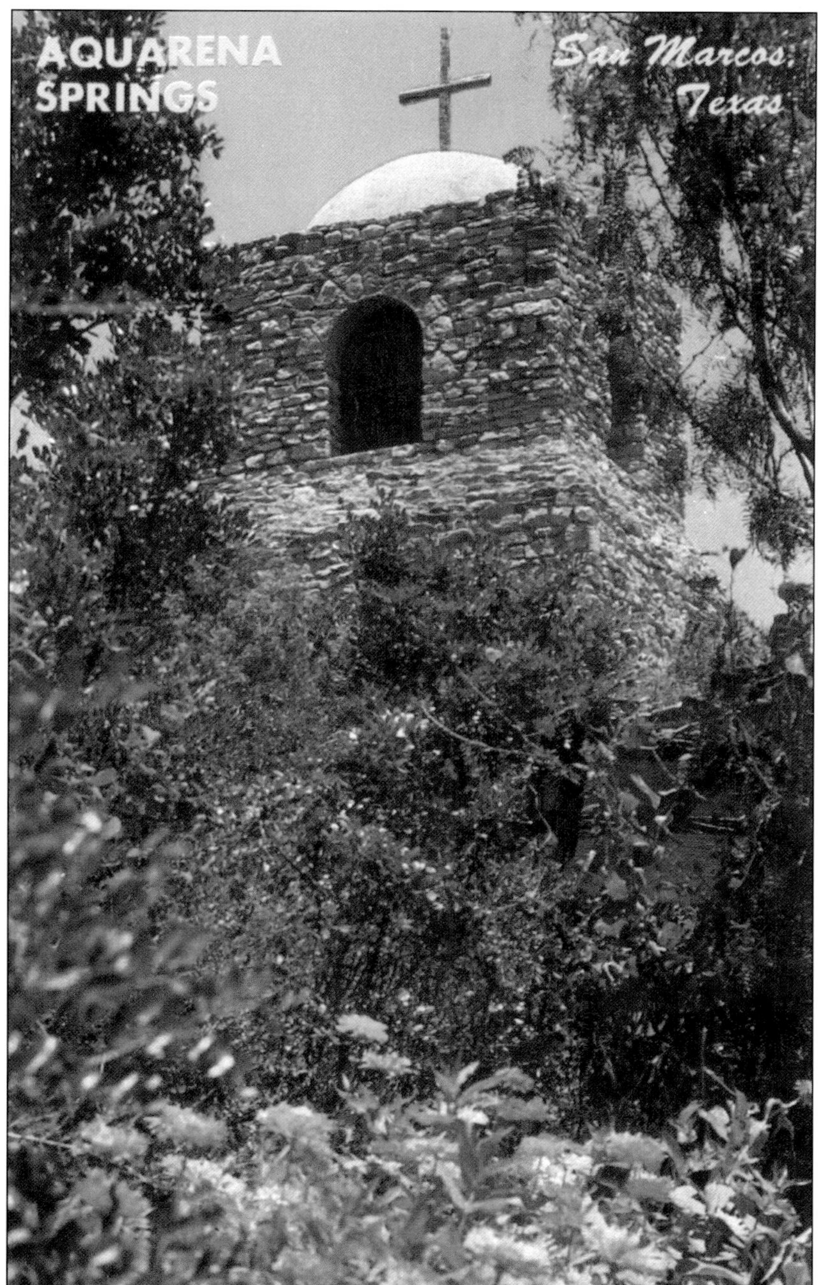

Beyond the natural beauty the Hanging Gardens afforded, their primary appeal was the opportunity to step back in time, whether by seeing corn meal milled as it was two centuries ago or watching an exhibition of the ancient art of glassblowing. The first sight to greet visitors after they disembarked from the sky ride and headed to the trails of the Hanging Gardens was a historic Spanish mission. In 1743, Spanish explorers stumbled upon the bubbling springs that Aquarena would later call home. Because it was St. Mark's Day, Franciscan monks called the river the San Marcos. The monks established San Xavier Mission and the Presidio of San Francisco Xavier in 1755. The reconstruction of the mission's bell tower on the original site in the gardens allowed Aquarena visitors to travel back 200 years as they entered the mission's cool interior.

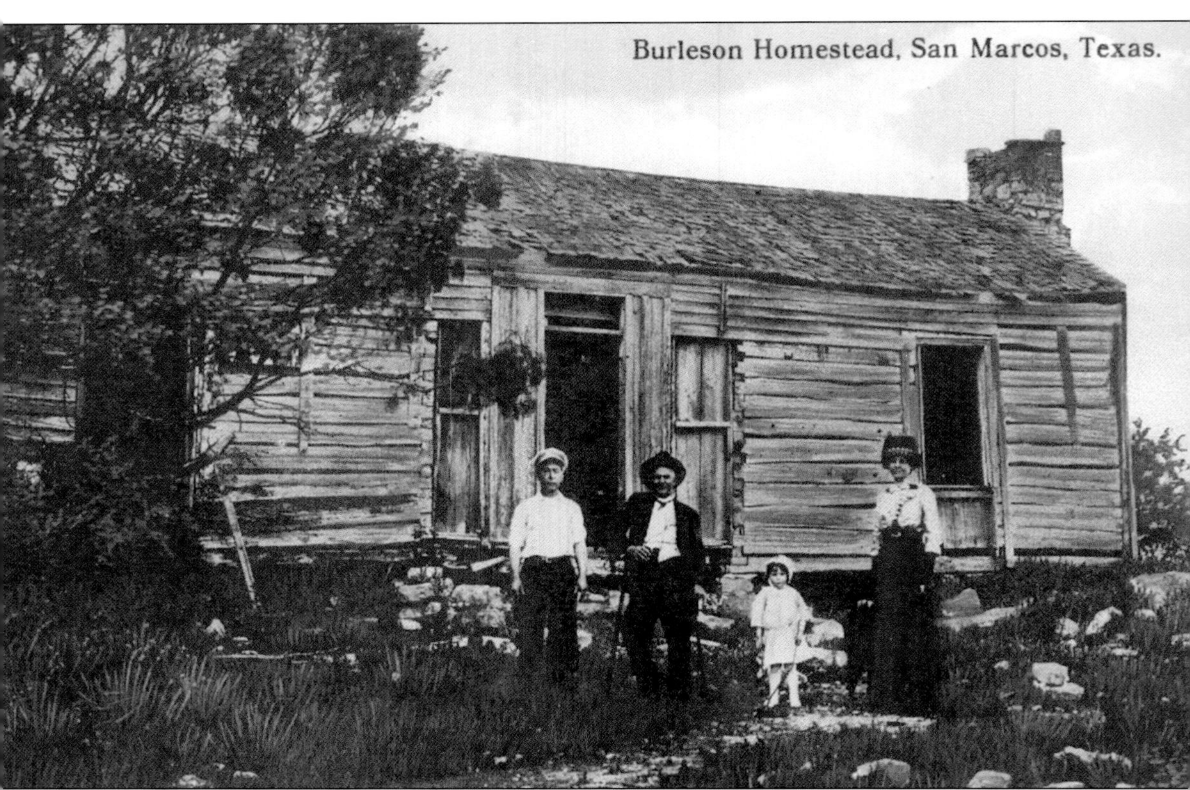

War hero Gen. Edward Burleson fought with Ben Milam in San Antonio and commanded the First Regiment at San Jacinto in the battle for Texas independence. He served as vice-president of the Republic of Texas under Sam Houston, and as a Texas state senator. Burleson acquired the San Marcos River headwaters and springs in 1845. In 1848, he and his sons built a two-room cabin on a hill overlooking the springs. A. B. Rogers acquired Burleson's homestead tract when he purchased the land at the headwaters in 1926. Research indicates that the original Burleson cabin fell down in a 1917 storm. In 1960, the storm-flattened cabin was dismantled, and its materials were stored until 1964, when a replica cabin was built near the original site in the Hanging Gardens. Visitors could wander through this cabin, and for several years, glassblower Richard Manley used the space for his demonstrations.

By far, one of the most memorable personalities at Aquarena Springs was Bohemian glassblower Richard Manley. Six days a week, Manley thrilled audiences in the Burleson cabin, and later in the Casa de Papel building, with his astounding artistry. Manley, who had performed as a glassblower at the 1938 World's Fair in New York, was so skilled that he could actually work blindfolded and often amazed visitors with a demonstration of this ability. Former Aquarena general manager Scott McGehee recalls that Manley traveled by bus from San Marcos to San Antonio each month to get glassblowing supplies. No trip to the Hanging Gardens was complete without a visit to Manley's studio. (Both photographs by Herman Kelly; courtesy TxDOT.)

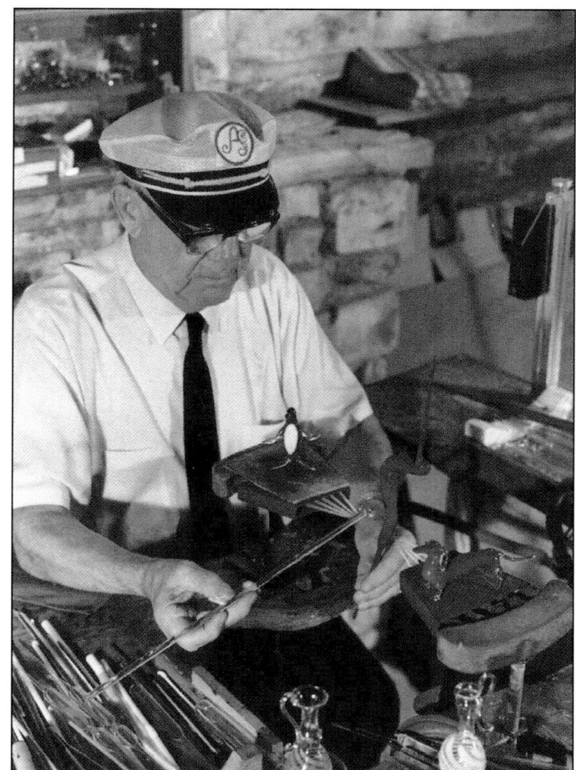

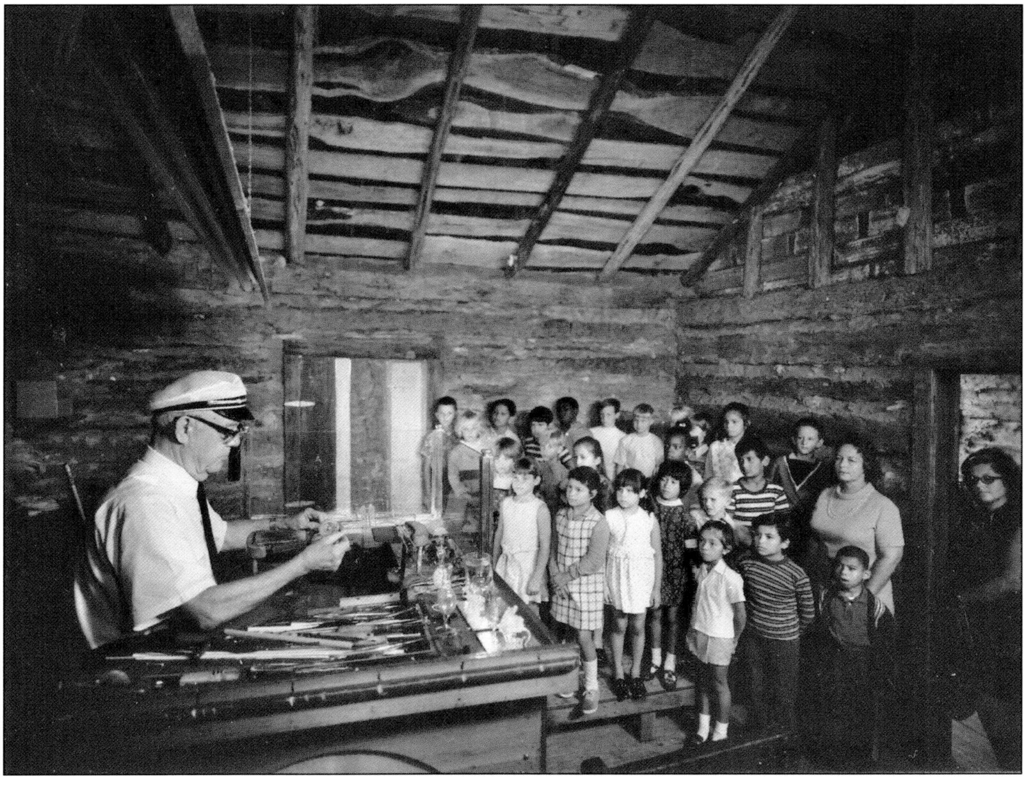

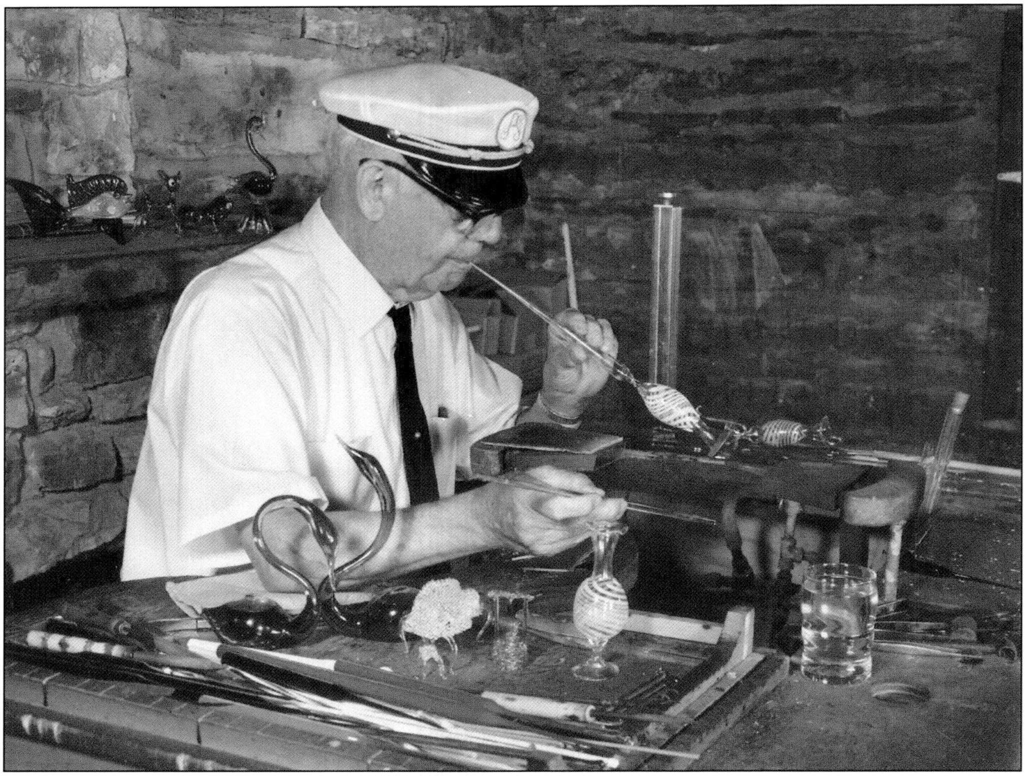

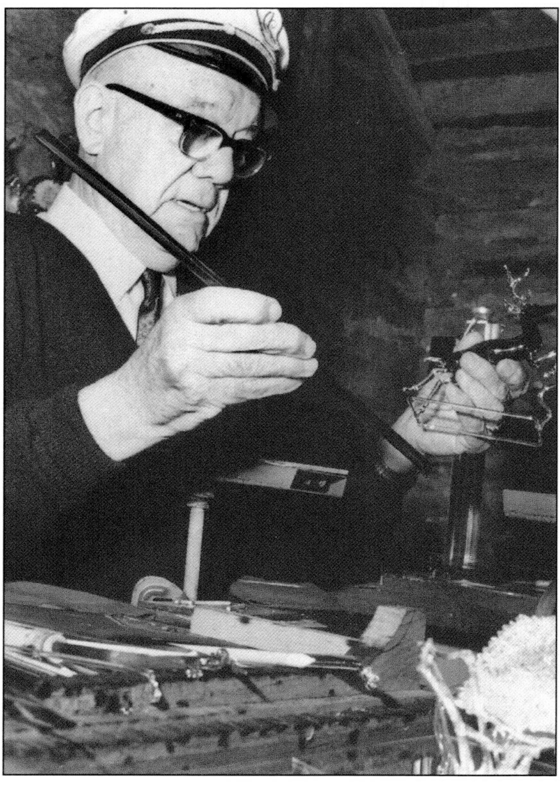

Richard Manley's glass creations, including colorful vases and animal figurines, were for sale and were eagerly scooped up by Aquarena visitors. Some of his pieces featured incredibly intricate detail. The delicate piano and stool in the above photograph are an example of this intricacy. One audience favorite was called "Satan's tears." Manley created a glass teardrop with a tiny filament of glass extending from the point at the top. When an invited audience member tweaked the thin strand, the entire piece disintegrated into dust. Another crowd-pleaser was the "goose that laid the golden egg." After fashioning a clear glass goose, Manley inserted a gold glass rod through a small opening and blew a golden "egg" into existence. Even as his eyesight failed, Manley continued to entertain and amaze audiences, blowing glass by instinct that looked a lot like magic. (Above, photograph by John Suhrstedt; courtesy TxDOT; left, courtesy SMHCC-San Marcos Public Library.)

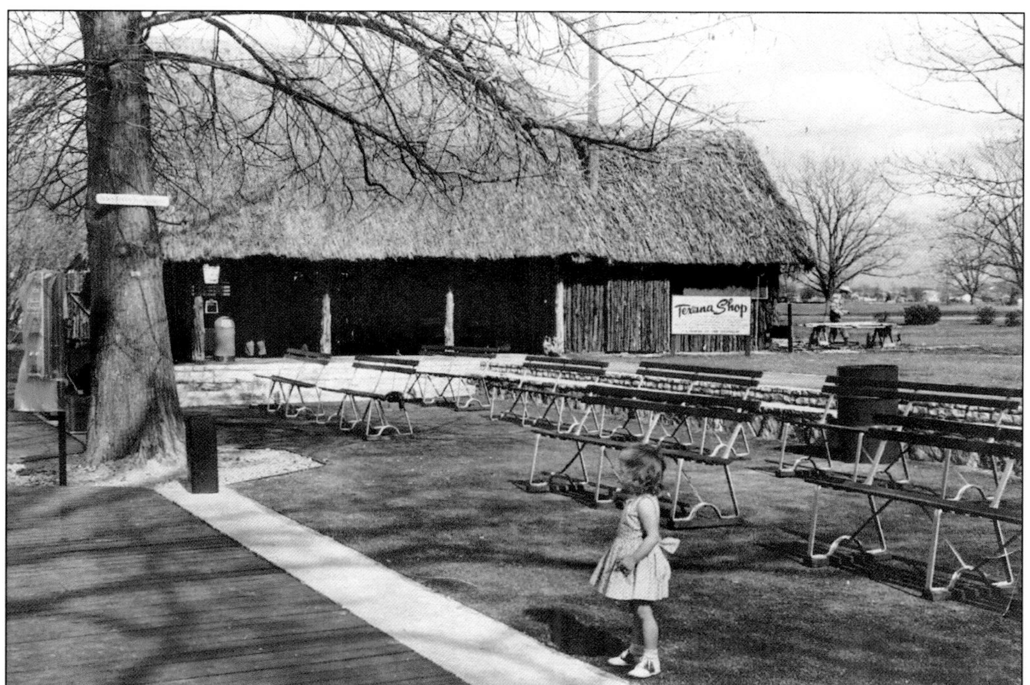

In the early days of Aquarena, pre-1958, guests could visit the thatched structure shown in these photographs if they wanted to shop for natural treasures from Texas and the Southwest. The Texana Shop building was styled after typical Mexican dwellings and was constructed of native reeds and cedar poles. Inside, Aquarena visitors could purchase cacti, shrub plantings, driftwood, or mineral rocks. The shop, situated adjacent to the glass bottom boat docks, offered guests a place to browse as they awaited boarding. Picnic tables outside the shop provided a place for families to have lunch or a cool drink and take a break from their strolls around the park grounds. Pictured above, the author enjoys one of her earliest visits to the park.

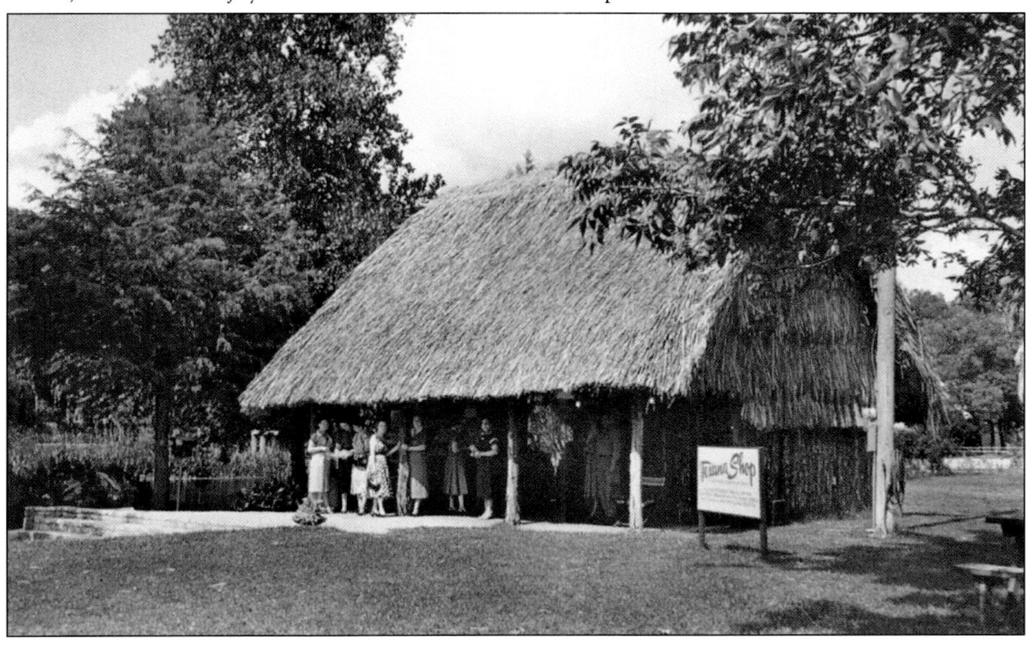

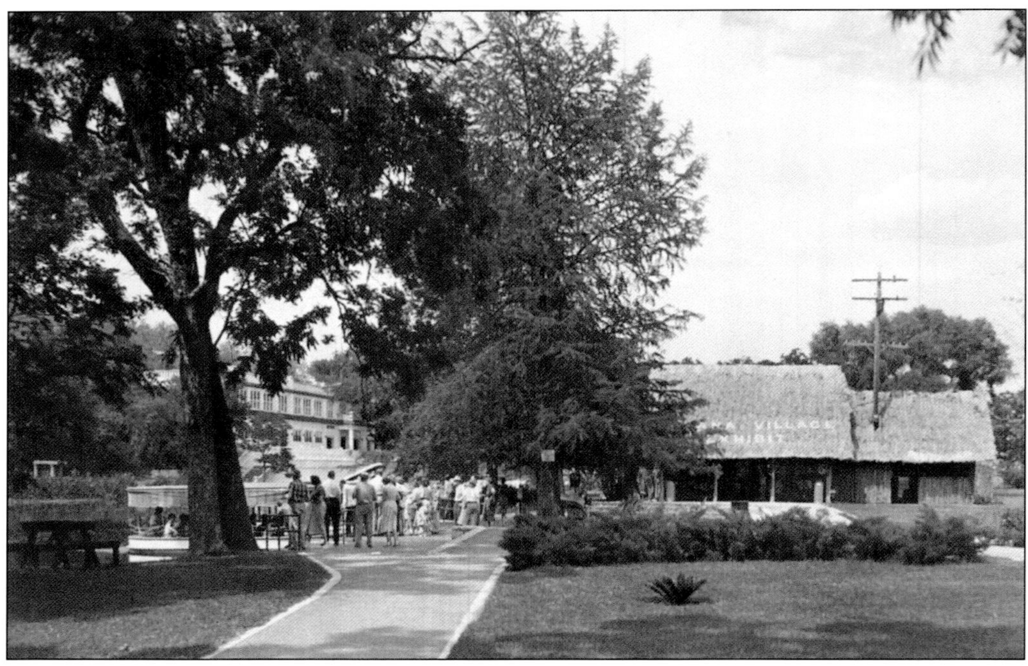

In 1958, Paul Rogers transformed the Texana Shop into Texana Village. The village was a remarkable frontier town exhibit for which Rogers and manager Don Russell amassed everything from complete buildings to the smallest items of jewelry or clothing from frontier times. The two men made numerous trips through west Texas and Mexico in search of items that could be incorporated into the exhibit. Visitors meandered through painstakingly reconstructed buildings, including a saloon, a barbershop, a general store, a blacksmith shop, a livery stable, and even a jail. In addition, Rogers moved San Marcos' oldest house, log by log, to Texana Village.

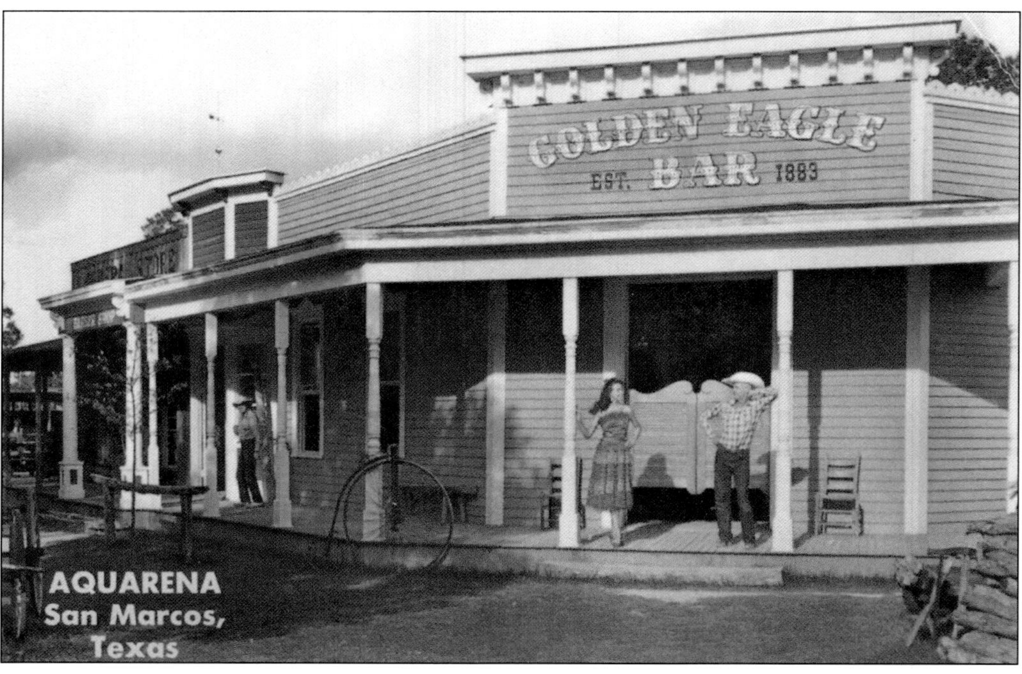

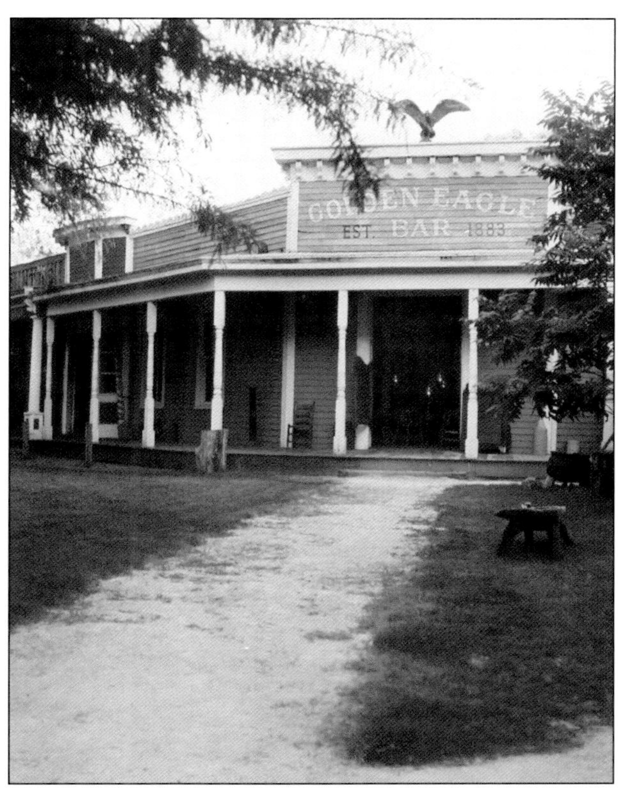

Visitors to the Golden Eagle Saloon would not have been surprised to see Jesse James walk into this frontier bar. In the meantime, they could slake their thirst with a glass of sarsaparilla. The back bar was imported from Norway and displayed intricate carving, lead glass, and a marble top. The front bar, where patrons were served, previously graced the White Elephant Saloon in Fredericksburg, Texas. Three men were rumored to have been shot while standing at this bar. The saloon's lumber came from the old Sam Maverick home in San Antonio. Maverick was the man who famously refused to brand his calves on the 19th-century range. Against one wall stood an old-fashioned player piano, which cranked out tinny-sounding tunes from a bygone frontier era. (Right, photograph by John Suhrstedt; both photographs courtesy TxDOT.)

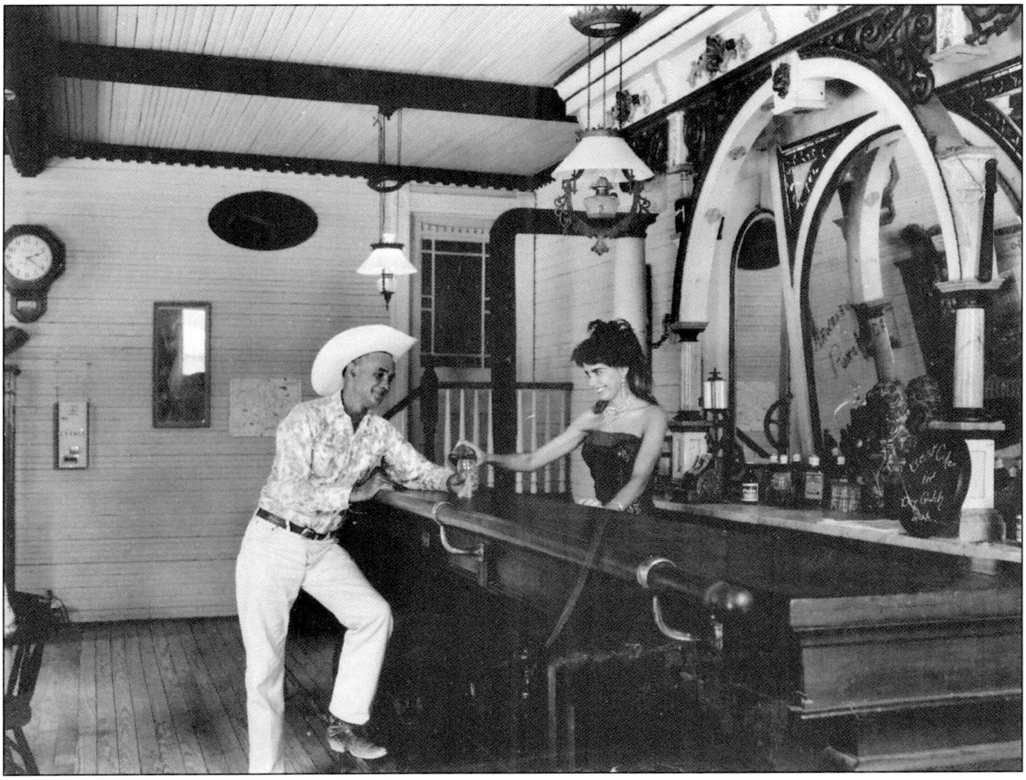

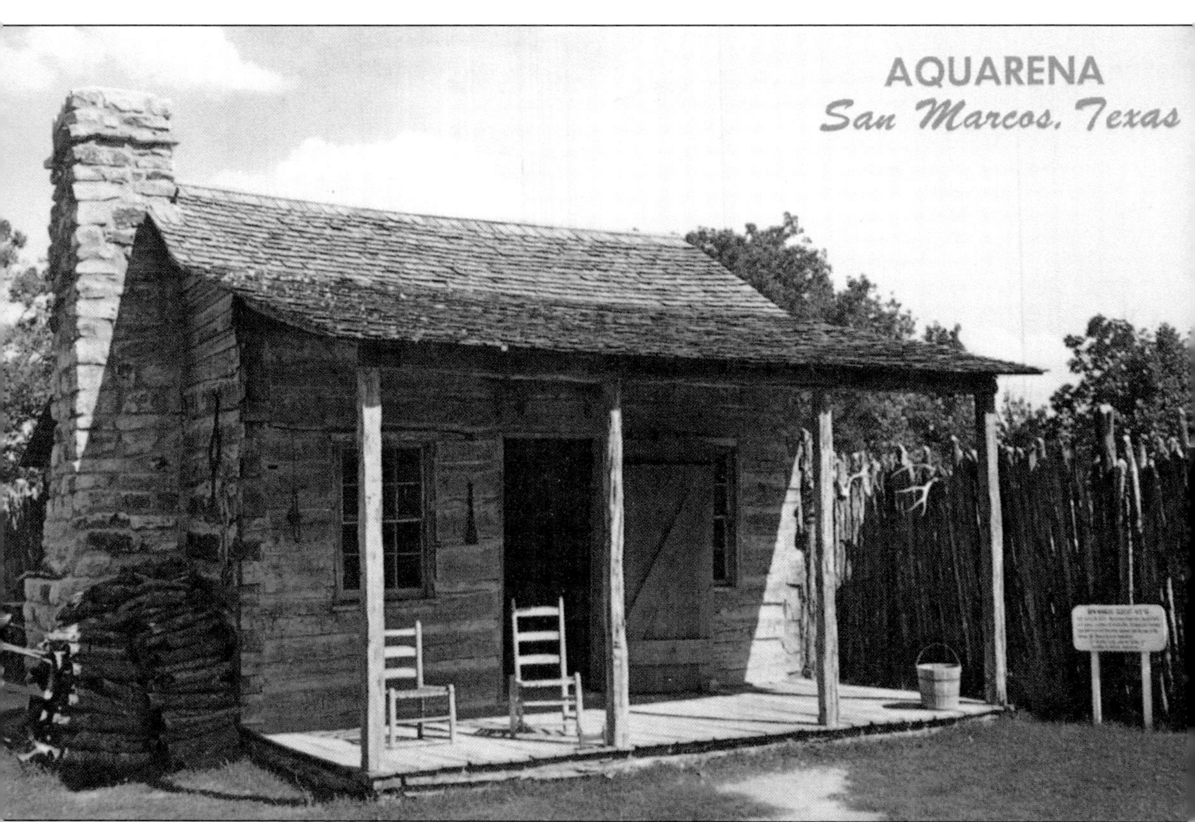

Upon entering Texana Village, visitors' attention was drawn to a log cabin that was the first house built in San Marcos. The Merriman Cabin was constructed in the 1840s for Dr. Eli T. Merriman and his family. Along with Gen. Edward Burleson and surveyor William Lindsey, Merriman was one of San Marcos' original town planners. In 1958, Paul Rogers and Don Russell supervised the relocation of the cabin from its downtown location to Texana Village. The cabin was disassembled log by log and reconstructed at the site. Russell said that every square foot of floor space was photographed and each separate piece numbered, so that nothing would be out of its original place. In 2000, Texas State University gave the cabin to the San Marcos Heritage Association. In conjunction with the City Parks and Recreation Department, the Heritage Association restored and relocated the cabin to Veramendi Plaza, not far from its original location. The cabin has been furnished with antiques appropriate to the 1847–1860 time period and is open to the public weekly for tours conducted by Heritage Association docents. (Photograph by Bill Kobert.)

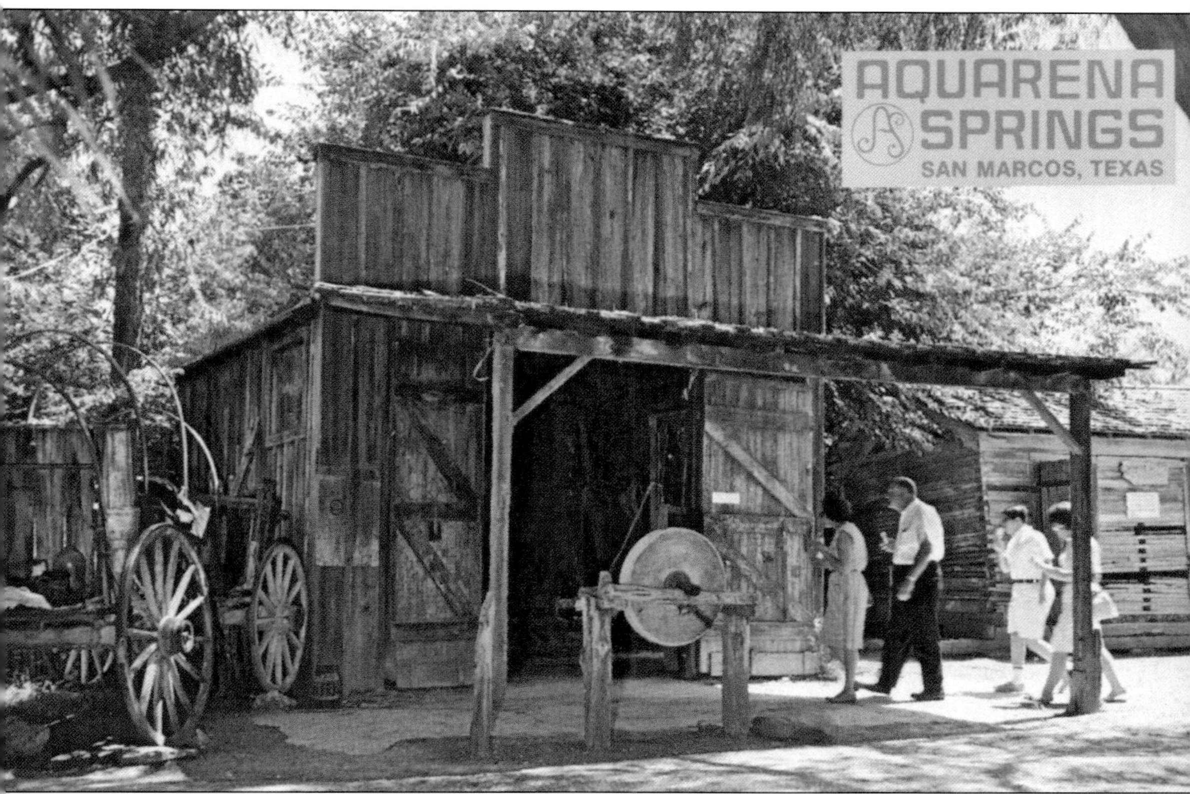

The aim of Texana Village was to provide as complete a picture of frontier town life as possible. Since the village included a stable for horses, a blacksmith shop was obviously a requirement. Like other structures, this shop, originally located on the main street of Fredericksburg, Texas, was taken apart board by board and carefully reconstructed in its new location. The shop was completely equipped with a forge, a set of metalworking tools, and an ancient but serviceable anvil. These items, along with the brand marks burned on the doors and walls, contributed to the realism of the setting. In the early hours of December 4, 1975, San Marcos firefighters were called to the blacksmith shop after a watchman reported a fire. An electric malfunction had started the fire, which destroyed the shop. Aquarena Springs president Gene Phillips said that a price tag could not be placed on the destroyed items because they were "one of a kind." Nevertheless, the shop was soon rebuilt and furnished as closely as possible to the original.

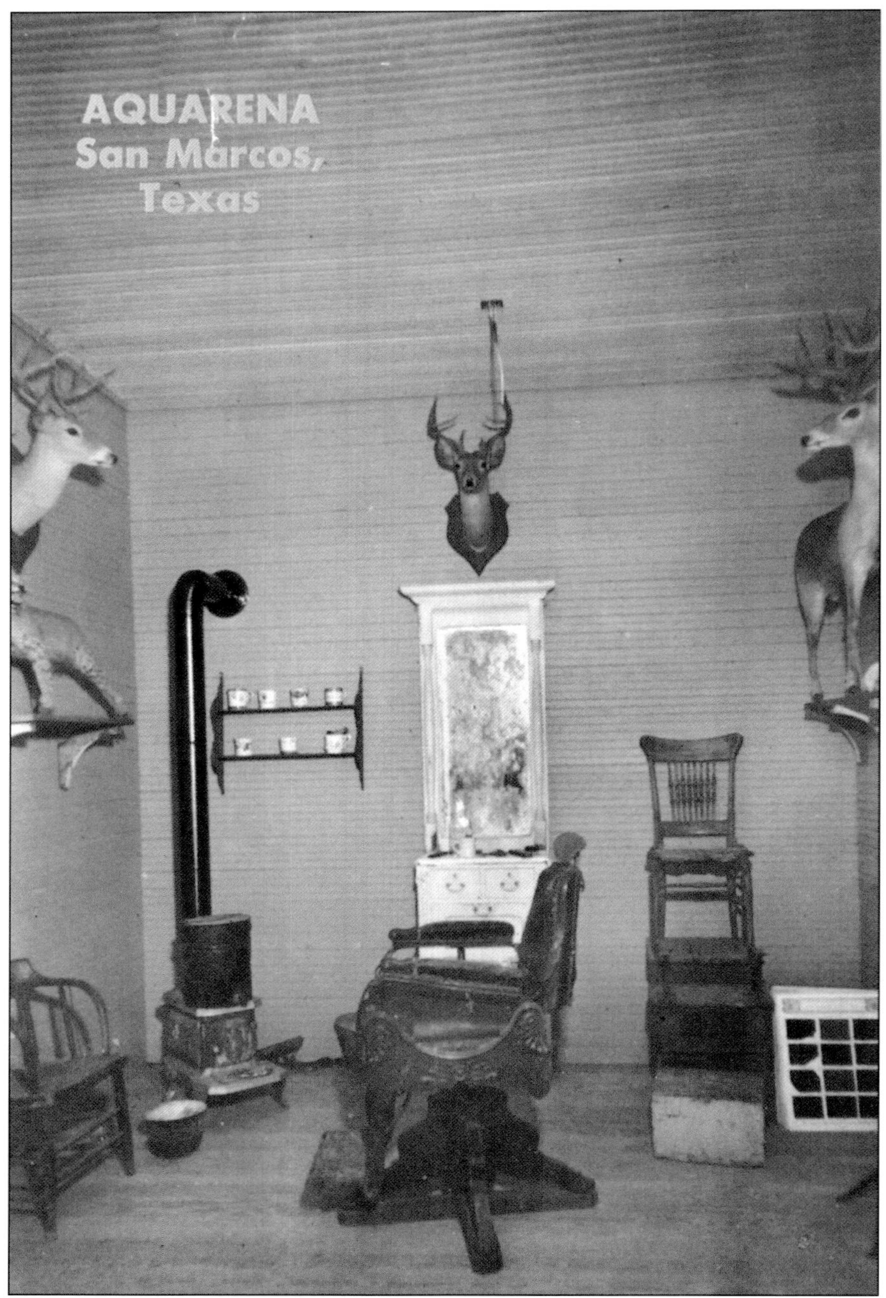

No frontier town would be complete without a barbershop to provide haircuts, shoe shines, and a place to engage in local gossip or political discussions. Kit Griffin's barbershop, purchased and moved to Texana Village by Paul Rogers following the death of its octogenarian owner, was a 19th-century structure from Tioga, Texas, in Grayson County. In this shop, both Sam King, Texana Village's first proprietor, and singing movie cowboy Gene Autry got their first haircuts, and both shined shoes at the shop's stand when they were boys. Visitors to the barbershop enjoyed taking a turn in the historic chairs and posing for souvenir photographs. The wood-burning stove in the corner and stuffed hunting trophies on the walls contributed to the realistic old-time atmosphere. (Photograph by Bill Kobert.)

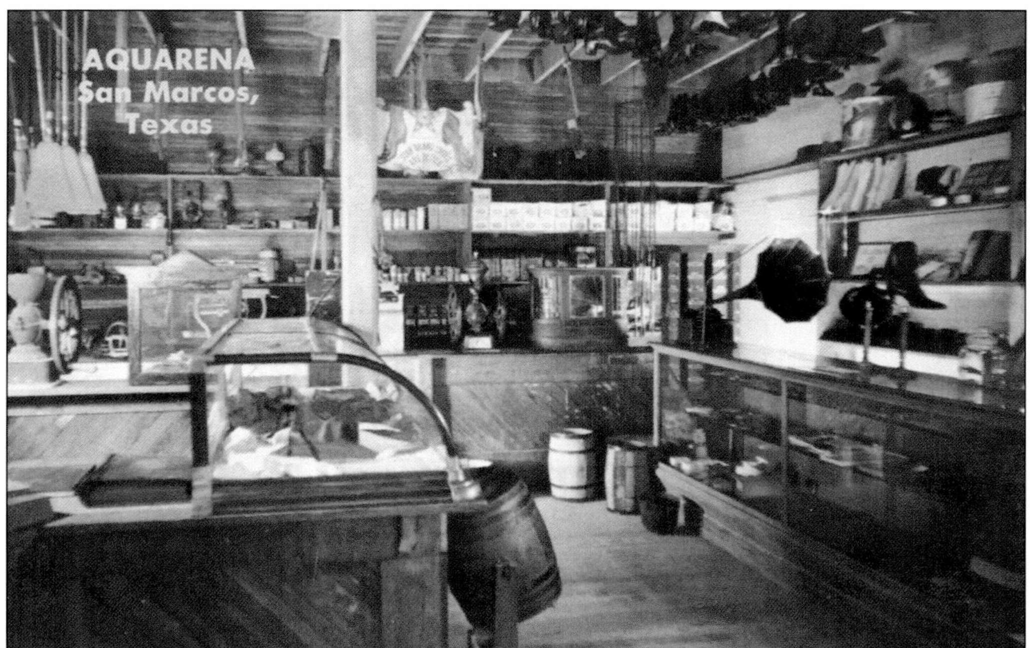

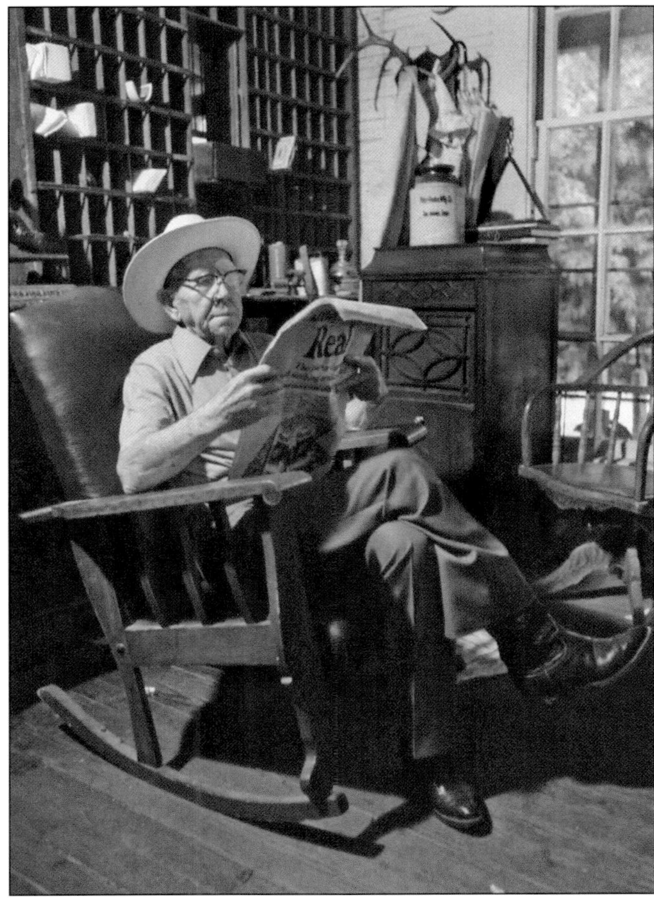

Adjoining the barbershop was a general store displaying the most complete collection of frontier artifacts in Texana Village. Visitors could wander among the shelves and display cases to see numerous high-button shoes, an ancient washing machine, manicure sets, sewing kits, costume jewelry, cabinets for bulk spices, an early vintage typewriter, and a Gramophone. An antique cash register and an old scale sat on the countertop. The store also housed a post office that had actually been used in Sattler, Texas. In the photograph at right, taken in 1977, W. E. ("Papa") Phillips awaits visitors to the general store so that he can regale them with fascinating, mostly true, stories. Guests always enjoyed listening to Phillips as he explained the exhibits and elaborated on San Marcos history. (Above, photograph by Bill Kobert; right, photograph by Greg White; courtesy TxDOT.)

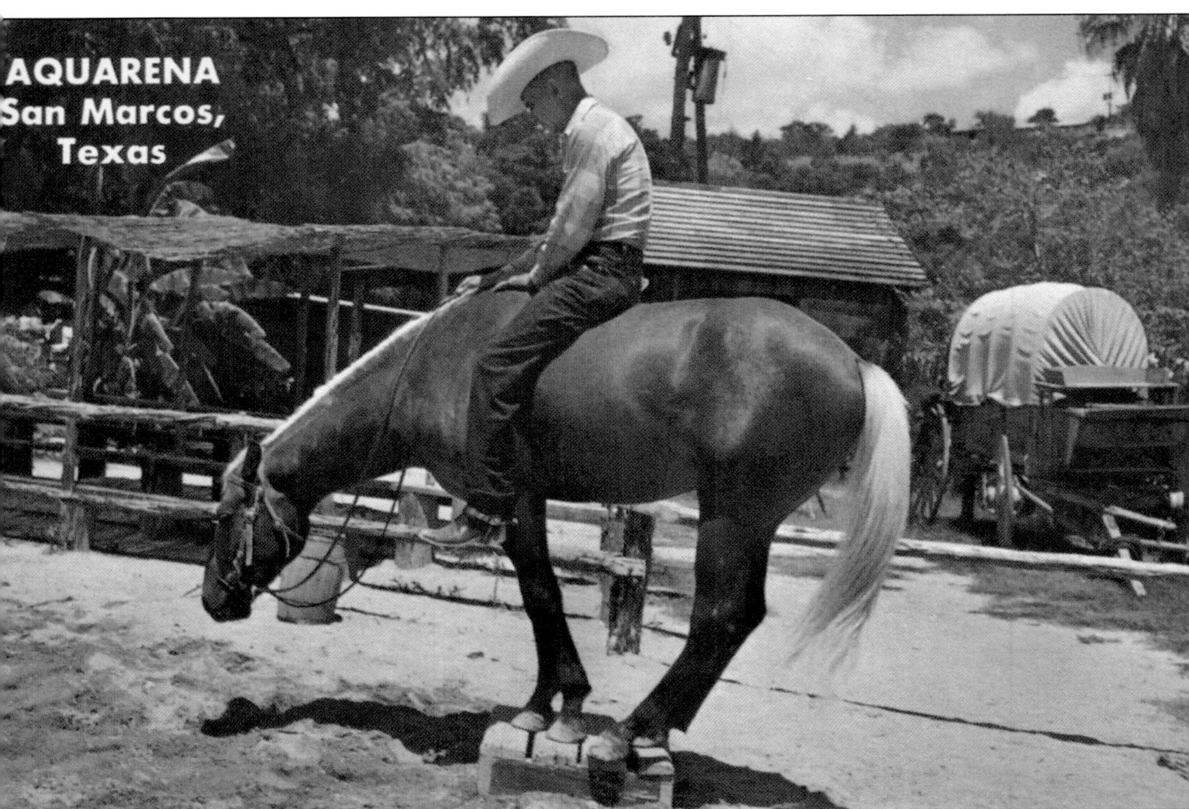

Next door to the general store was a corral in which Texana Village proprietor Sam King ran a horse show. King's shows were a highlight of Texana Village tours in the late 1950s and early 1960s. Here one of King's horses demonstrates impressive balancing skills. When the horse show closed in the mid-1960s, the corral became home to a herd of goats. Visitors enjoyed watching and feeding them, particularly a large black goat named Guillermo, who had a voracious appetite for cigarettes. Three of the goats—named Boo, Nervous, and Don Knotts—were an unusual breed known as "scare goats." In response to a sudden loud noise, these goats would collapse, falling down with their muscles rigid. The goats would recover after a few seconds. Some say that these goats were used by herders to protect other livestock, such as sheep, from predators by involuntarily sacrificing themselves, allowing the more valuable livestock to escape. The goats were safe in Texana Village, but children delighted in clapping their hands to elicit this strange response. (Courtesy Carole McCarley.)

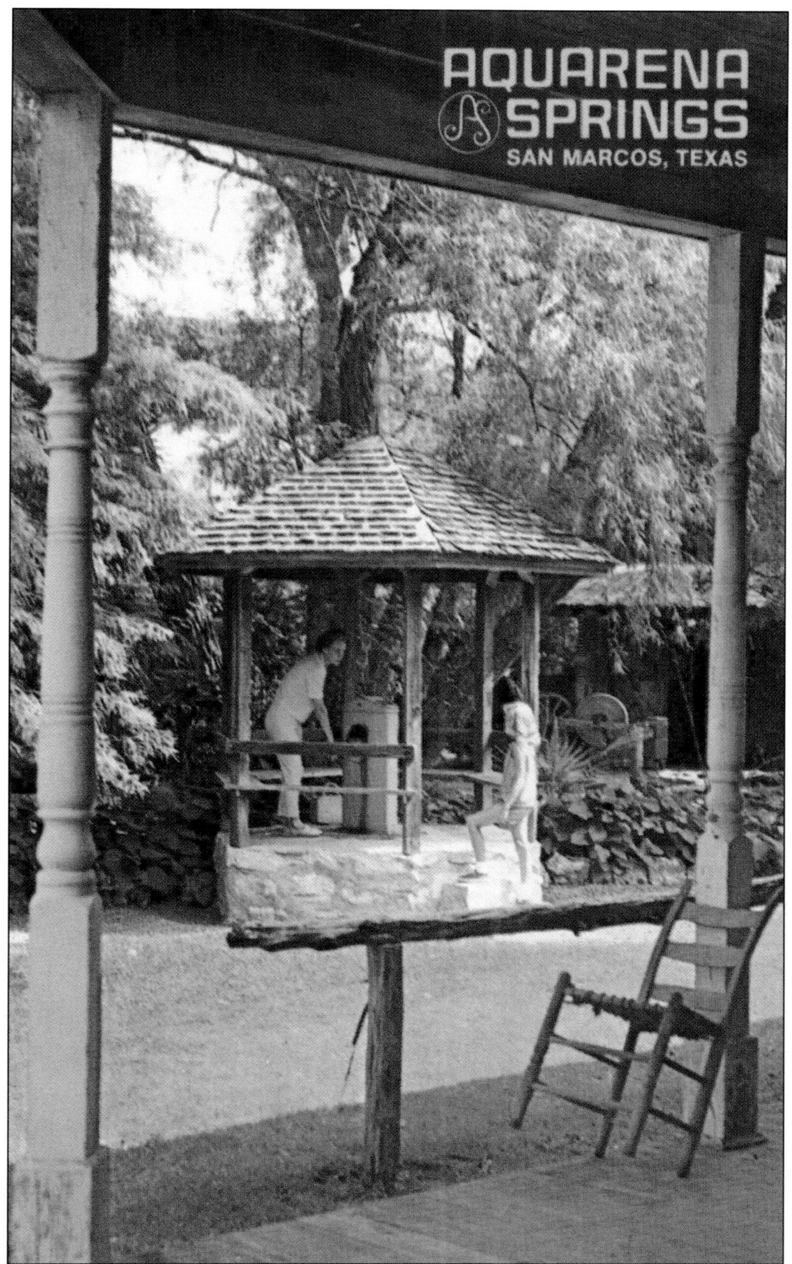

From the porch outside the saloon, guests had a view of a gazebo containing a *c.* 1900 water pump, yet another authentic frontier artifact in Texana Village. The open area where the pump was located served as the site of a yearly party at Texana Village, at which Texas legislators and politicians were wined and dined and reminded of the importance of promoting Texas tourism. Aquarena billed Texana Village as offering "the six gun pulse quickening excitement of the old West," and nothing was more pulse quickening than Black Bart, a life-size and very lifelike wax cowboy gunman. For a dime, visitors were provided with a three-shooter pistol, which allowed them to aim electronic rays at Bart's midsection. If a shot missed, a recorded, gravelly voice snarled an insult: "You miserable polecat. You didn't even come close." A good shot evoked, "Yeeow! You got me. That was pretty good shooting for a dude."

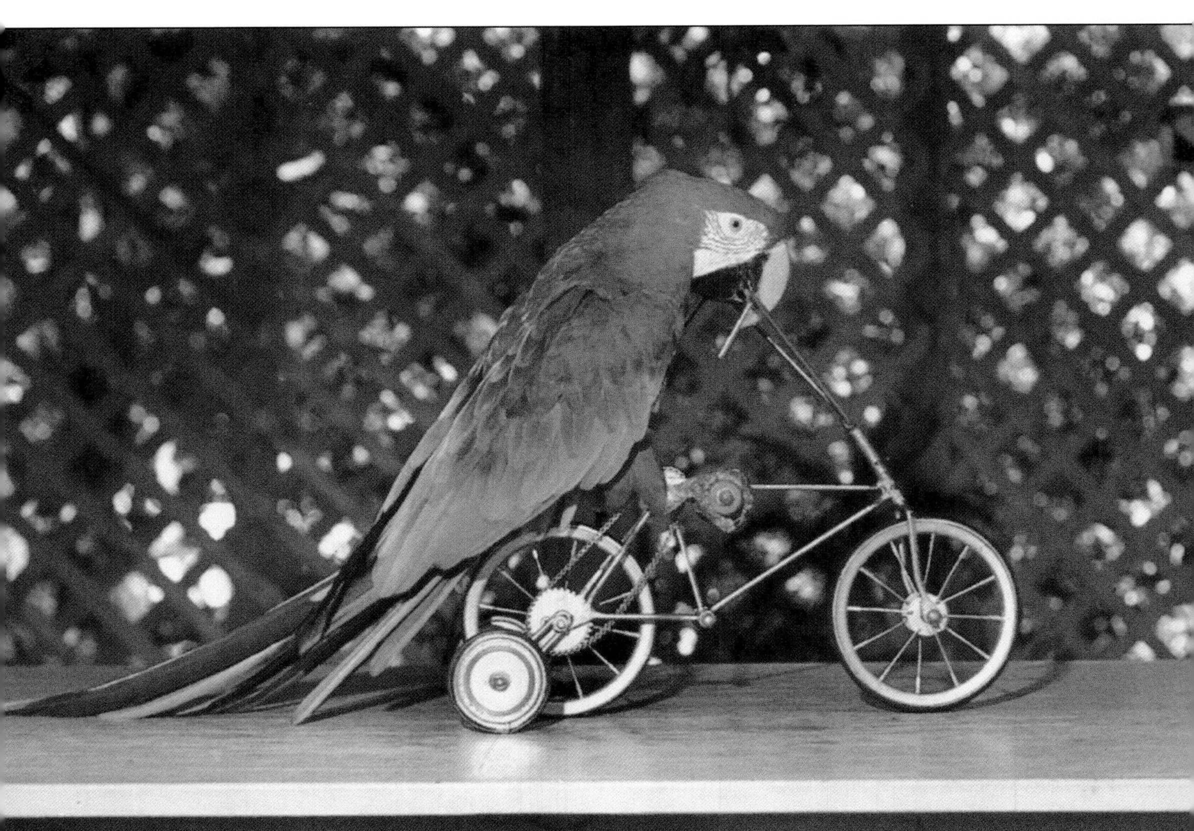

In addition to its frontier exhibits, Texana Village housed an alligator pond, a turtle pool, and numerous exotic birds. For several years, guests could enjoy the Bird of Paradise show in the village. Here Bertha the Bicycling Bird performs for an audience. Former visitors to Texana Village will surely remember the small arcade area just outside the entrance, complete with fun-house mirrors and various animal entertainers. Skilled animals included a piano-playing chicken, a dancing chicken, and a basketball-playing chicken that pecked at Ping-Pong balls, driving them into a small hoop. A rabbit fire chief raced out of his cage, jumped in the back of a toy fire engine, and pulled a lever that set off a siren. One of the most popular performers was the chicken that played tic-tac-toe. In 1983, Austin humor columnist John Kelso lamented that he was unable to defeat the chicken. When confronted, assistant manager Scott McGehee grinned and said, "I can't tell you secrets. Let's put it this way. Have you ever beat a computer?"

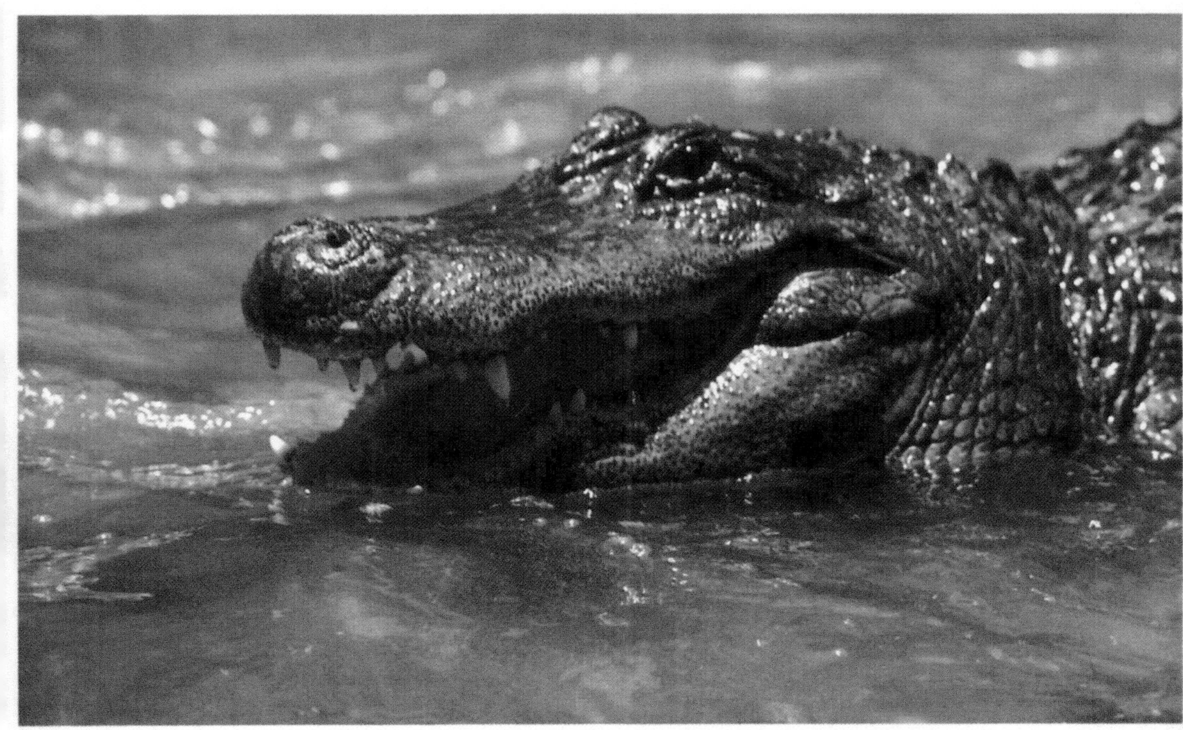

Alligator Basks in Sunshine in Reptile Exhibit, Hillside Gardens

Aquarena Springs housed a collection of 24 alligators in Texana Village, and visitors enjoyed getting a close-up view of these enormous creatures. In May 1970, thunderstorms dropped 15 inches of water on San Marcos and inundated the town. The river overflowed its banks, and all of Aquarena was under water. In this chaos, the alligators were able to make their escape from Texana Village into the San Marcos River. Aquarena officials contacted Tom Allen, a reptile expert and one of the stars of the television show *Mutual of Omaha's Wild Kingdom*. Allen flew to Texas to help recapture the fugitive alligators. Scott McGehee, Aquarena attractions supervisor at the time, recalls accompanying Allen and then president Don Russell as they set out by boat. When asked if all the alligators were finally accounted for, McGehee replies, "Yes. Plus one." Following this event, the alligators were moved to the Hanging Gardens on the hill to prevent a future recurrence.

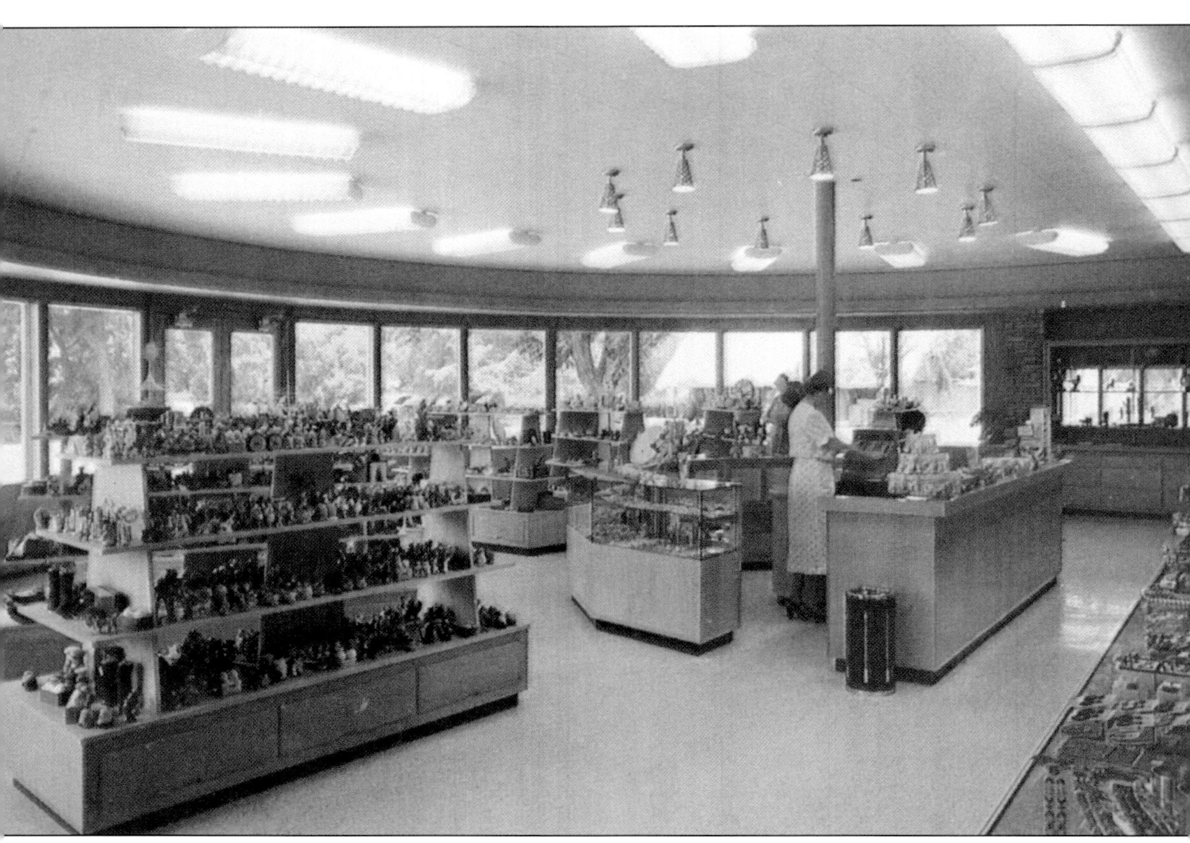

The gift shop, which was added to the park in 1955, was not to be missed on any trip to Aquarena Springs. A 1956 brochure touted the shop as "one of the finest in the Southwest." Visitors purchased tickets for the park's attractions at the ticket booth inside the shop, and parents invariably had to drag their children away from the enticing merchandise after tickets were obtained. Parents and children alike welcomed the air-conditioned space after a long day exploring Aquarena. Former visitors recall the aroma of cedar in the shop, where customers could purchase souvenir cedar boxes, coasters, or figurines, all with the "Aquarena Springs" name. Ashtrays, tea sets, coasters, and trays were for sale and would later become sought-after collectibles. Of course, T-shirts featuring Ralph the Swimming Pig were a popular choice. Children tended to be drawn to items that had nothing to do with Aquarena itself, such as eyeglasses with attached nose and mustache. (Photograph by Gene Aiken.)

Directly across the breezeway from the gift shop was the Aquarena Springs restaurant. Opened as a snack shop in 1950, the restaurant was expanded and remodeled in 1955 to accommodate more than 125 diners and was expanded again in 1960 when the new hotel opened. By the mid-1970s, the restaurant had been updated to incorporate the park's aquatic theme. Guests could dine in an ancient pirate's powder house, on the creaking deck of a ship, or in a bamboo-lined Polynesian village. The menu offered fresh shrimp, a catfish buffet, and a fish platter. The restaurant served breakfast, lunch, and dinner, with live music provided on weekend evenings, and was popular with local residents as well as tourists. The children's menu, picturing Ralph the Swimming Pig, offered kid-friendly choices. (Right, photograph by Greg White; courtesy TxDOT.)

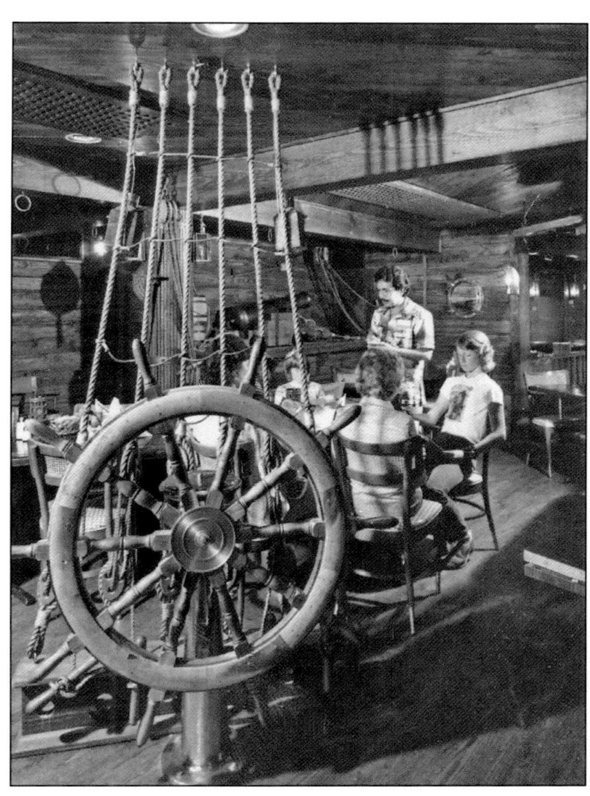

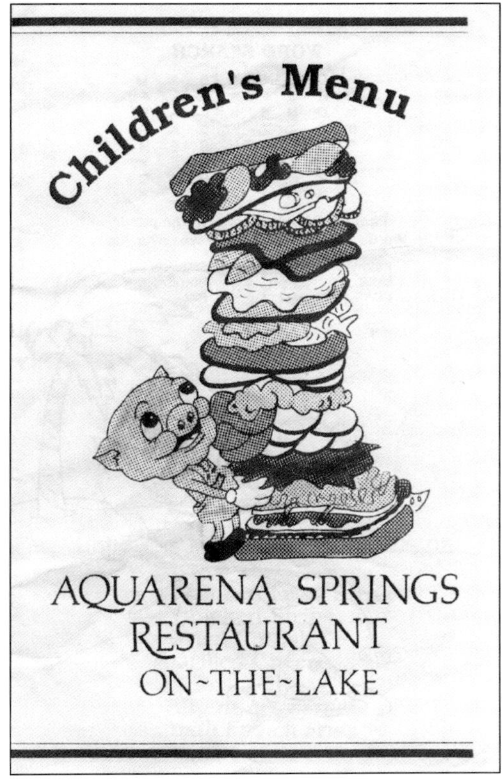

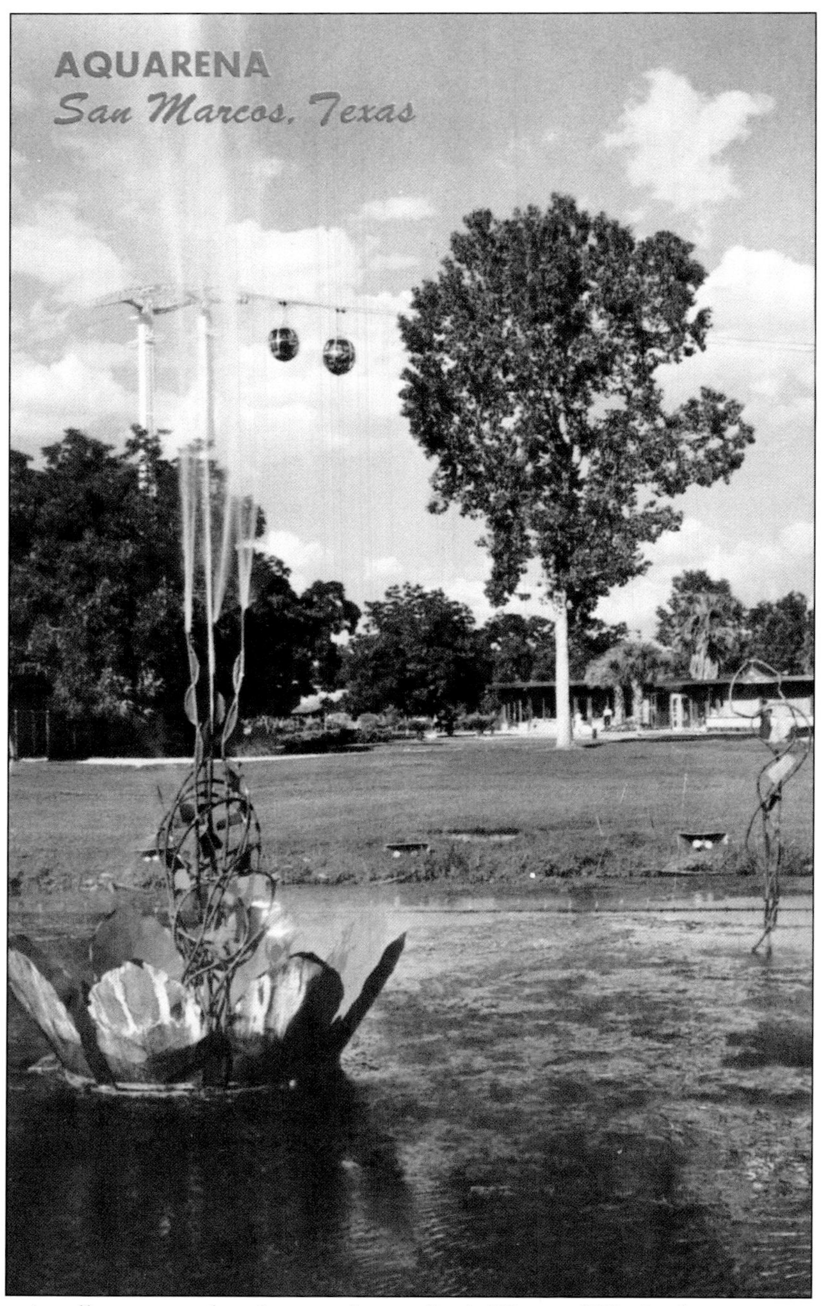

In 1962, nationally renowned sculptor and artist Buck Winn, of Wimberley, was commissioned to create an impressive new fountain system to be built on the edge of Spring Lake near the new sky ride launch pad. Winn commented, "We wanted to get away from the stereotyped fountains with bronze figures of women pouring water out of a jar or frogs spitting water." Instead, Winn utilized tubes and pipes to carry the flow of water, forming the artistic figures and lending motion to the water creation. The main parts of the fountain included a water curtain along the bank of the lake that was nearly 10 feet high and 80 feet long. Behind the curtain, a central water jet periodically shot a stream of water 30 feet into the air, "Just like Old Faithful," Paul Rogers said. At the base of the main fountain was a continuous ball of mist enclosed by large copper petals.

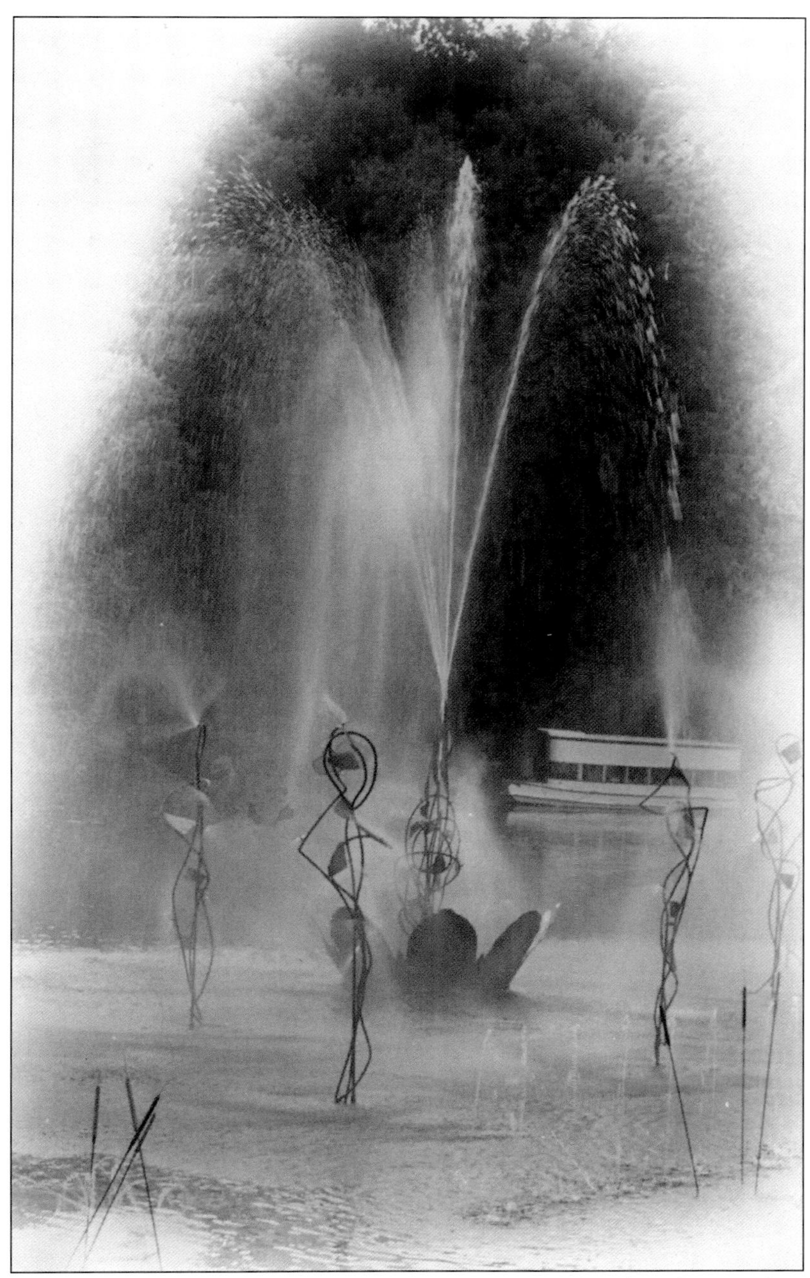

Arranged on both sides of the fountain's copper centerpiece were free-form figures of copper tubing and brightly colored panels of glass. These 10-foot-tall figures, evoking the impression of dancing Aquamaids, revolved slowly and had a single jet of water shooting from the top. Also spread throughout the arrangement were copper cattails with sprays of water serving as leaves and with ceramic cattail heads and copper birds adding additional color. During the day, the sun helped light the waters with colors from the glass panels, and at night, the waters were illuminated with colored, artificial lights. The fountain was named Rainbow Fountain because of its multicolored components as well as the effect created at sunset, when the sun's rays caused a rainbow to appear just above the water's surface. At night, seen from the Aquarena Springs restaurant, the brightly lit fountain was dazzling. (Courtesy SMHCC-San Marcos Public Library.)

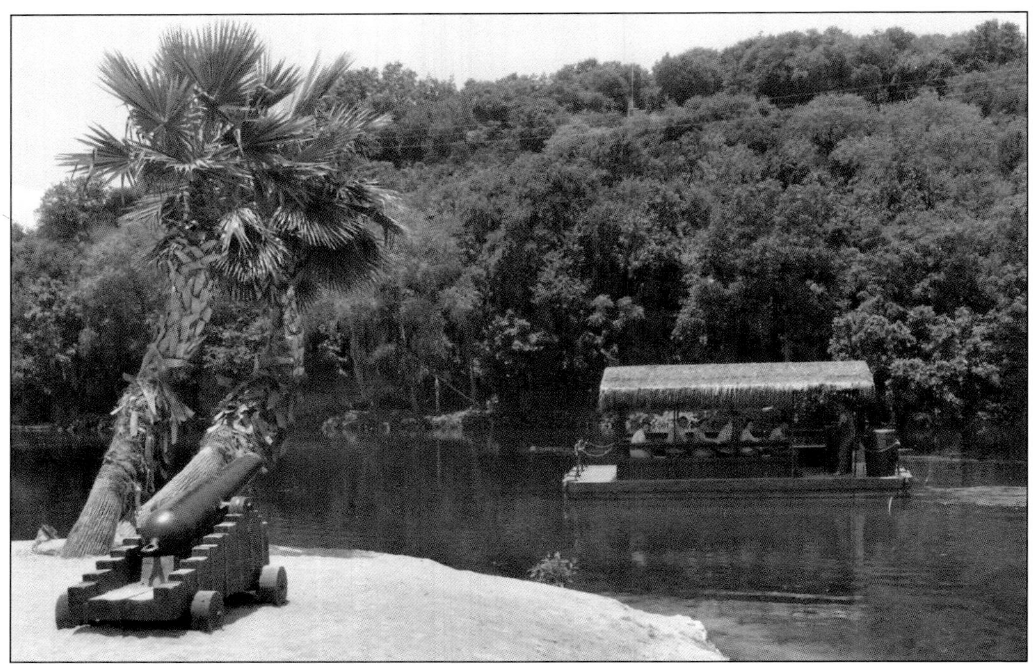

In the mid-1960s, Pirates Cove and a ferryboat were added to the park. Visitors now had an alternate route from the park's headquarters to the Hanging Gardens. A landing was added on the river's west bank. Pres. Don Russell explained, "A lot of people are afraid of the sky ride, so they go over on the ferry and get off on Dead Man's Landing." Tickets specified "Swiss Sky Ride or Ferry Boat," so visitors could choose to use either method of transportation on each part of their journey to and from the Hanging Gardens. Many guests chose to take the sky ride to the gardens and ride the ferry back, passing close to the Rainbow Fountain and feeding the ducks and swans from the big sack of corn kept on board. (Both photographs by John Suhrstedt; courtesy TxDOT.)

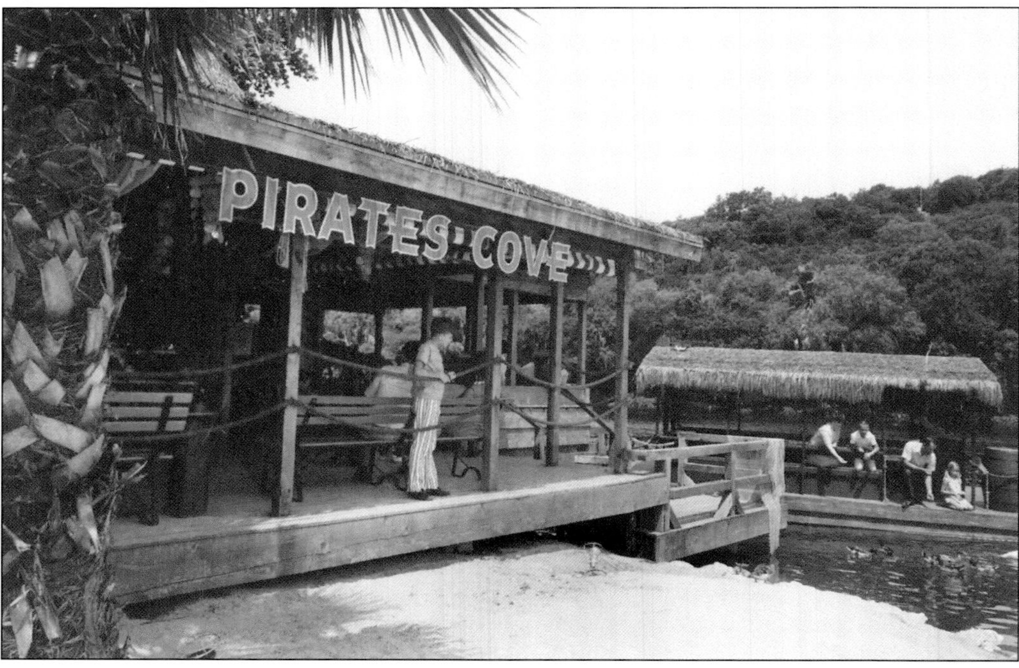

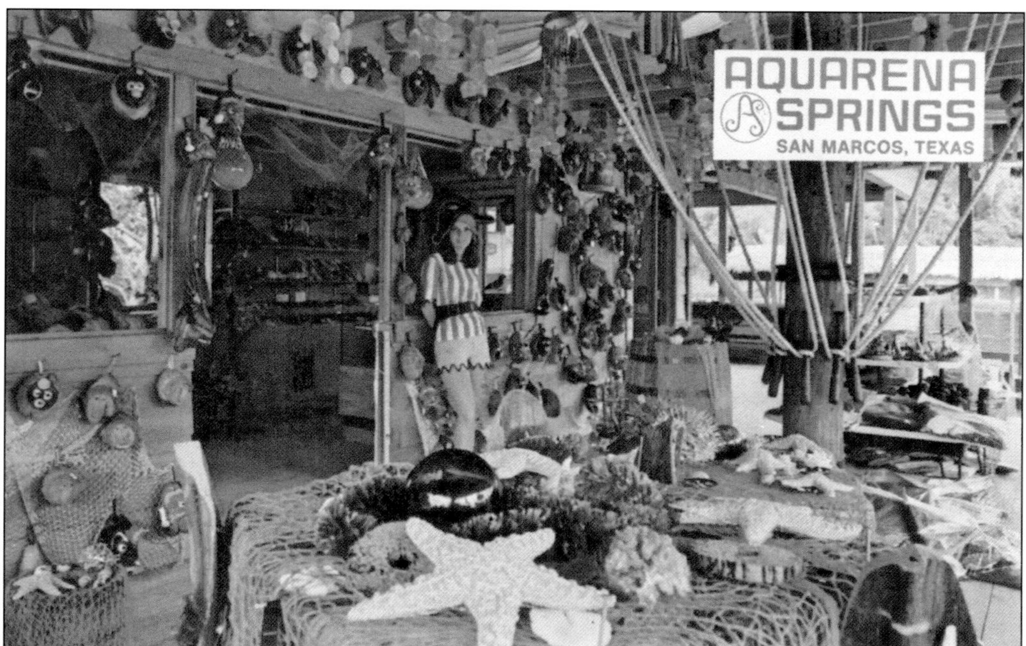

Returning from the Hanging Gardens, ferry passengers disembarked at Pirates Cove, an aquatic shop reminiscent of ancient swashbuckling days. Here visitors could see shells from around the world and purchase sea-themed souvenirs. Potter-in-residence John Stovall created works that were popular with tourists. A beach outside the shop greeted guests with an old-fashioned anchor and an old cannon, examined at right by Lolly Balzer, her husband Robert, and their two children, Lisa and Doug. Visitors who wanted a personalized souvenir of their walk back in time could pose in late-19th-century costumes for a photographic portrait from Smiling Eyes Photo Gallery. Started by photographer M. August Mosel, the gallery was later operated by photographer Wally Hayes. (Right, photograph by John Suhrstedt; courtesy TxDOT.)

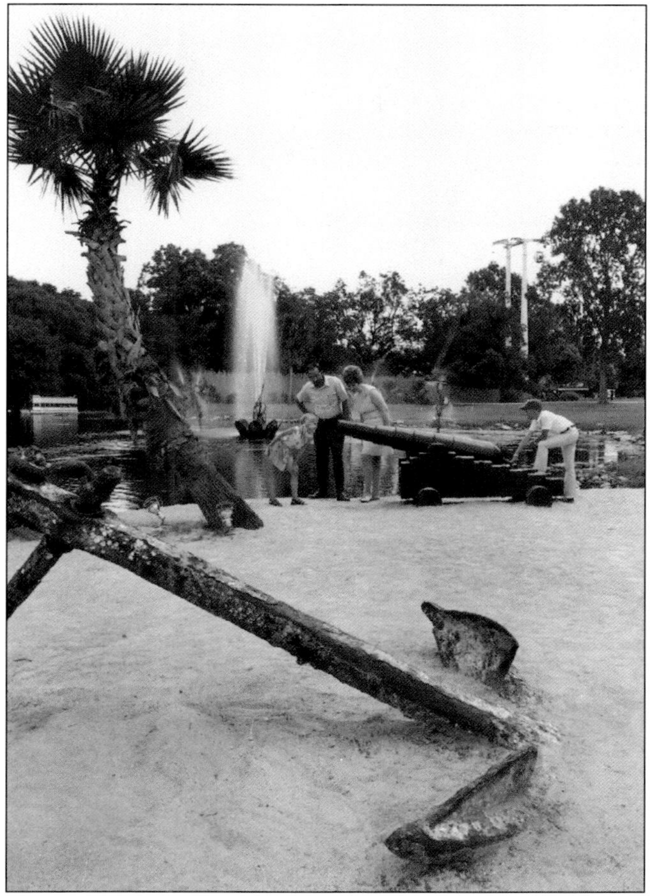

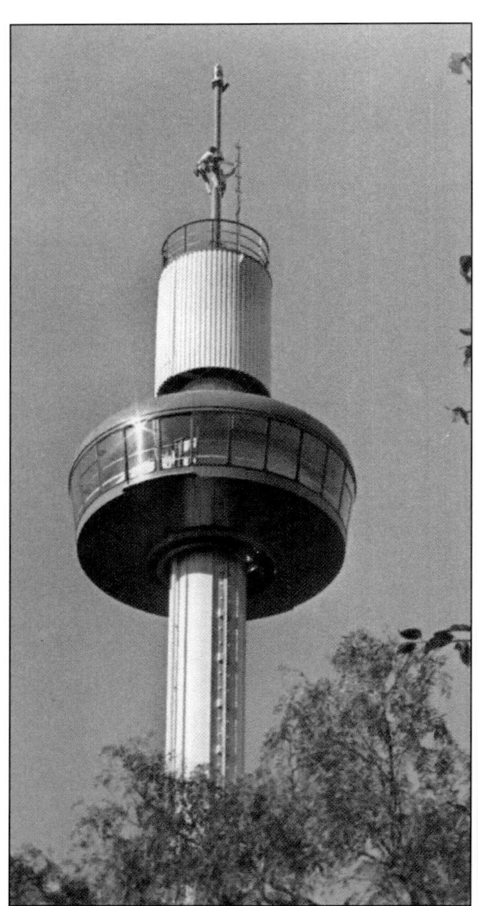

In 1978, Lion Country Safari in Atlanta, Georgia, was going out of business and intended to sell their giant gyro tower for scrap. Engineer Fred Biegler, who had worked on the Aquarena sky ride, heard about the tower, and before long, the tower was destined for Aquarena Springs. Then president Gene Phillips said construction of a gyro tower had been a dream of the late Paul Rogers, who had seen such a tower on a visit to Switzerland. Under Biegler's direction, the tower was cut down outside Atlanta and transported to San Marcos on a dozen 18-wheel trucks. Aquarena hired Intaman of Switzerland, the company that built it, to erect the 220-foot tower on an 80-foot cliff in the Hanging Gardens. At a cost of about $500,000, the tower would be the second Swiss-made attraction at the park. (Left, courtesy SMHCC-San Marcos Public Library.)

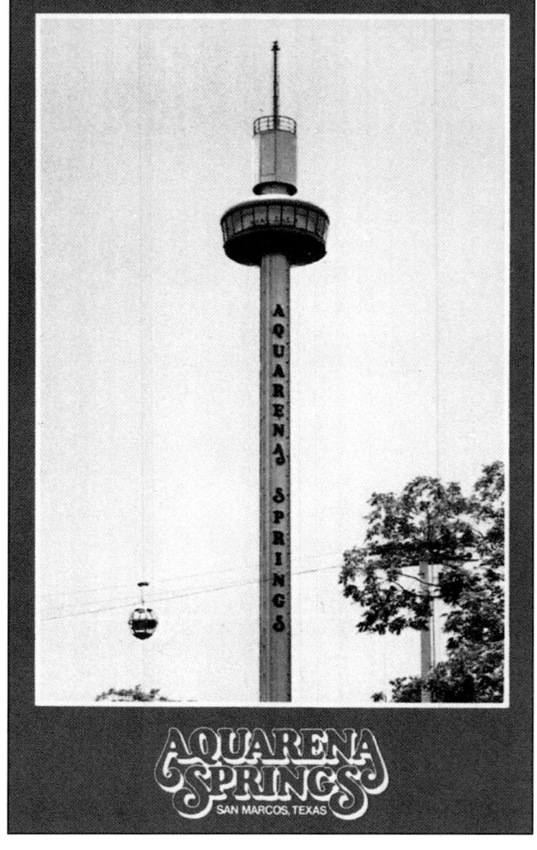

The new gyro tower, named the Sky Spiral, opened in 1979. The tower consisted of a slender steel tube, 7 feet in diameter. A donut-shaped cabin encircled the tube and revolved slowly during both the ascent and descent so that tourists could see in all directions without moving about the cabin. From the top of the tower, in addition to the city of San Marcos, visitors had a spectacular view of the Balcones Fault, Devil's Backbone, the San Marcos and Blanco Rivers, and prairies to the east. Before the tower opened, assistant manager Scott McGehee and supervisor Sonny Marston purchased fireworks and staged an impromptu display from the top of the tower. This began a yearly tradition of a citywide Fourth of July fireworks display in San Marcos.

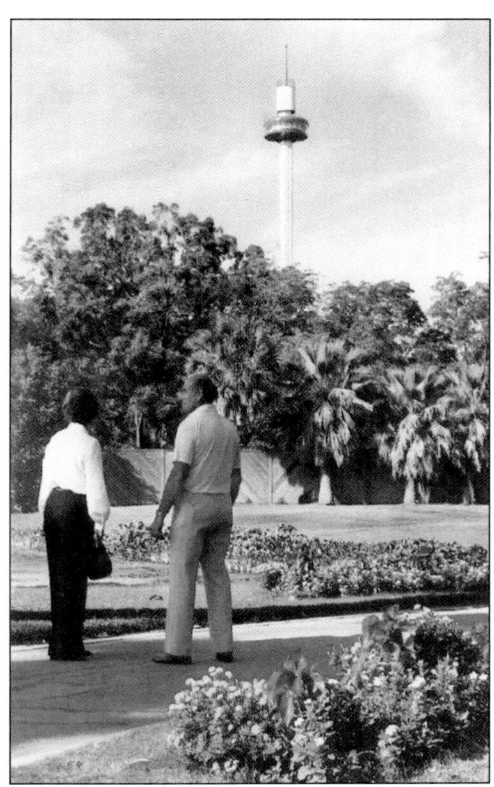

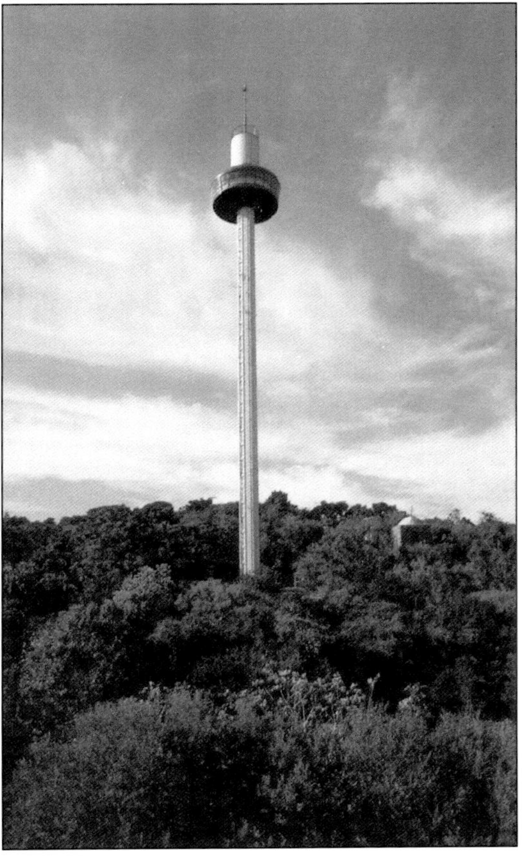

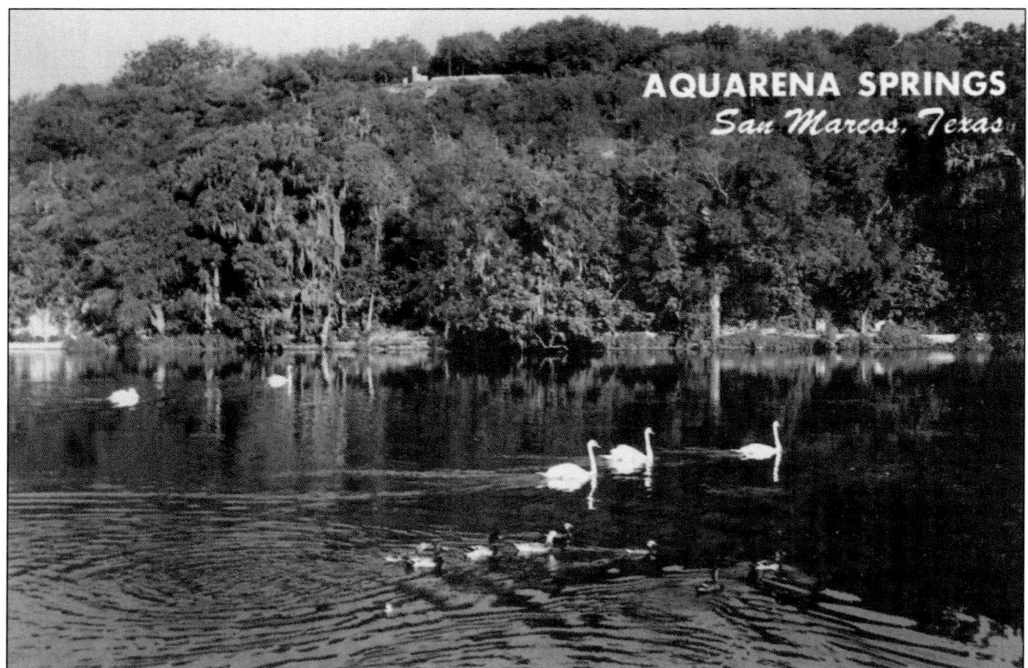

Despite all the technical wonders at Aquarena Springs, visitors never ceased to be enthralled by the denizens of the San Marcos River, particularly swans and mallard ducks. Beyond their role in the submarine theater performances, the ducks roamed the entire Spring Lake area, enjoying their natural habitat and, at night, frequently flying from the springs to the chlorinated hotel swimming pool and lounging on the deck chairs as if they were tourists. The mallards often played follow-the-leader to the swans, which glided in V-formation, stopping occasionally to pull up salads from the river's underwater gardens. Fish and duck food were available at intervals along the river, and visitors willing to spend a nickel could quickly attract appreciative aquatic diners.

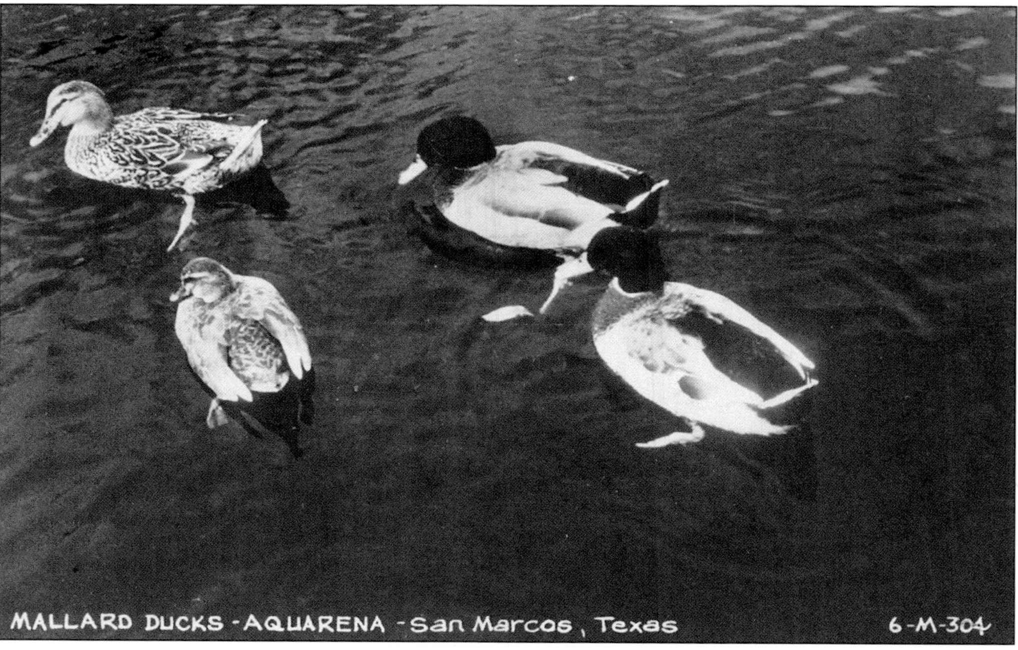

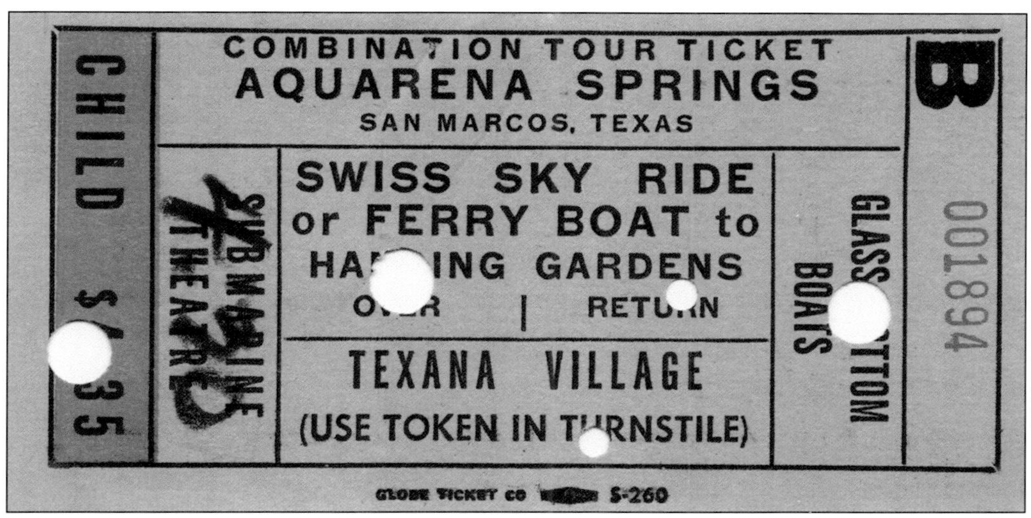

In the 1950s, Aquarena attracted yearly crowds ranging from 200,000 to 300,000. In later decades, the numbers swelled to well over half a million annually. Year after year, numerous school, church, civic, and scouting groups, many from out of state, traveled to Aquarena for outings, attracted not only by the recreational amusements but also by the educational opportunities afforded by the springs. Aquarena's convenient location between Austin and San Antonio on U.S. Highway 81, later Interstate Highway 35, made it easily accessible to travelers. Visitors could purchase tickets to individual attractions or a combination ticket allowing access to the entire park.

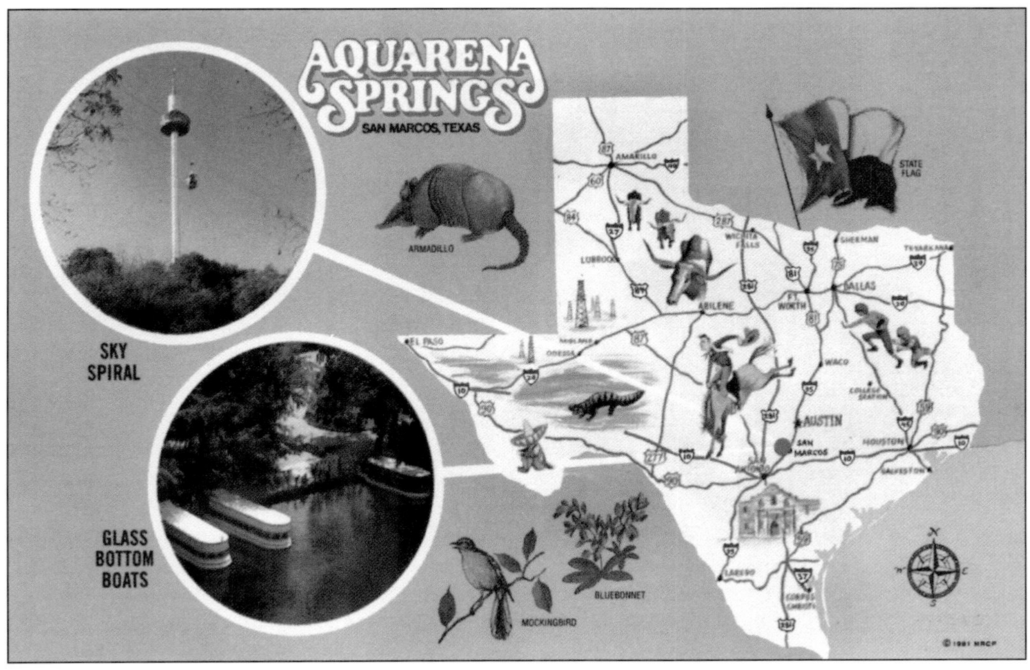

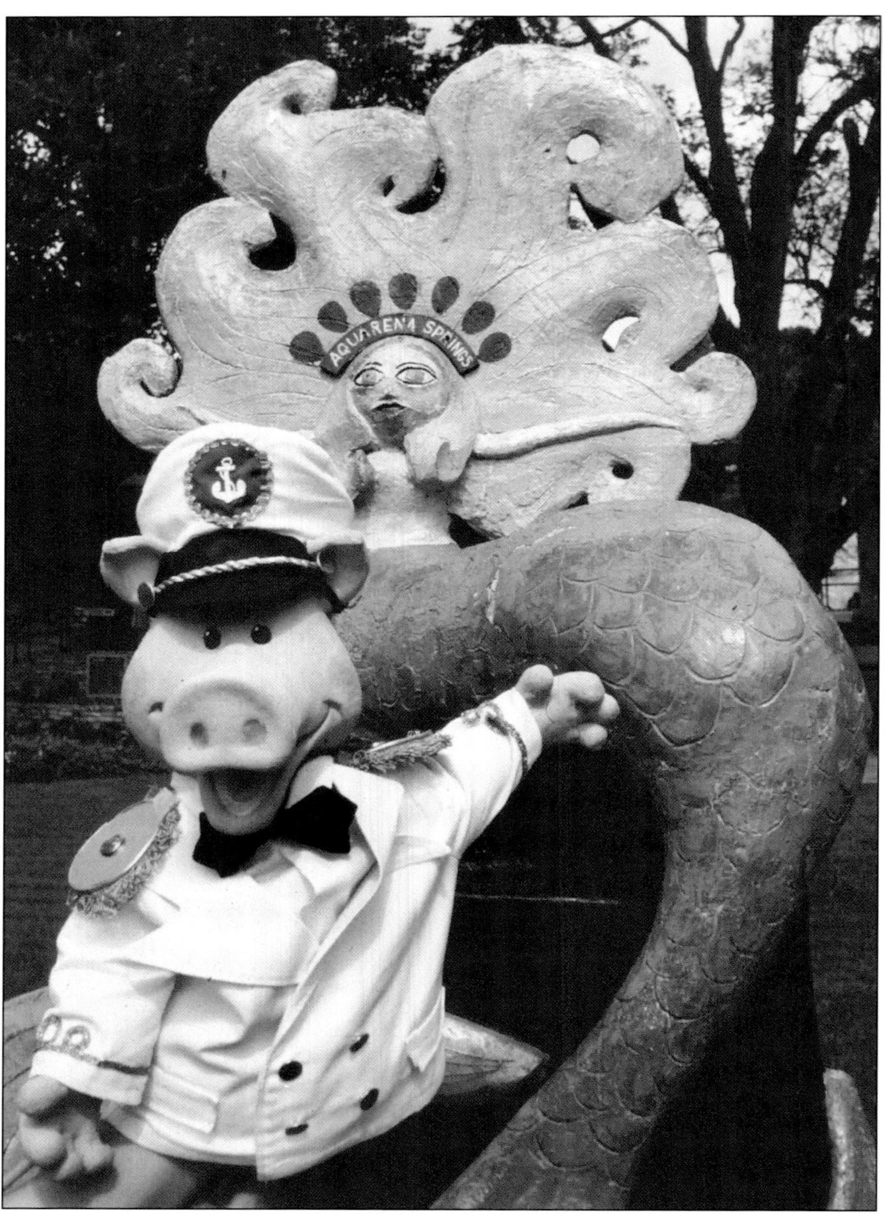

In this photograph, a Ralph the Swimming Pig hand puppet poses in front of the larger-than-life Aquamaid statue on the Aquarena Springs grounds. This Ralph puppet was a spokesperson in a television advertisement encouraging Texas tourists to consider taking the short trip to Aquarena Springs on their next vacation. A mid-1950s chamber of commerce magazine noted that the foundation for this popular resort "was completed about six million years ago, when an upheaval in the earth created the Balcones Escarpment, a ridge of lush hill country around San Marcos. During this upheaval, the springs which now feed Spring Lake were uncovered." A. B. and Paul Rogers acknowledged and appreciated the unique setting in which they built their dream, and it was the San Marcos River beyond all else that inspired each evolution of Aquarena from the 1920s to the 1980s. In the next decades, stewardship of the river would more and more become the focus of Aquarena, and appreciation of the river would be encouraged in ways even the two dreamers could not have imagined. (Courtesy Ron Coley.)

Six

The Vision, Continued

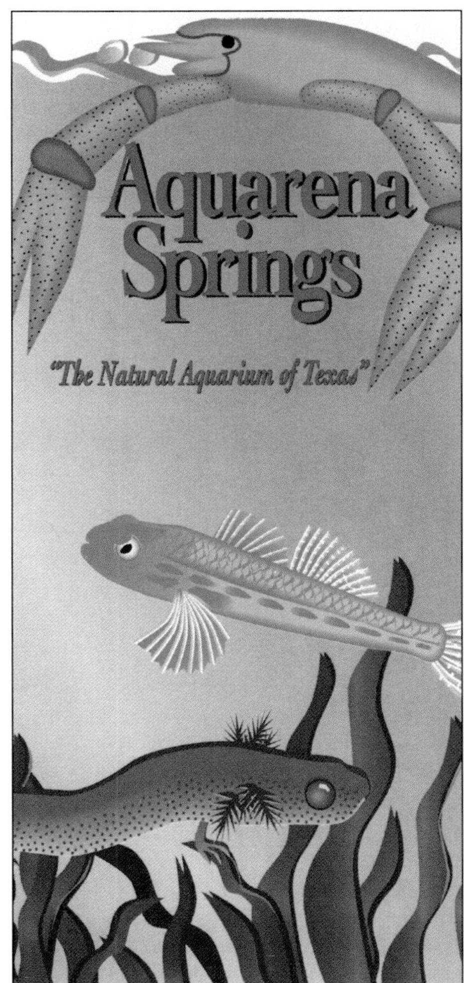

In 1985, the Rogers family sold Aquarena Springs to a private investor, John Baugh. However, it was the 1994 sale of the park to Southwest Texas State University (now Texas State University) that would usher in a dramatic and important transition. Under Texas State's stewardship, Aquarena has evolved from a theme park to an important center for environmental education, research, and preservation.

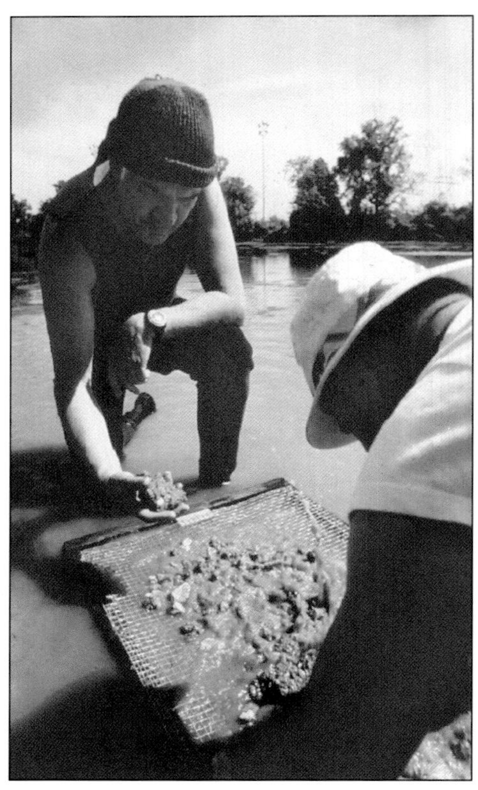

In 1978, archaeologist and retired anthropology professor Dr. Joel Shiner began excavation in the deeply stratified San Marcos River bottom. For 10 years, Shiner worked in Spring Lake, sifting through the ancient past of the river. His work uncovered the longest continuous record of Native American occupation of any locality in North America, including indications of a tribe not previously described. This group, which Shiner labeled the Spring Lake Indians, settled the springs along the Balcones Escarpment 10,000 to 12,000 years ago. Sifting through a gravel pile left over from dredging for the submarine theater, Shiner unearthed the first Clovis point projectile to be discovered in Texas. Below, Shiner holds a fragment of a giant bison tooth that was so well preserved it still contained intact dentin. (Both courtesy Ron Coley.)

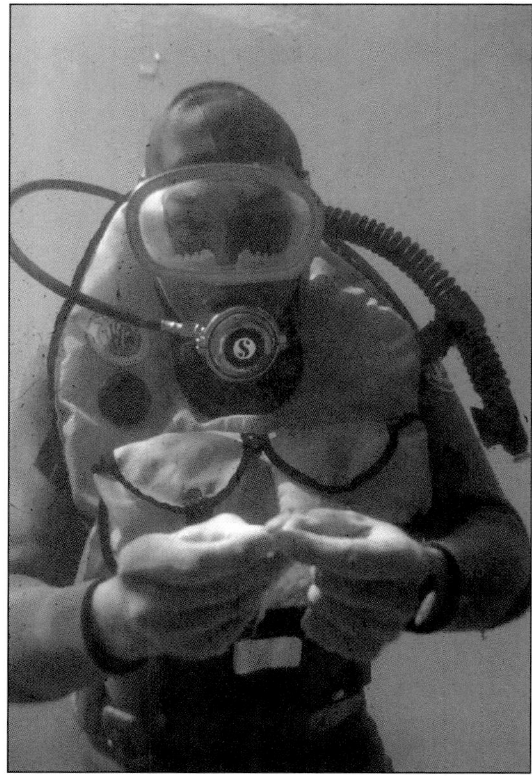

In his excavations, Dr. Shiner used an "airlift," a vacuum device that lifted soft soil, sediment, and silt but left rocks and artifacts behind. After the vacuuming, a second diver marked the location of artifacts and built a box around them. At right, Shiner uses the airlift. Below, Shiner and his assistants inspect the rocks and artifacts after the vacuuming. When divers discovered an item of interest, they carefully marked its location in the underwater "box" before removing it, tagging it, and putting it into an identification bag. (Both courtesy Ron Coley.)

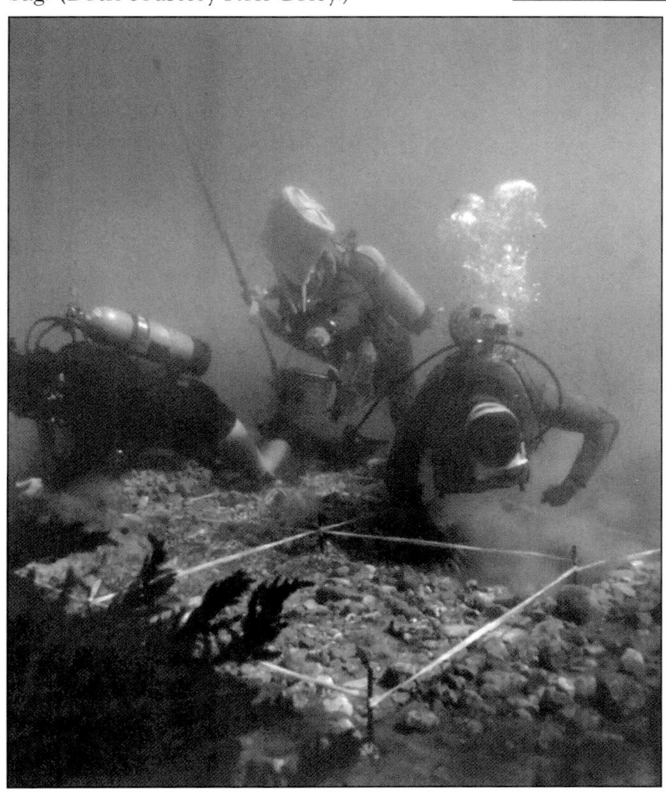

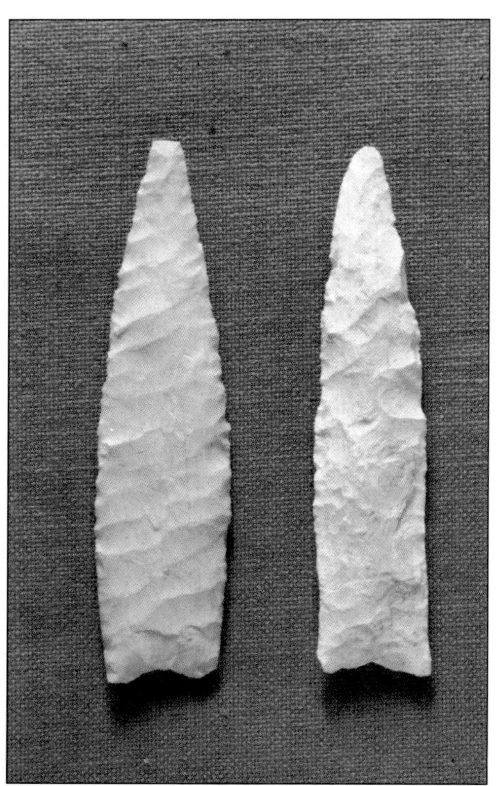

These points were not classifiable into any known category. Joel Shiner christened them "Spring Lake points." After exploring only one-twentieth of the excavation site, Shiner had already pulled more than 200,000 artifacts from the river. Some of his finds included bones and teeth from several extinct species, including mammoths, mastodons, camels, three-toed horses, and bison twice the size of a modern buffalo. (Courtesy Ron Coley.)

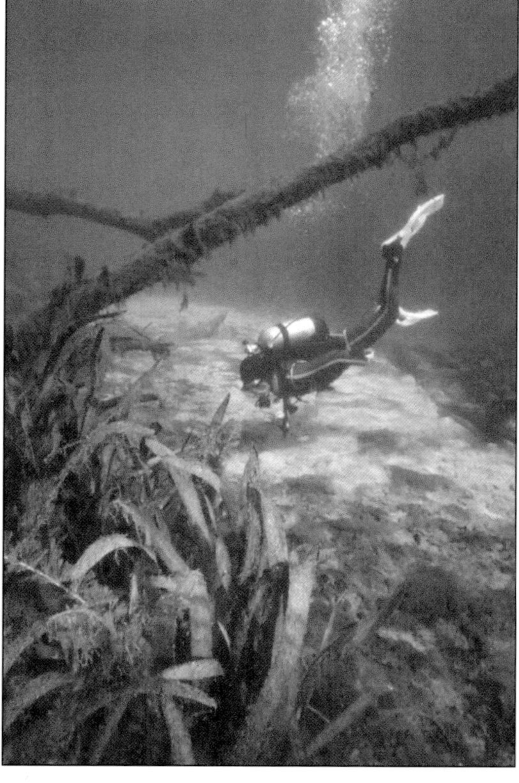

Joel Shiner's excavations concluded shortly before his death in 1988. When Texas State University acquired Aquarena in 1994, they embarked on a 10-year project of ridding the river of nonnative plants that were choking off parts of Spring Lake. Underwater gardener Ethan Chappell, along with two student helpers and 5,000 volunteers, removed hydrilla one piece at a time, replacing it with broad-leafed eelgrass. (Courtesy Ron Coley.)

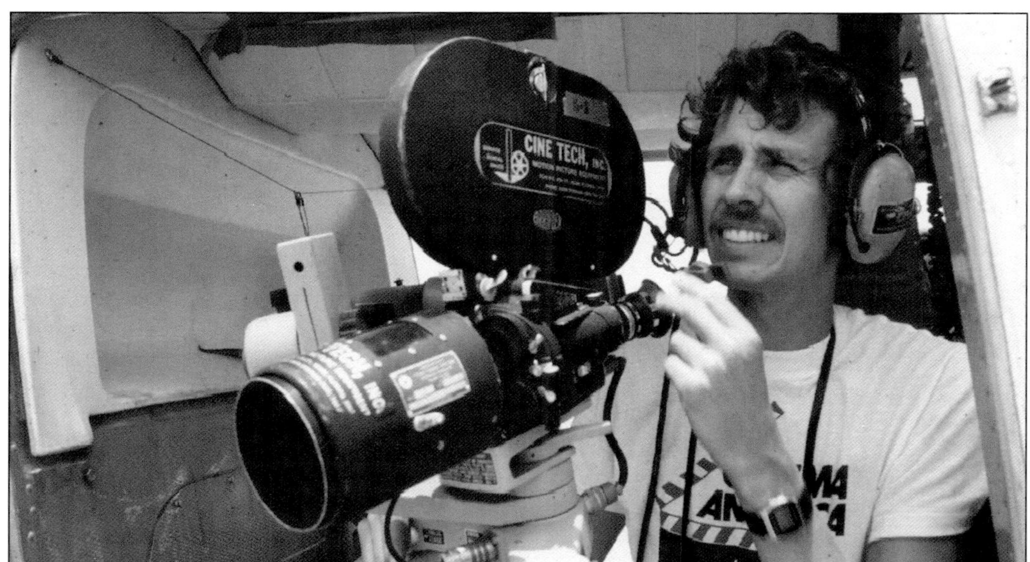

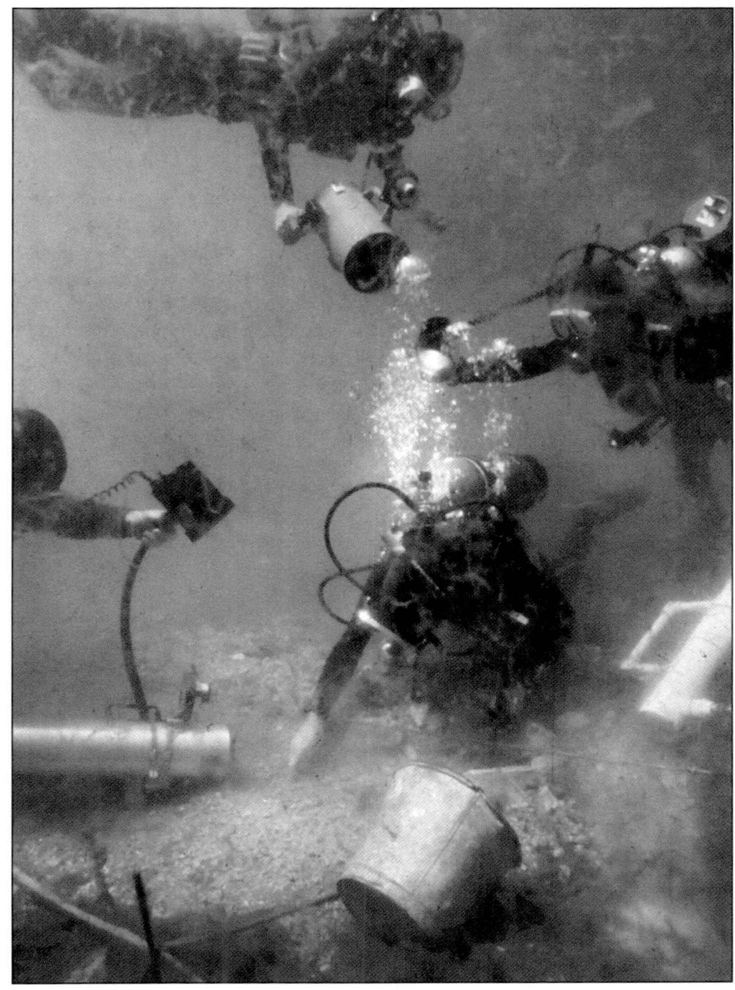

The year 1983 saw the debut of *River of Innocence*, a documentary about the San Marcos River. Produced and directed by Ron Coley, the film was a four-year project undertaken for the KUHT public television station in Houston. The film was shown nationally on PBS for 10 years and for another 10 years on local PBS stations. Central Texas singer-songwriter Shake Russell wrote the theme song, and a concert at San Marcos' Sewell Park is a centerpiece of the film. In the photograph at right, the underwater film crew captures Joel Shiner's work. Visitors to Aquarena could view the documentary on a new deck dubbed the "River of Innocence Theater" while Shiner's excavation continued just beneath them. (Both courtesy Ron Coley.)

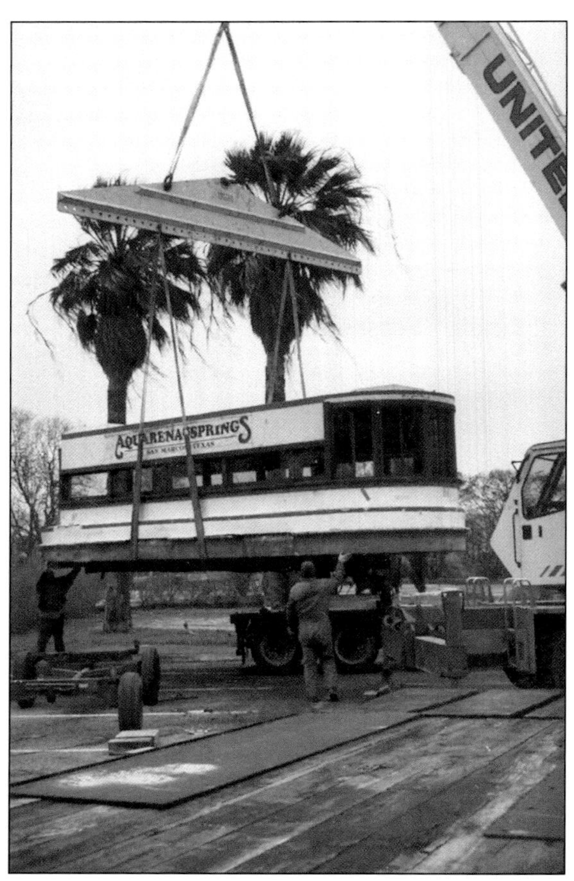

Although some of Aquarena's tourist attractions would go by the wayside as it evolved into an educational center, the glass bottom boats would remain a vital part of the park. The boats, as always, afforded visitors an opportunity to view the rich life in Spring Lake. However, by 1999, the boats were in a state of complete disrepair. Texas State University embarked on a two-year project to refurbish three of Aquarena's boats. Since there were no old drawings to go by, one of the boats was completely disassembled, and a blueprint was created from the pieces. This reverse engineering process took a year to complete. (Both courtesy Aquarena Center.)

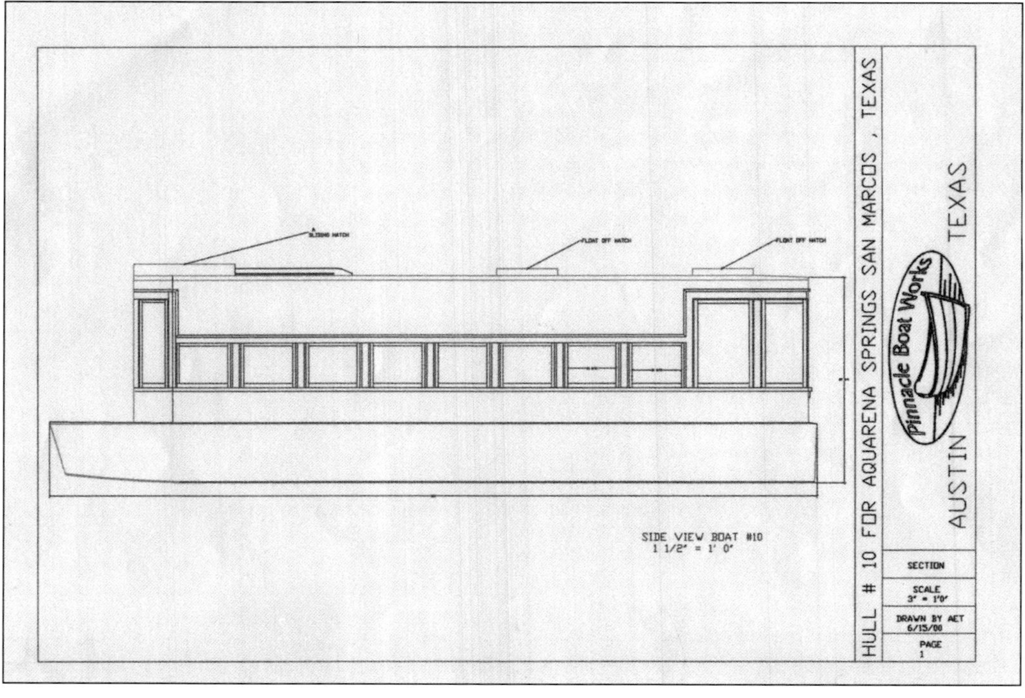

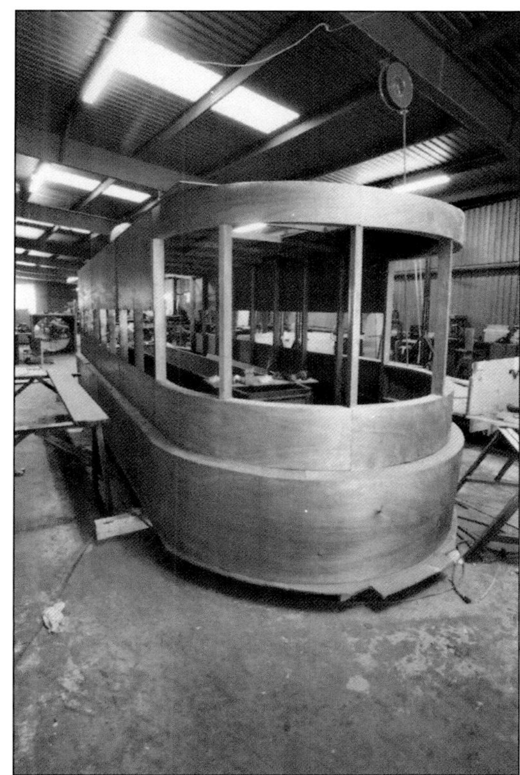

Using a process called lofting, pieces for the hull and keel of the boat were drawn and cut, using the old glass bottom boat No. 10 as a pattern. When the project began, boat 10 was largely comprised of rotten wood, all of which was replaced. In the photograph at right, the refurbished skin of boat 10 has been completed, and the inside awaits restoration. The photograph below shows the restored boat 10 at the dock in 2001 while another boat glides in the background. Currently, five magnificently refurbished boats allow visitors to Aquarena Center to enjoy educational tours over the springs once more. (Both courtesy Aquarena Center.)

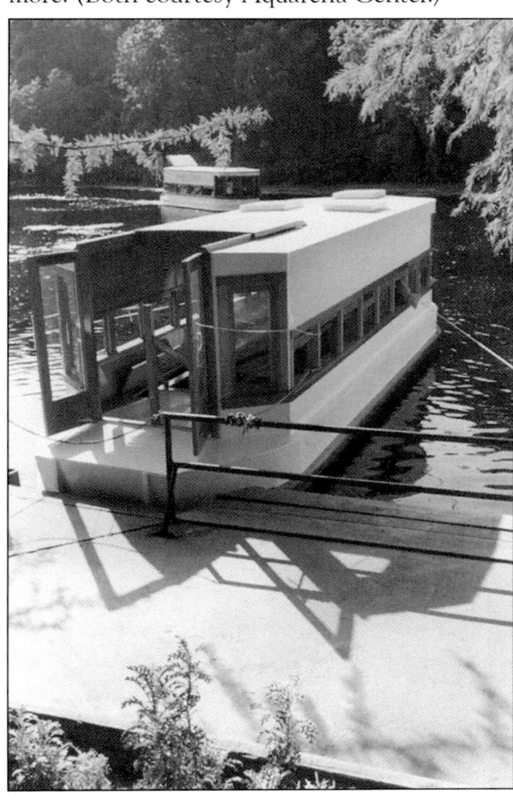

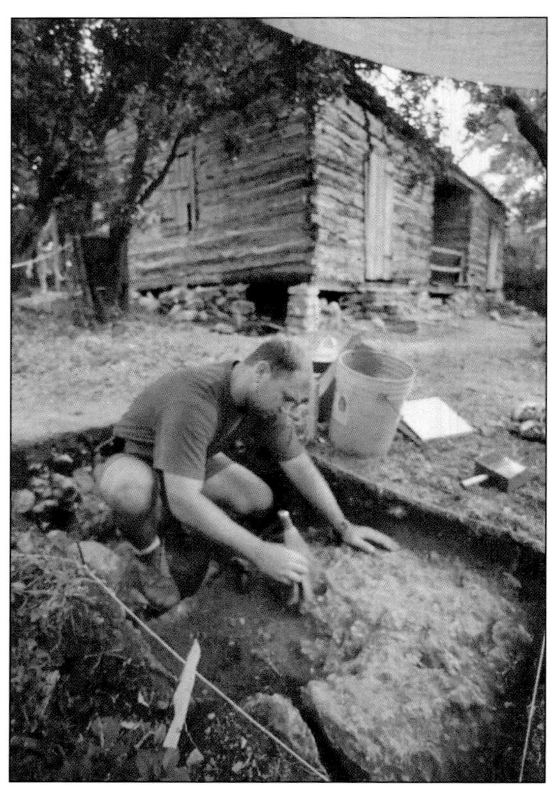

In the spring of 2000, Texas State University requested that the university's Center for Archaeological Studies, under the direction of C. Britt Bousman, conduct a study of the original Edward Burleson homestead above Aquarena Springs. That summer, the Department of Anthropology's field school, under the direction of Katherine Brown, excavated the site with the purpose of, according to Bousman, "determining if the original site still contained intact archaeological deposits, if the replica constructed in the 1960s was placed on the original site and foundation, and if the information provided by the excavation could be used for the accurate representation and interpretation of this site." The excavation revealed that the original foundation was about 50 feet from the 1960s cabin. In the photograph below, workers examine the original outdoor kitchen. (Both courtesy Ron Coley.)

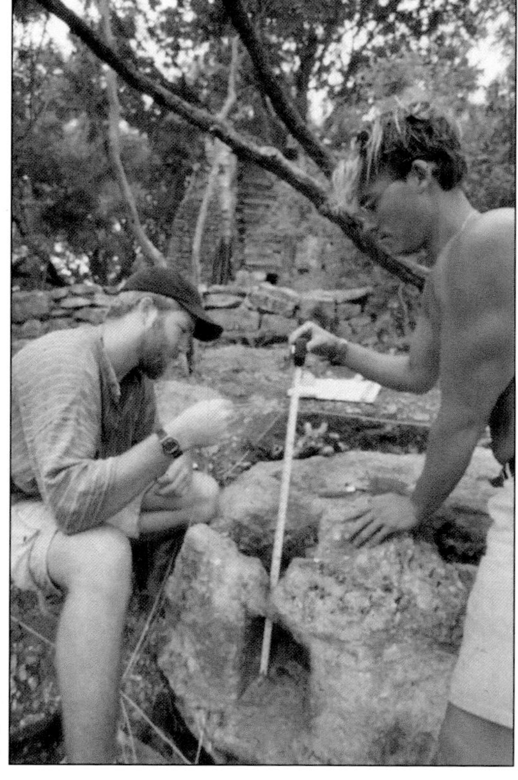

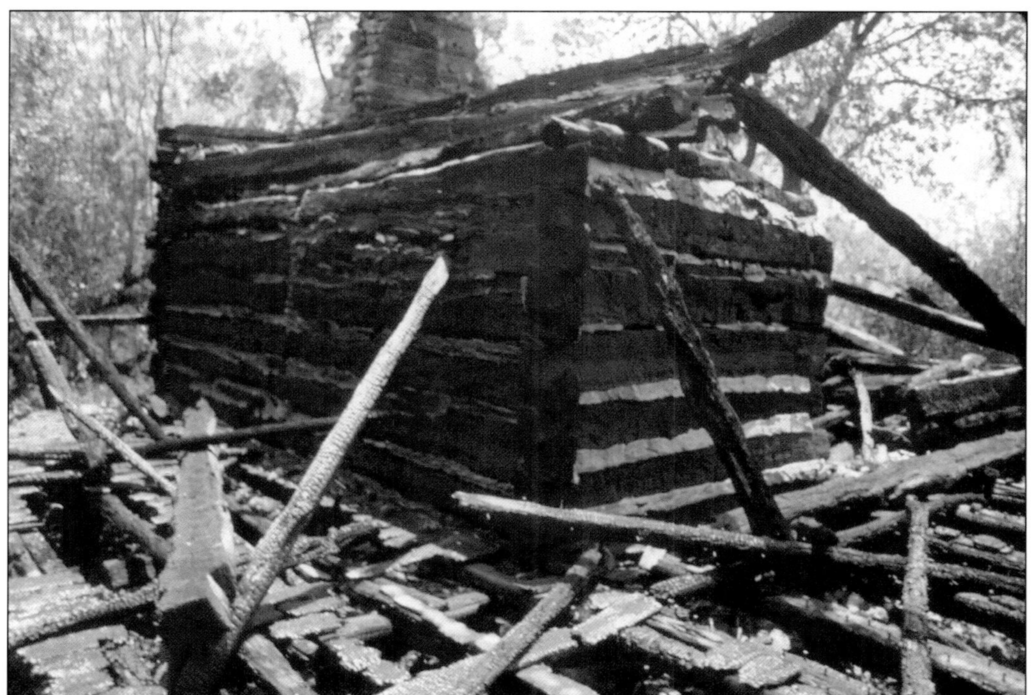

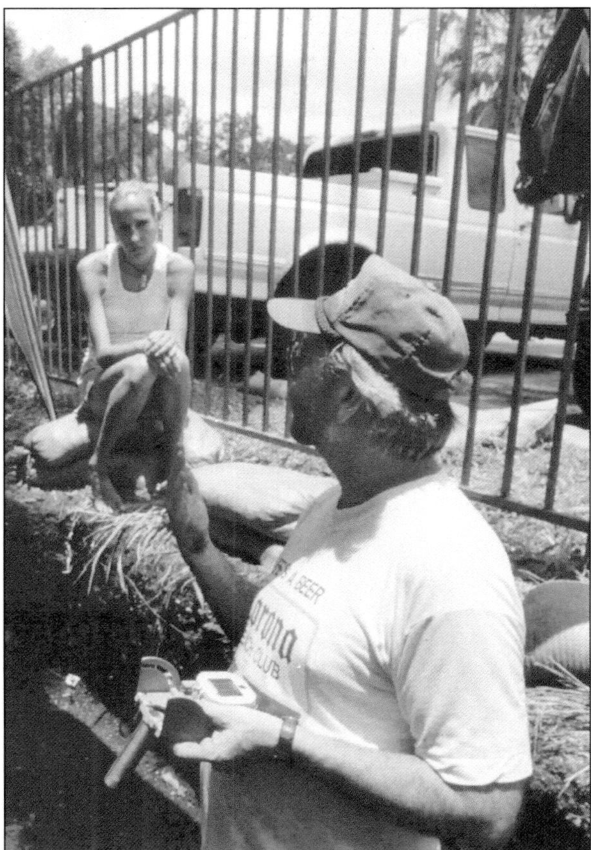

The year 2006 saw important changes at Aquarena Springs. In that year, a fire destroyed the 1964 Burleson home replica, and efforts to raise money for a restoration of the cabin on its original site were redoubled. Also in that year, Texas State University and the Army Corps of Engineers entered an agreement for a wetlands restoration project, which would restore the site of the Aquarena theme park to its natural state, with native grasses covering the property. Plans included trails with interpretive stations for educational programs, along with a new visitor center. Plans to locate the new center in a pecan grove near the parking lot were abandoned when Dr. Britt Bousman discovered extensive evidence of ancient and prehistoric occupation at the site, including a 7,000-year-old spear point from the Calf Creek culture. (Both courtesy Ron Coley.)

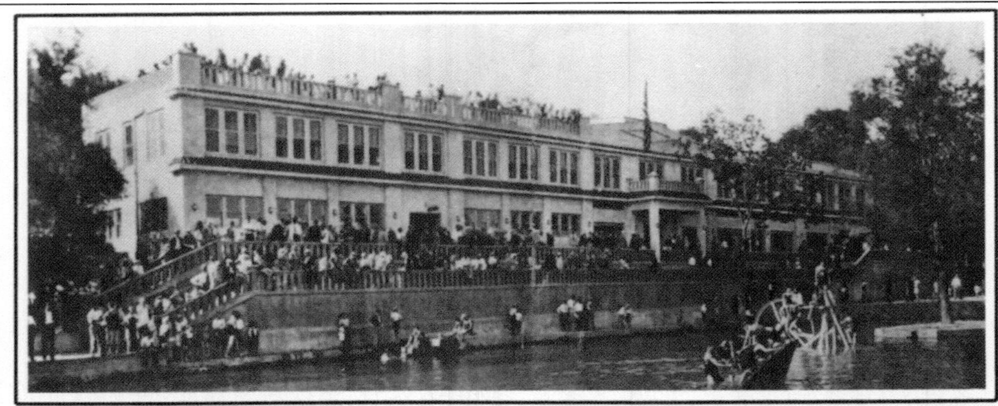

"Rogers' Spring Lake Park Hotel" opened to a crowd on April 22, 1929. Today, Aquarena Springs Inn is still a favored stopping place for Texans and visitors.

Seventy-seven years after the 1929 grand opening of the Spring Lake Park Hotel, the Texas Rivers Center celebrated its own grand opening at the same site. According to Texas State University, the Texas Rivers Center "represents a partnership that brings together the River Systems Institute with branches of the Texas Parks and Wildlife Department and the National Park Service." The 2006 grand opening marked the completion of a "$3.1 million renovation project that began in 1999 with a master plan to transform a former landmark resort hotel into a major facility devoted to the study and protection of water resources." (Below, photograph by Don Anders; courtesy Texas State University.)

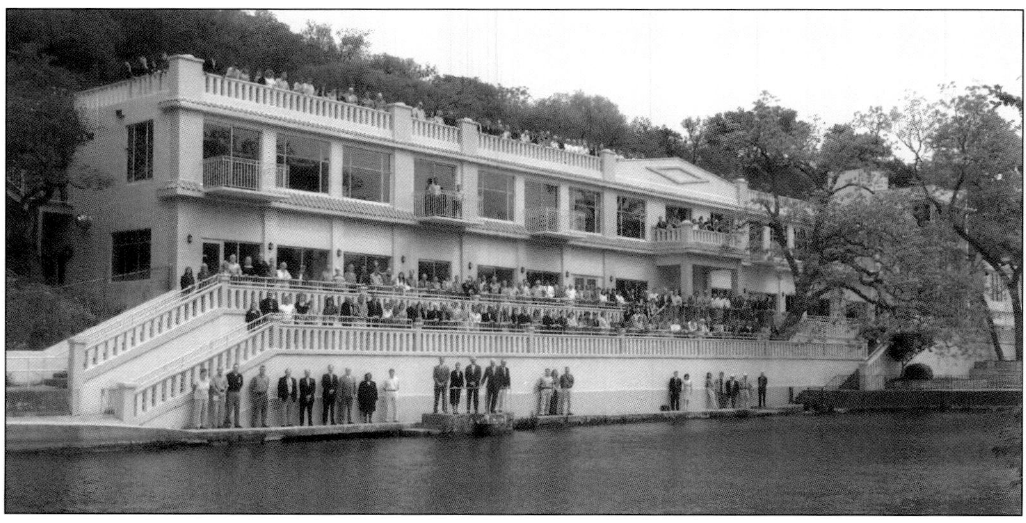

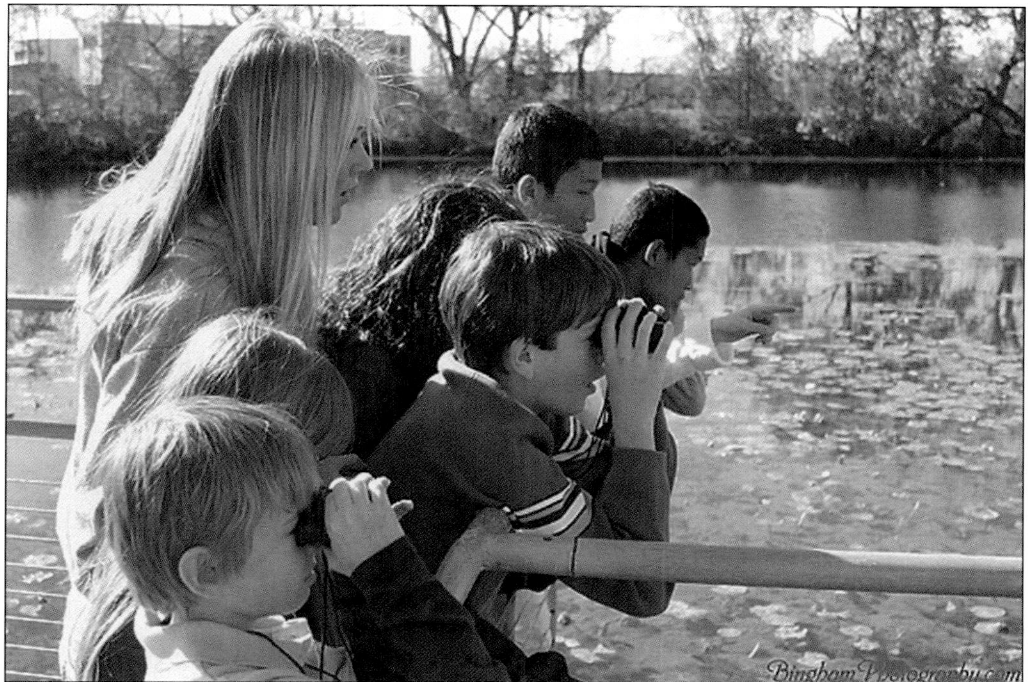

The River Systems Institute at Texas State University, San Marcos, is committed to "studying, preserving, and interpreting the remarkable aquatic system that surrounds it as it extends that attention and concern to freshwater systems across the state, the nation, and the world." The institute oversees Aquarena Center, which "offers interpretive programs focusing on the unique freshwater ecosystem of Spring Lake and the importance of aquifers, rivers, and aquatic systems." In the above photograph, students explore the river from the wetlands boardwalk. The photograph below shows that the old sky ride landing has become the backdrop for an outdoor classroom. (Above, courtesy Richard G. Bingham II; below, courtesy Ron Coley.)

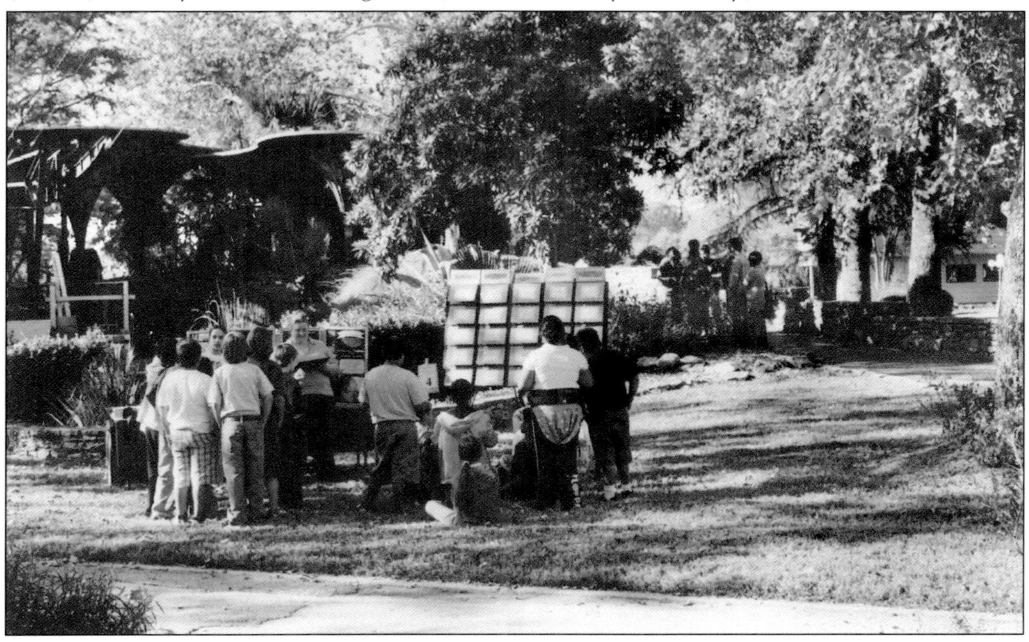

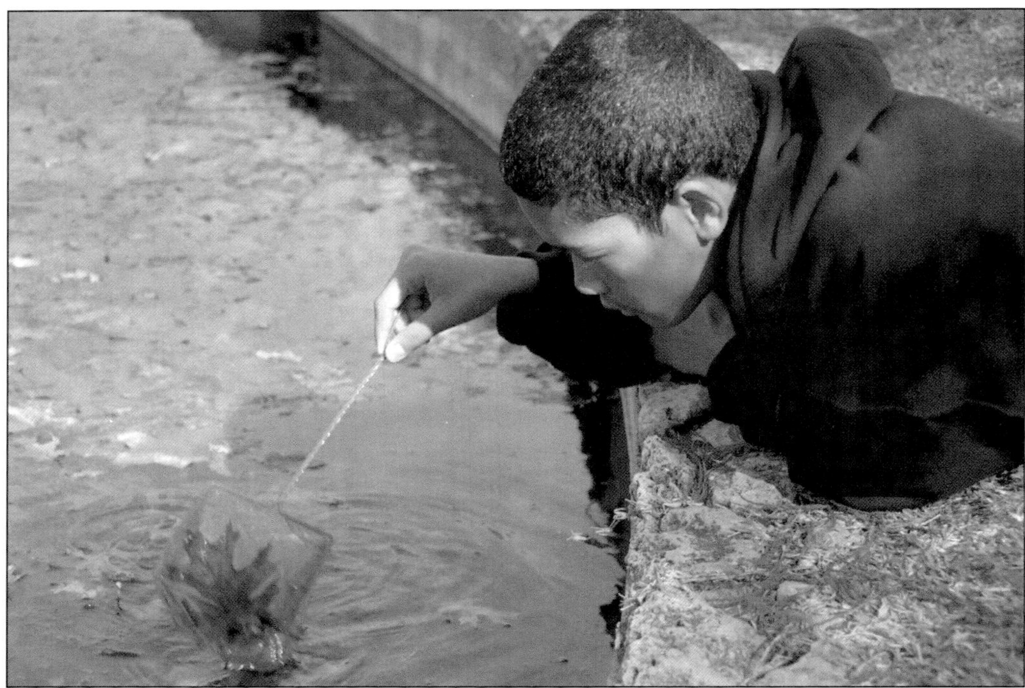

The aquatic environmental educational opportunities provided by the River Systems Institute and Aquarena Center attract more than 100,000 visitors annually. Aquarena Center describes itself as "a living laboratory unmatched in the world for exploring the interconnections between all living things and water." Visitors can learn about and observe eight federally listed endangered or threatened species, including the San Marcos salamander, the Texas blind salamander, the fountain darter, and Texas wild rice. The center offers educational opportunities for all ages, specializing in customized, interpreter-led field trips, including private group tours, school field trips, scouting programs, and summer day camps. (Above, courtesy Paul Johnston; below, courtesy Ron Coley.)

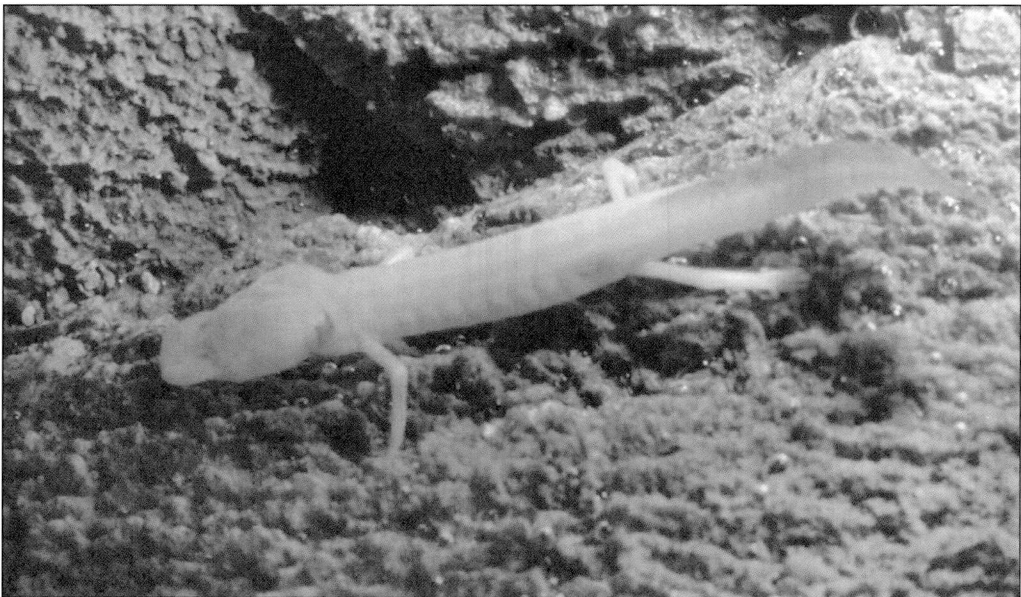

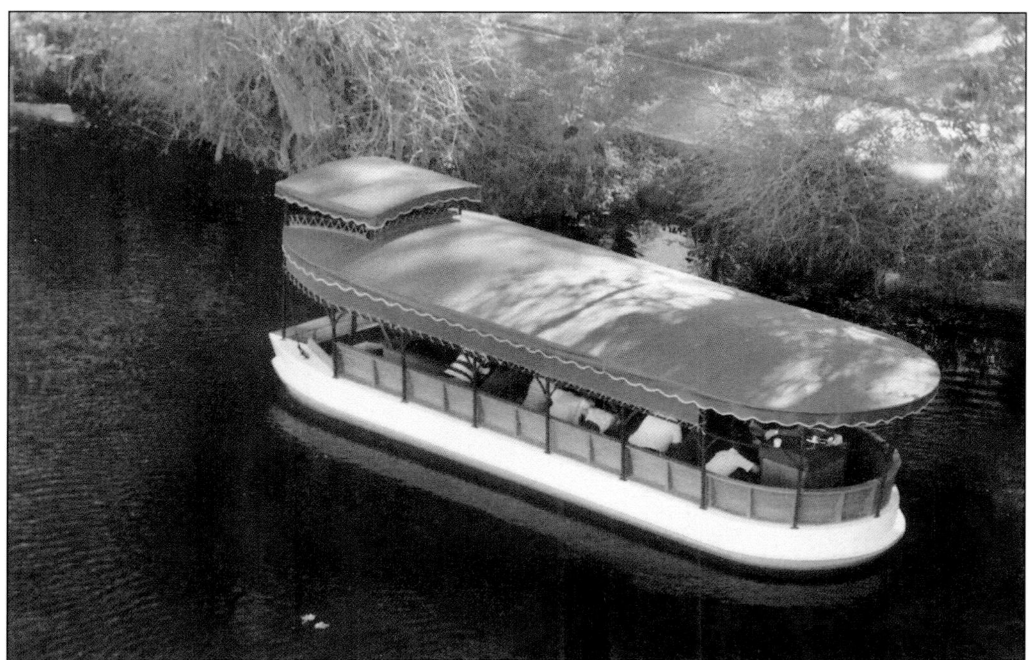

The current glass bottom boat fleet is comprised of five boats, one of which has been outfitted with a canvas top reminiscent of the early 1940s version built by Paul Rogers. Today guests learn about the freshwater ecosystem of Spring Lake and are educated about conservation and preservation. As part of the Texas Rivers Center partnership, Texas State University deposited 33,108 acre-feet of its San Marcos River water rights into the Texas Water Trust in perpetuity for environmental flows. Recently, Aquarena unveiled five glass bottom kayaks that allow individuals to take their own guided, personalized ecotours. (Both courtesy Ron Coley.)

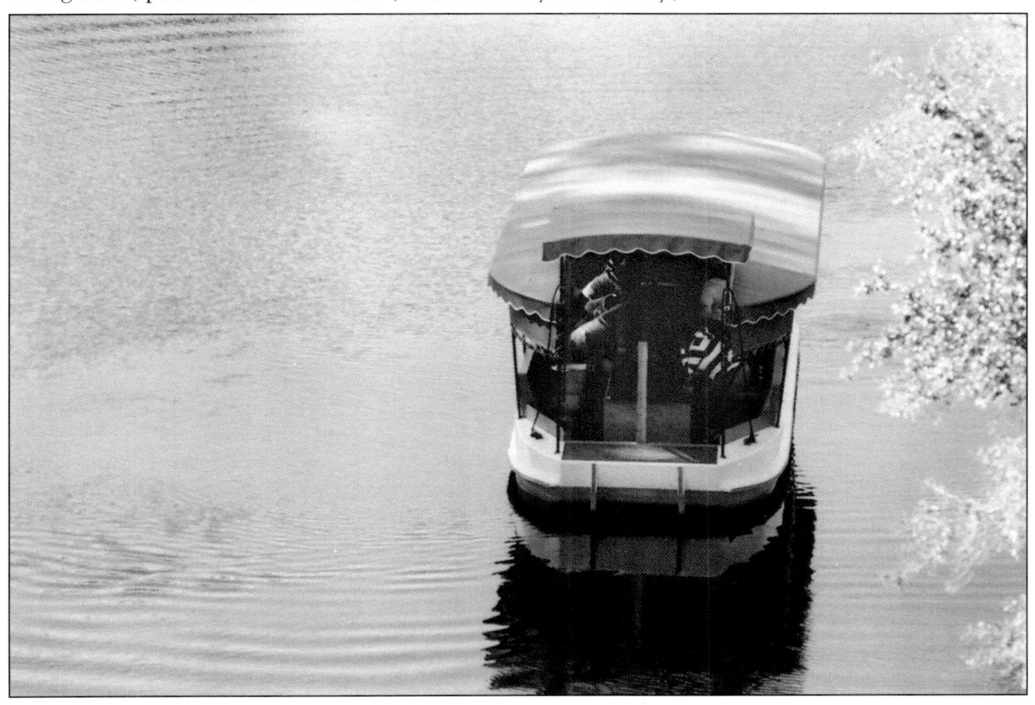

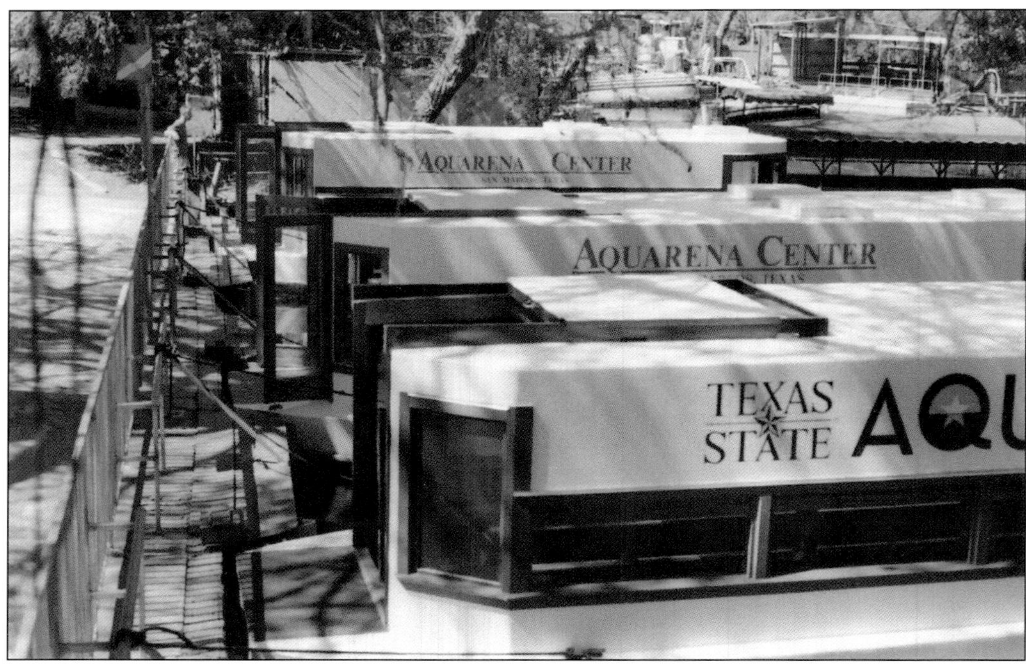

The above photograph shows the glass bottom boat fleet. The boat in the foreground displays the Texas state logo, which will soon adorn the other boats as well. To celebrate Earth Day 2009, Aquarena Center debuted its first solar-powered glass bottom boat, underscoring the River Systems Institute's commitment to environmental stewardship. A spokesman expressed the hopes that passengers on the new boat would be inspired to "use that experience to build a greener world." Arthur Birch Rogers and Paul Jackson Rogers could never have imagined boats run by solar power, but they would no doubt appreciate the respect and care being shown to the river they both loved and wanted to share with the world. (Both courtesy Ron Coley.)

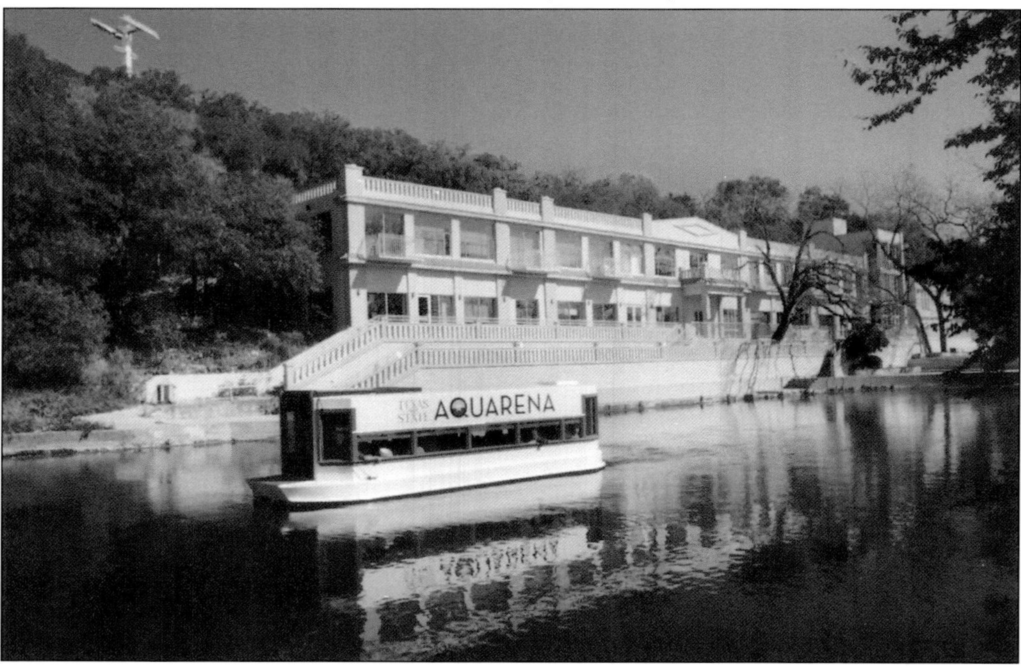

CONTINUING A TRADITION

TEXAS STATE AQUARENA

The handmade wooden boats built in the 1950s may hold the key to preserving Texas's freshwater systems. More than 125,000 people, mostly schoolchildren, visit Aquarena Center each year, and riding in the glass bottom boats is the highlight of their visits. These experiences help create an appreciation for water resources that can lead to a lifetime of responsible natural resources stewardship.

Aquarena's ability to preserve these historical treasures is beyond the capacity of the program's existing support. Many repairs have had to be postponed, making the challenge even more daunting. Just five of the 10 original boats remain. Funding is critical if they are to continue to educate and fascinate future conservationists. The materials and craftsmanship involved in the boats' upkeep create financial demands that Aquarena cannot meet alone.

A reliable source of funding will guarantee the boats' continued operation. The River Systems Institute at Texas State University has established a "Perpetual Endowment" for these boats. Their fate is critical to the future of the water resources of Texas and river systems across the globe.

The author and the Rogers family are donating all their proceeds from this book to the boat endowment.

Please give to

Aquarena Center Glass Bottom Boat Endowment (Account No. 6-7968)

Mail checks to

Texas State University Development Foundation
601 University Drive/480 J. C. Kellam
San Marcos, Texas 78666